METHUEN'S HANDBOOKS OF ARCHAEOLOGY

Greek Terracottas

In this series

ENGLISH COINS
G. C. BROOKE

GREEK PAINTED POTTERY
R. M. COOK

GREEK AND ROMAN JEWELLERY
R. A. HIGGINS

MOSAICS
H. P. L'ORANGE and P. J. NORDHAGEN

ROMAN COINS
HAROLD MATTINGLY

A SURVEY OF PRIMITIVE MONEY
A. H. QUIGGIN

GREEK COINS
CHARLES SELTMAN

GREEK AND ROMAN GOLD AND SILVER PLATE
D. E. STRONG

A. Women gossiping. Made at Myrina. Unknown provenance. Late second century B.C. British Museum

Greek Terracottas

R. A. HIGGINS

Deputy Keeper of Greek and Roman Antiquities
in the British Museum

METHUEN & CO LTD
11 NEW FETTER LANE LONDON EC4

First published 1967

Printed in Great Britain by
Butler & Tanner Ltd., Frome and London

Distribted in the U.S.A.
by Barnes & Noble Inc.

To Jenny, Michael, Nicolas, Thomas and Katherine

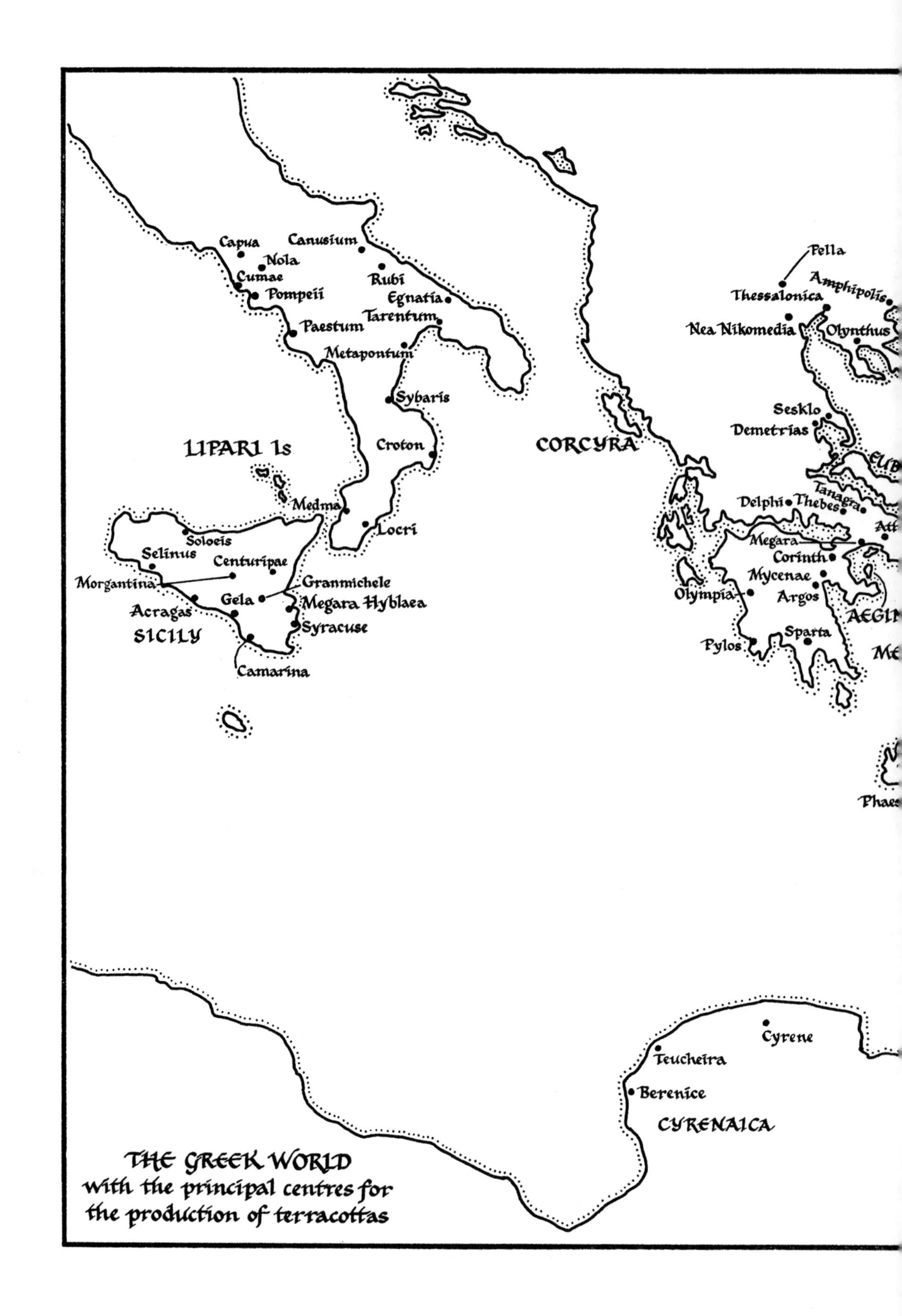
Capua
Canusium
Nola
Cumae
Rubi
Pompeii
Egnatia
Tarentum
Paestum
Metapontum
Sybaris
LIPARI Is
Croton
CORCYRA
Medma
Locri
Soloeis
Selinus
Centuripae
Morgantina
Granmichele
Gela
Megara Hyblaea
Acragas
Syracuse
SICILY
Camarina
Pella
Amphipolis
Thessalonica
Nea Nikomedia
Olynthus
Sesklo
Demetrias
Tanagra
Delphi
Thebes
Megara
Corinth
Mycenae
Olympia
Argos
Pylos
Sparta
Cyrene
Teucheira
Berenice
CYRENAICA
THE GREEK WORLD
with the principal centres for
the production of terracottas

Amisos
SAMOTHRACE
Ilion (Troy)
Assos
Pergamon
LESBOS
Myrina
Kyme
Sardis
Smyrna
CHIOS
Ephesus
SAMOS
Priene
DELOS
Miletus
Halicarnassus
CALYMNA
Cnidus
NAXOS
Xanthus
COS
Ialysus
Lindus
THERA
Camirus
RHODES
Knossos
Olous
Petsofa
Gortyn
Tarsus
Salamis (Enkomi)
Kition
Curium
Amathus
CYPRUS
Sidon
Alexandria
Naucratis
FAYOUM

Contents

Text Figures

List of Plates

NOTE: It is wise to be sceptical of all alleged find-spots except in the case of excavation pieces; but one can be over-cautious. Where a terracotta listed below has been properly excavated, the fact is stated. In other cases I have only queried the alleged find-spot if it has seemed to me doubtful or inherently improbable.

COLOUR PLATES

MONOCHROME PLATES

E] Plaster mould (with modern impression). Provenance unknown. Hellenistic period. British Museum. Cat. no. E 56. L. 9 cm.
Photo: British Museum

2. NEOLITHIC, ABOUT 5000–3000 B.C. *pages 6–8*
A] Female idol. Excavated Knossos. Heraclion Museum. Zervos, *Crète*, fig. 56. Evans, *Palace*, i, fig. 12:1. Ht 9·3 cm.
Photo: Cahiers d'Art
B] Female idol. Excavated Knossos. Heraclion Museum. Zervos, *Crète*, fig. 59. Evans, *Palace*, i, fig. 12:6. Ht 4·4 cm.
Photo: Cahiers d'Art
C, D] Goddess. Excavated Lerna. Argos Museum. *Hesperia*, xxv (1956), 175. Ht 18·2 cm.
Photo: American School of Classical Studies
E] Mother-goddess. Excavated Sesklo. Athens, National Museum. Tsountas, *Dimini and Sesklo*, pl. 31. Ht 16 cm.
Photo: Constantopoulos

3. MIDDLE MINOAN, 2000–1550 B.C. *pages 9–10*
A] Deer. Excavated Porti. Heraclion Museum. Marinatos and Hirmer, pl. 14 (top). Ht 19·5 cm.
Photo: Hirmer Verlag
B] Bull or cow. Excavated Phaestos. Heraclion Museum. Marinatos and Hirmer, pl. 19 (bottom). Ht 21 cm.
Photo: Hirmer Verlag
C] Man. Excavated Petsofa. Heraclion Museum. Marinatos and Hirmer, pl. 15 (bottom). Ht 17·5 cm.
D] Woman. Excavated Chamaizi. Heraclion Museum. Bibliography as above. Ht 23 cm.
E] Woman. Excavated Petsofa. Heraclion Museum. Bibliography as above. Ht 14·3 cm.
Photo (C–E): Hirmer Verlag

4. MYCENAEAN, 1400–1200 B.C. *pages 13–16*
A] Seated goddess. From Mycenae. 1400–1200 B.C. Paris, Louvre Museum. Cat. no. A 3. Ht 9 cm.
Photo: Chuzeville
B] Standing goddess. Excavated Pylos. 1420–1400 B.C. Pylos Museum. Lord W. Taylour, *The Mycenaeans* (London, 1964), 81, pl. 26. Ht 12·5 cm.
Photo: American School of Classical Studies
C] Throne. Excavated Argive Heraeum. 1400–1200 B.C. Athens, National Museum. Blegen, *Prosymna*, ii, fig. 619. Ht 13·5 cm.
Photo: Constantopoulos
D] Bull. Excavated Ialysus. 1400–1200 B.C. British Museum. Cat. no. B 3. L. 10·5 cm.
Photo: British Museum

E] Chariot-group. Excavated Ialysus. 1400–1200 B.C. British Museum. Cat. no. B 2. Ht 7·5 cm.
Photo: British Museum
F] Standing goddess, ϕ type. From Melos (?). 1400–1300 B.C. British Museum. Cat. no. B 12. Ht 8 cm.
Photo: British Museum
G] Standing goddess. τ type. From Athens. 1400–1200 B.C. British Museum. Cat. no. B 7. Ht 10 cm.
Photo: British Museum
H] Standing goddess, ψ type. From Athens. 1300–1200 B.C. British Museum. Cat. no. B 5. Ht 10·5 cm.
Photo: British Museum

5. LATE MINOAN AND MYCENAEAN, 1500–1100 B.C. *pages 11–16*
A] Bull (rhyton). Excavated Pseira. 1500–1450 B.C. Heraclion Museum. Marinatos and Hirmer, pl. 90 (top). L. 25·5 cm.
Photo: Hirmer Verlag
B] Horse. Excavated Ialysus. Twelfth century B.C. Rhodes Museum. *Ann.* xiii–xiv (1930–1), 295. Ht 24 cm.
Photo: Rhodes Museum
C] Bull. Excavated Phaestos. Twelfth century B.C. Heraclion Museum. Marinatos and Hirmer, pl. 134 (bottom). Ht 37 cm.
Photo: Hirmer Verlag
D] Goddess. Excavated Gazi. Twelfth century B.C. Heraclion Museum. Marinatos and Hirmer, pl. 130. Ht 77·5 cm.
Photo: Hirmer Verlag

6. GREEK ISLANDS, TENTH TO EIGHTH CENTURIES B.C. *pages 17–20*
A, B] Centaur (vase). Excavated Cos, Fadil Cemetery (Tomb 7). Tenth century B.C. Cos Museum. No. 1104. Ht. 12·3 cm.
Photo: Prof. L. Morricone
C] Shrine. From Archanes, near Knossos. Late ninth century B.C. Heraclion Museum. Marinatos and Hirmer, pl. 139. Ht 22 cm.
Photo: Hirmer Verlag
D] Woman. Excavated Camirus. About 700 B.C. British Museum. Cat. no. 5. Ht 20 cm.
Photo: British Museum
E] Doll. Excavated Cos, Seraglio Cemetery (Tomb 14). Eighth century B.C. Cos Museum. No. 586. *Boll. d'Arte*, xxxv (1950), 320. Ht 15·6 cm.
Photo: Prof. L. Morricone
F] Woman. Excavated Samos. 720–700 B.C. Samos Museum. *AM* lxvi (1941), pl. 3, no. 873. Ht 18 cm.
Photo: German Archaeological Institute, Athens

7. ATTICA, TENTH TO EIGHTH CENTURIES B.C. *pages 20–23*

A] Woman. From Attica. Eighth century B.C. Oxford, Ashmolean Museum. No. 1934. 320. Ht 18 cm.
Photo: Ashmolean

B] Bird. From Athens. Eighth century B.C. Oxford, Ashmolean Museum. No. 1894. 13c. Ht 3·6 cm.
Photo: Ashmolean

C] Doll. Excavated Athens, Cerameicus. 925–900 B.C. Cerameicus Museum. *Kerameikos*, iv, pl. 31 (centre). Ht (without legs) 8·4 cm.
Photo: German Archaeological Institute, Athens

D] Stag (vase). Excavated Athens, Cerameicus. 925–900 B.C. Cerameicus Museum. *Kerameikos*, iv, pl. 26. Ht 26·6 cm.
Photo: German Archaeological Institute, Athens

E] Woman. From Eleusis. Eighth century B.C. Oxford, Ashmolean Museum. No. 1945. 327. Ht 15·8 cm.
Photo: Ashmolean

F, G] Seated goddess. Unknown provenance. Eighth century B.C. New York, Metropolitan Museum of Art, Fletcher Fund, 1931. Acc. no. 31.11.8. Ht 12·3 cm.
Photo: Metropolitan Museum

8. ATTICA, EIGHTH CENTURY B.C. *pages 22–23*

A] Mule with amphoras (toy). Unknown provenance. British Museum. Reg. no. 1921. 11–29.2. Ht 19 cm.
Photo: British Museum

B] Chariot-group. From Athens. Vienna, Kunsthistorisches Museum. No. V 399. Ht 30 cm.
Photo: Kunsthistorisches Museum

9. BOEOTIA AND LACONIA, EIGHTH CENTURY B.C. *pages 23–24*

A] Woman's head. Laconian. Excavated Amyclae. 720–700 B.C. Athens, National Museum. No. 4382. *AM* lv (1930), 156, Beil. XLII–XLIII. Ht 8 cm.
Photo: German Archaeological Institute, Athens

B] Man's head. Laconian. Excavated Amyclae. 720–700 B.C. Athens, National Museum. No. 4381. *AM* lv, as above. Ht 11·5 cm.
Photo: German Archaeological Institute, Athens

C] Doll. Boeotian. From Thebes. Eighth century B.C. Copenhagen, Danish National Museum. Cat. no. 110. Ht (without legs) 15 cm.
Photo: Danish National Museum

D] Doll. Boeotian. From Thebes. Late eighth century B.C. Paris, Louvre Museum. Cat. no. B 53. Ht 33 cm.
Photo: Chuzeville

E] Doll. Boeotian. Unknown provenance. Late eighth century B.C. Boston, Museum of Fine Arts, No. 98. 891. Total ht 30 cm. Ht without legs 23·5 cm.
Photo: Museum of Fine Arts

D] Standing goddess (scent-bottle?). From Etruria. Early sixth century B.C. Rome, Conservatori Museum. Castellani, iii, 20. Ht 20 cm.
Photo: Conservatori Museum

E] Standing goddess (scent-bottle). From Locri. 575–550 B.C. Amsterdam, Allard Pierson Museum. No. 1809. Ht 19 cm.
Photo: Allard Pierson Museum

F] Standing goddess (scent-bottle). Excavated Camirus. 575–550 B.C. British Museum. Cat. no. 49. Ht 23 cm.
Photo: British Museum

13. EASTERN GREECE, SIXTH CENTURY B.C. *pages 32–37*

A] Seated goddess (scent-bottle). Excavated Naucratis. 550–525 B.C. British Museum. Cat. no. 63. Ht 14 cm.
Photo: British Museum

B] Seated goddess. Excavated Camirus. Later sixth century B.C. British Museum. Cat. no. 68. Ht 14·5 cm.
Photo: British Museum

C] Kneeling boy (scent-bottle). Excavated Camirus. Late sixth century B.C. British Museum. Cat. no. 82. Ht 16 cm.
Photo: British Museum

D, E] Standing goddess (scent-bottle). Excavated Camirus. 550–525 B.C. British Museum. Cat. no. 57. Ht 26 cm.
Photos: British Museum

F] Standing goddess. Excavated Camirus. 550–525 B.C. British Museum. Cat. no. 58. Ht 25·5 cm.
Photo: British Museum

14. EASTERN GREECE, SIXTH CENTURY B.C. *pages 32–37*

A] Siren (scent-bottle). Excavated Camirus. 550–525 B.C. British Museum. Cat. no. 75. Ht 12·5 cm.
Photo: British Museum

B] Dwarf (scent-bottle). Excavated Camirus. 550–500 B.C. British Museum. Cat. no. 86. Ht 15 cm.
Photo: British Museum

C] Standing goddess (scent-bottle). Unknown provenance. 550–500 B.C. Oxford, Ashmolean Museum. No. G 4. Ht 20·8 cm.
Photo: Ashmolean

D] Standing man. From Rhodes. 550–500 B.C. Amsterdam, Allard Pierson Museum. No. 3580. Ht 19·5 cm.
Photo: Allard Pierson Museum

E] Standing goddess. From Sicily. Late sixth century B.C. The Hague, Schneider-Herrmann Collection. *Bull. Ant. Besch.*, xiv (1939), 3, fig. 1. Ht 24·5 cm.
Photo: Schneider-Herrmann

15. EASTERN GREECE AND ISLANDS, SEVENTH AND SIXTH CENTURIES B.C. *pages 37–41*

A] Dedalic plaque. Excavated Samos. Late seventh century B.C. Samos Museum. *AM* lxvi (1941), pl. 32, no. 496. Ht 11·5 cm.
Photo: German Archaeological Institute, Athens

B] Female head. Excavated Samos. Late seventh century B.C. Samos Museum. *AM* lxvi (1941), pl. 26, no. 723. Ht 7·5 cm.
Photo: German Archaeological Institute, Athens

C] Relief: man with dog. Lemnian. Unknown provenance. Late sixth century B.C. British Museum. Cat. no. 902 (incorrectly catalogued as Corinthian). Ht 10·5 cm.
Photo: British Museum

D] Seated goddess. Excavated Thasos. 600–550 B.C. *Archaeology*, xiii (1960), 101, fig. 8. Ht 17 cm.
Photo: French School at Athens

E] Dedalic plaque. Excavated Ephesus. Mid seventh century B.C. British Museum. Cat. no. 529. Ht 13 cm.
Photo: British Museum

F] Dedalic plaque. Excavated Ephesus. Late seventh century B.C. British Museum. Cat. no. 530. Ht 12·5 cm.
Photo: British Museum

G] Standing woman. Excavated Samos. Early sixth century B.C. Samos Museum. *AM* lxv (1941), pl. 35, no. 662. Ht 26·5 cm.
Photo: German Archaeological Institute, Athens

H] Female mourner. Excavated Thera. Mid seventh century B.C. Thera Museum. *AM* lxxiii (1958) Beil. 83. Ht 32 cm.
Photo: German Archaeological Institute, Athens

16. ATTICA, SIXTH CENTURY B.C. *pages 43–44*

Kneeling boy (scent-bottle). Excavated Athens, Agora. About 540 B.C. Agora Museum. *Hesperia*, vi (1937), 426, pl. X. Ht 25·5 cm.
Photo: Agora Excavations

17. ATTICA, SEVENTH AND SIXTH CENTURIES B.C. *pages 42–44*

A] Horse. Excavated Athens, Agora. Seventh century B.C. Agora Museum. No. T 204. *Hesperia*, ii (1933), 617, fig. 83. Ht 16·5 cm.
Photo: Agora Excavations

B] Female head. Excavated Athens, Agora. Mid seventh century B.C. Agora Museum. No. T 1203. *Hesperia*, vi (1937), 378, fig. 44. Ht 4·5 cm.
Photo: Agora Excavations

C] Warrior. Excavated Athens, Agora. Seventh century B.C. Agora Museum. No. T 194. *Hesperia*, ii (1933), 616, fig. 82. Ht 8·1 cm.
Photo: Agora Excavations

D] Mourning woman. Excavated Athens, Cerameicus. Early sixth century B.C. Cerameicus Museum. Karo, *An Attic Cemetery*, pl. 16. Ht 12·4 cm.
Photo: German Archaeological Institute, Athens

E] Seated woman. Excavated Athens. Cerameicus. 540–530 B.C. Cerameicus Museum. No. 682. Ht 23 cm.
Photo: German Archaeological Institute, Athens

18. BOEOTIA, SIXTH CENTURY B.C. *pages 45–46*

A, B] Standing goddess. Unknown provenance. Early sixth century B.C. British Museum. Cat. no. 765. Ht 16 cm.
Photos: British Museum

C] Standing goddess. From Tanagra. Mid sixth century B.C. British museum. Cat. no. 778. Ht 15 cm.
Photo: British Museum

D] Standing goddess. From Tanagra. Mid sixth century B.C. British Museum. Cat. no. 776. Ht 13 cm.
Photo: British Museum

E] Standing goddess. From Tanagra. Mid sixth century B.C. British Museum. Cat. no. 779. Ht 21 cm.
Photo: British Museum

F] Seated goddess. From Thebes. Late sixth century B.C. British Museum. Cat. no. 647 (incorrectly catalogued as Attic). Ht 23 cm.
Photo: British Museum

G] Standing goddess. From Tanagra. About 575 B.C. British Museum. Cat. no. 768. Ht 28 cm.
Photo: British Museum

19. BOEOTIA, SIXTH CENTURY B.C. *pages 45–46*

A, B] Seated goddess. From Tanagra. Early sixth century B.C. British Museum. Cat. no. 769. Ht 21 cm.
Photos: British Museum

C] Standing goddess. From Thebes. Late sixth century B.C. British Museum. Cat. no. 791. Ht 28 cm.
Photo: British Museum

D] Squatting monkey. From Lake Copais. Mid sixth century B.C. British Museum. Cat. no. 774. Ht 9 cm.
Photo: British Museum

E] Horseman. From Tanagra. Mid sixth century B.C. British Museum. Cat. no. 782. Ht 13·5 cm.
Photo: British Museum

F] Standing goddess. From Tanagra. About 600 B.C. Paris, Louvre Museum. Cat. no. B 100. Ht 18·5 cm.
Photo: Chuzeville

20. CORINTH, SEVENTH AND SIXTH CENTURIES B.C. *pages 47–49*

A] Seated woman. Excavated Corinth. Late seventh century B.C. Corinth Museum. *Corinth*, xv, pt 2, pl. 9, no. viii, 9. Ht 11·9 cm.
Photo: Corinth Excavations

B] Seated goddesses. From Thebes. Late seventh century B.C. British Museum. Cat. no. 897. Ht 16·5 cm.
Photo: British Museum

C] Standing woman. Excavated Perachora. 675–650 B.C. Athens, National Museum. *Perachora*, i, pl. 88, no. 15. Ht 16·4 cm.
Photo: British School at Athens

D] Seated woman. Excavated Solygeia. Mid sixth century B.C. Corinth Museum. *Archaeology*, xv (1962), 191. Ht 14 cm.
Photo: Tombazi

E] Standing woman. Excavated Camirus. Early sixth century B.C. British Museum. Cat. no. 898. Ht 17 cm.
Photo: British Museum

F] Seated woman. Excavated Solygeia. Mid sixth century B.C. Corinth Museum. *Archaeology*, xv (1962), 191. Ht 14 cm.
Photo: Tombazi

21. LACONIA AND ARGOS, SEVENTH AND SIXTH CENTURIES B.C. *pages 50–52*

A] Female head. Excavated Sparta, Acropolis. Early seventh century B.C. Athens, National Museum. Jenkins, *Dedalica*, pl. I:i. Ht 10·5 cm.
Photo: Hellenic Society

B] Dedalic plaque (lower part missing). Excavated Sparta, Orthia Sanctuary. About 660 B.C. British Museum. Cat. no. 1026. Ht 5 cm.
Photo: British Museum

C] Dedalic plaque (bust-length). Excavated Sparta, Orthia Sanctuary. Early seventh century B.C. British Museum. Cat. no. 1024. Ht 6·5 cm.
Photo: British Museum

D] Dedalic plaque (bust-length). Excavated Sparta, Orthia Sanctuary. Mid seventh century B.C. Oxford, Ashmolean Museum. No. 1923. 163. Ht 5·1 cm.
Photo: Ashmolean

E] Artemis standing (with lion). Excavated Sparta, Orthia Sanctuary. Late seventh century B.C. Sparta Museum. Dawkins, *Artemis Orthia*, pl. XXXII:2. Ht 14·17 cm.
Photo: Hellenic Society

F] Seated woman. Argive. From Boeotia. Mid sixth century B.C. Paris, Louvre Museum. Cat. no. B 75. Ht 25 cm.
Photo: Chuzeville

G] Plaque. Excavated Sparta, Orthia Sanctuary. About 600 B.C. Oxford, Ashmolean Museum. No. 1923. 164. Ht 7·7 cm.
Photo: Ashmolean

22. SICILY AND SOUTH ITALY, SEVENTH ABD SIXTH CENTURIES B.C. *pages 52–55*

A] Standing woman. Excavated Locri. Mid sixth century B.C. Reggio Museum. *Critica d'Arte*, vi (1941), pl. XXVIII, fig. 9 (right). Ht 17·5 cm.
Photo: Soprintendenza alle antichità della Calabria

B] Dedalic plaque. Excavated Metapontum. Late seventh century B.C. Reggio Museum. *JHS* lix (1939), 219, fig. 5. Ht 5·5 cm.
Photo: Helenic Society

C] Standing man. From Tarentum. Early sixth century B.C. Oxford, Ashmolean Museum. No. 1886. 744. *JHS* vii (1886), 25, fig. 3. Ht 14·5 cm.
Photo: Ashmolean

D] Standing man. Excavated Metapontum. Early sixth century B.C. Reggio Museum. *JHS* lix (1939), 221, fig. 6. Ht 14 cm.
Photo: Hellenic Society

E] Standing woman. From Sicily. Late sixth century B.C. British Museum. Cat. no. 1089. Ht 39 cm.
Photo: British Museum

F] Dedalic plaque. From Tarentum. Late seventh century B.C. Oxford, Ashmolean Museum No. 1886. 737. *JHS* vii (1886), 25, fig. 2. Ht 18 cm.
Photo: Ashmolean

23. CRETE (KNOSSOS), FIFTH AND FOURTH CENTURIES B.C. *pages 59–61*

A] Standing woman. Probably from Crete. Mid fourth century B.C. British Museum. Reg. no. 1953. 10–1.1. Ht 12·5 cm.
Photo: British Museum

B] Pitcher-bearer. Excavated Knossos. Mid fifth century B.C. Heraclion Museum. Ht 15 cm.
Photo: British School at Athens

C] Standing woman. Unknown provenance. Mid fourth century B.C. Paris, Cabinet des Médailles. No. L 1193. Ht 16·5 cm.
Photo: Cabinet des Médailles

D] Seated woman. 'From Asia Minor'. 450–400 B.C. British Museum. Cat. no. 567 (incorrectly catalogued as Aeolian). Ht 10·5 cm.
Photo: British Museum

E] Seated woman. Excavated Knossos. Early fourth century B.C. Heraclion Museum. Ht 10·5 cm.
Photo: British School at Athens
F] Seated woman. Unknown provenance. Early fourth century B.C. British Museum. Cat. no. 940 (incorrectly catalogued as Corinthian). Ht 12 cm.
Photo: British Museum

24. IONIA(?) AND RHODES, FIFTH CENTURY B.C. *pages 61–65*
A] Standing woman. Excavated Lindus. Ionian (?). Early fifth century B.C. Copenhagen, Danish National Museum. No. 10543. *Lindos*, i, no. 2147. Ht 14·6 cm.
Photo: Danish National Museum
B] Seated woman. Excavated Camirus. Rhodian. Early fifth century B.C. British Museum. Cat. no. 121. Ht 12 cm.
Photo: British Museum
C] Seated woman. Excavated Camirus. Rhodian. Late fifth century B.C. British Museum. Cat. no. 290. Ht 15 cm.
Photo: British Museum
D] Standing woman. Excavated Camirus. Rhodian. Early fifth century B.C. British Museum. Cat. no. 113. Ht 15 cm.
Photo: British Museum
E] Standing woman. Excavated Camirus. Rhodian. Mid fifth century B.C. British Museum. Cat. no. 206. Ht 23·5 cm.
Photo: British Museum
F] Standing woman. Excavated Camirus. Rhodian. Mid fifth century B.C. British Museum. Cat. no. 213. Ht 19 cm.
Photo: British Museum

25. RHODES, FIFTH AND FOURTH CENTURIES B.C. *pages 61–64*
A] Boy on mule. Excavated Camirus. Mid fifth century B.C. British Museum. Cat. no. 255. Ht 13 cm.
Photo: British Museum
B] Woman carrying basket. Excavated Lindus. Mid fourth century B.C. Copenhagen, Danish National Museum. No. 10780. *Lindos*, i, no. 3016. Ht 13 cm.
Photo: Danish National Museum
C] Negro boy. Excavated Camirus. Mid fifth century B.C. British Museum. Cat. no. 264. Ht 12 cm.
Photo: British Museum
D] Woman with child. Excavated Lindus. Mid fourth century B.C. Copenhagen, Danish National Museum. No. 10765. *Lindos*, i, no. 2991. Ht 14·5 cm.
Photo: Danish National Museum

E] Woman dancing. Excavated Lindus. Mid fourth century B.C. Copenhagen, Danish National Museum. No. 10755. *Lindos*, i, no. 2971. Ht 13·5 cm.
Photo: Danish National Museum
F] Man standing. Excavated Lindus. About 380 B.C. Copenhagen, Danish National Museum. No. 10718. *Lindos*, i, no. 2875. Ht 15·6 cm.
Photo: Danish National Museum

26. RHODES, FIFTH CENTURY B.C. *page 64*
A] Female protome. Excavated Camirus. About 500 B.C. British Museum. Cat. no. 134. Ht 24·5 cm.
Photo: British Museum
B] Female protome. Excavated Camirus. Early fifth century B.C. British Museum. Cat. no. 139. Ht 30 cm.
Photo: British Museum
C] Female protome. Unknown provenance. Mid fifth century B.C. British Museum. Cat. no. 239. Ht 36 cm.
Photo: British Museum
D] Female protome. Excavated Camirus. Late fifth century B.C. British Museum. Cat. no. 294. Ht 18 cm.
Photo: British Museum

27. HALICARNASSUS, ETC., FIFTH AND FOURTH CENTURIES B.C. *pages 65–69*
A] Standing woman. Excavated Halicarnassus. Early fifth century B.C. British Museum. Cat. no. 336. Ht 15·5 cm.
Photo: British Museum
B] Standing man. From Cos. Early fifth century B.C. British Museum. Cat. no. 345. Ht 11·5 cm.
Photo: British Museum
C] Seated woman with child. From Calymna. Early fourth century B.C. British Museum. Cat. no. 460. Ht 11 cm.
Photo: British Museum
D] Standing woman. Excavated Halicarnassus. Mid fourth century B.C. British Museum. Cat. no. 495. Ht 14·5 cm.
Photo: British Museum
E] Standing man. Excavated Halicarnassus. Mid fifth century B.C. British Museum. Cat. no. 364. Ht 17 cm.
Photo: British Museum
F] Pitcher-bearer. Excavated Halicarnassus. Late fifth century B.C. British Museum. Cat. no. 391. Ht 21 cm.
Photo: British Museum

G] Pitcher-bearer. Excavated Halicarnassus. Late fifth century B.C. British Museum. Cat. no. 408. Ht 17 cm.
Photo: British Museum
H] Standing man. Excavated Halicarnassus. Late fifth century B.C. British Museum. Cat. no. 433. Ht 13·5 cm.
Photo: British Museum

28. MELIAN RELIEFS, MID FIFTH CENTURY B.C. *page 70*
A] Peleus and Thetis. Excavated Camirus. British Museum. Cat. no. 615. Ht 17 cm.
Photo: British Museum
B] Eos and Kephalos. Excavated Camirus. British Museum. Cat. no. 614. Ht 16 cm.
Photo: British Museum

29. ATTICA, 500 B.C. *page 72*
Seated goddess. From Athens. Berlin, Staatliche Museen. TC 2493. Ht 23 cm.
Photo: Staatliche Museen

30. ATTICA, FIFTH CENTURY B.C. *pages 72–76*
A] Female half-figure. Excavated Athens, Cerameicus. Mid fifth century B.C. Cerameicus Museum. Karo, *An Attic Cemetery*, pl. 24. Ht 15·4 cm.
Photo: German Archeological Institute, Athens
B] Doll. Unknown provenance. Mid fifth century B.C. Copenhagen, Danish National Museum. No. 12952. Ht 15·5 cm.
Photo: Danish National Museum
C] Seated woman. From Thebes. Mid fifth century B.C. Oxford, Ashmolean Museum. No. 1893. 95. Ht 21·3 cm.
Photo: Ashmolean
D] Standing woman. Excavated Athens, Acropolis. About 500 B.C. Acropolis Museum. Cat. no. 3. Ht 31·5 cm.
Photo: Hellenic Society
E] Standing woman. From Aegina. About 450 B.C. British Museum. Cat. no. 669. Ht 24 cm.
Photo: British Museum
F] Standing woman. From Lake Copais. About 440 B.C. British Museum. Cat. no. 674. Ht 23 cm.
Photo: British Museum

31. ATTICA, FIFTH AND FOURTH CENTURIES B.C. *pages 72–76*
A] Comic actor as woman. From Athens. Mid fourth century B.C. British Museum. Cat. no. 746. Ht 14 cm.
Photo: British Museum
B] Comic actor. Excavated Knossos. Mid fourth century B.C. Heraclion Museum. Ht 9·7 cm.
Photo: British School at Athens

C] Doll. From Athens. Mid fourth century B.C. British Museum. Cat. no. 734. Ht (complete) 19 cm.
Photo: British Museum
D] Standing woman. From Melos. Mid fourth century B.C. British Museum. Cat. no. 726. Ht 15·5 cm.
Photo: British Museum
E] Seated woman. From Athens. About 400 B.C. Paris, Louvre Museum. Cat. no. C 5. Ht 13 cm.
Photo: Chuzeville
F] Woman carrying basket. Unknown provenance. Late fifth century B.C. Copenhagen, Danish National Museum. No. 12953. Ht 17·5 cm.
Photo: Danish National Museum

32. BOEOTIA, AROUND 500 B.C. *page 77*
A] Scribe. From Thebes. Paris, Louvre Museum. Cat. no. B 114. Ht 11 cm.
Photo: Chuzeville
B] Butcher. From Thebes. Paris, Louvre Museum. Cat. no. B 122. Ht 12 cm.
Photo: Chuzeville
C] Woman grinding corn. From Tanagra. Athens, National Museum. No. 4044. Ht 11·5 cm.
Photo: Alison Frantz
D] Cook. Unknown provenance. Berlin, Staatliche Museen. No. 31.464. Ht 10 cm.
Photo: Staatliche Museen
E] Woman holding pan with cakes. From Tanagra. Athens, National Museum. No. 4756. Ht 14·5 cm.
Photo: Alison Frantz
F] Carpenter. Unknown provenance. Copenhagen, Danish National Museum. Cat. no. 157. Ht 8·5 cm.
Photo: Danish National Museum
G] Horse and rider. From Tanagra. British Museum. Cat. no. 805. Ht 11 cm.
Photo: British Museum

33. BOEOTIA, FIFTH CENTURY B.C. *pages 77–80*
A] Cock-horse. From Thebes. Early fifth century B.C. Paris, Louvre Museum. Cat. no. B 108. Ht 15 cm.
Photo: Chuzeville
B] Man on goose. From Tanagra. Early fifth century B.C. British Museum. Cat. no. 806. Ht 12 cm.
Photo: British Museum
C] Standing woman. Unknown provenance. Mid fifth century B.C. British Museum. Cat. no. 816. Ht 30 cm.
Photo: British Museum

D] Standing woman. From Lake Copais. Late fifth century B.C. British Museum. Cat. no. 846. Ht 38·5 cm.
Photo: British Museum
E] Standing youth. From Thespiae. Mid fifth century B.C. British Museum. Cat. no. 825. Ht 25·5 cm.
Photo: British Museum

34. BOEOTIA, FOURTH CENTURY B.C. *pages 77–80*
A] Aphrodite. From Lake Copais. About 380 B.C. British Museum. Cat. no. 864. Ht 22 cm.
Photo: British Museum
B] Artemis. Unknown provenance. Mid fourth century B.C. British Museum. Cat. no. 889. Ht 20 cm.
Photo: British Museum
C] Woman dancing. Unknown provenance. Mid fourth century B.C. British Museum. Cat. no. 881. Ht 19 cm.
Photo: British Museum
D] Leda. From Athens. Mid fourth century B.C. British Museum. Cat. no. 880. Ht 26 cm.
Photo: British Museum
E] Youth with dogs. Unknown provenance. About 380 B.C. British Museum. Cat. no. 871. Ht 32 cm.
Photo: British Museum
F] Standing woman. From Tanagra. About 350 B.C. Athens, National Museum. No. 4541. Ht 27·5 cm.
Photo: Alison Frantz

35. CORINTH, FIFTH AND FOURTH CENTURIES B.C. *pages 81–84*
A] Doll. From Corinth. Mid fourth century B.C. British Museum. Cat. no. 973. Total ht 18 cm.
Photo: British Museum
B] Seated woman. Excavated Corinth. Early fifth century B.C. Corinth Museum. *Corinth*, XV, pt 2, pl. 17, no. XI, 3. Ht 8·5 cm.
Photo: Corinth Excavations
C] Doll. From Corinth. Early fifth century B.C. British Museum. Cat. no. 909. Total ht 13 cm.
Photo: British Museum
D] Artemis. Unknown provenance. Early fifth century B.C. British Museum. Cat. no. 907. Ht 14 cm.
Photo: British Museum
E] Standing woman. Excavated Corinth. Early fifth century B.C. Corinth Museum. *Corinth*, XV, pt 2, pl. 15, no. X, 1. Ht 14·2 cm.
Photo: Corinth Excavations

F] Standing woman. From Melos. Early fifth century B.C. British Museum. Cat. no. 903. Ht 14 cm.
Photo: British Museum

36. CORINTH, FIFTH AND FOURTH CENTURIES B.C. *pages 81–84*

A] Relief: cock. From Melos. Early fifth century B.C. British Museum. Cat. no. 917. Ht 9 cm.
Photo: British Museum

B] Relief: gorgon. From Melos. Early fifth century B.C. Copenhagen, Danish National Museum. Cat. no. 244. Ht 7·5 cm.
Photo: Danish National Museum

C] Satyr with fox. From Aegina. Mid fifth century B.C. Copenhagen, Danish National Museum. Cat. no. 319. Ht 8·5 cm.
Photo: Danish National Museum

D] Comic actor. From Corinth. Mid fourth century B.C. British Museum. Cat. no. 963. Ht 12 cm.
Photo: British Museum

E] Squatting satyr. From Tanagra. Mid fifth century B.C. British Museum. Cat. no. 932. Ht 9·5 cm.
Photo: British Museum

F] Mule carrying fish. Fiom Tanagra. Mid fourth century B.C. British Museum. Cat. no. 968. Ht 11 cm.
Photo: British Museum

G] Seated girl. From Benghazi. Mid fourth century B.C. British Museum. Cat. no. 974. Ht 8 cm.
Photo: British Museum

H] Monkey with pestle. From Tanagra. Late fifth century B.C. British Museum. Cat. no. 958. Ht 9 cm.
Photo: British Museum

37. SICILY, FIFTH AND FOURTH CENTURIES B.C. *pages 85–87*

A] Seated woman. Unknown provenance. Early fifth century B.C. British Museum. Reg. no. 1956. 7–19.1. Ht 21·5 cm.
Photo: British Museum

B] Standing woman. Excavated Selinus. Early fourth century B.C. Palermo Museum. *MA* xxxii (1927), pl. LXXVII:1. Ht 22·5 cm.
Photo: Palermo Museum

C] Seated woman. Excavated Gela. Early fifth century B.C. British Museum. Cat. no. 1113. Ht 18 cm.
Photo: British Museum

D] Standing woman. From Camarina. 470–460 B.C. British Museum. Cat. no. 1143. Ht 19 cm.
Photo: British Museum

E] Standing woman. Excavated Selinus. Late fifth century B.C. Palermo Museum. *MA* xxxii (1927), pl. LXXIV:1. Ht 19·5 cm.
Photo: Palermo Museum
F] Standing woman. Unknown provenance. 450–440 B.C. British Museum. Cat. no. 1139. Ht 19 cm.
Photo: British Museum

38. LOCRI, FIFTH CENTURY B.C. *pages 88–90*
A] Seated woman. Excavated Medma. 480–460 B.C. Reggio Museum. *NS* 1913, Suppl., 92, fig. 104. Ht 39·5 cm.
Photo: Soprintendenza alle Antichità della Calabria
B] Relief: sacred chest. From Naples. 470–450 B.C. British Museum. Cat. no. 1226. Ht 16 cm.
Photo: British Museum
C] Relief: Persephone and Hades (made up of fragments and casts). From Locri. 480–460 B.C. Reggio Museum. *Atti Magna Grecia*, i (1954), pl. XXIII. Ht 26 cm.
Photo: Dr P. Zancani-Montuoro
D] Relief: Persephone, Hades and Dionysus (made up of fragments and casts). From Locri. 480–460 B.C. Reggio Museum. Ht 24 cm.
Photo: Dr P. Zancani-Montuoro

39. TARENTUM, FIFTH AND FOURTH CENTURIES B.C. *pages 90–91*
A] Reclining man. From Tarentum. Mid fourth century B.C. Oxford, Ashmolean Museum. No. 1886. 746. Ht 14 cm.
Photo: Ashmolean
B] Woman seated. Unknown provenance. Early fourth century B.C. British Museum. Cat. no. 1305. Ht 23 cm.
Photo: British Museum
C] Reclining man. From Tarentum. Early fifth century B.C. Paris, Louvre Museum. No. B 145. Ht 24 cm.
Photo: Chuzeville
D] Seated woman. From Tarentum. Early fifth century B.C. British Museum. Cat. no. 1235. Ht 23 cm.
Photo: British Museum

40. TARENTUM AND PAESTUM, FIFTH AND FOURTH CENTURIES B.C. *pages 90–93*
A] Aphrodite on goose. Tarentine. Unknown provenance. Early fourth century B.C. British Museum. Cat. no. 1308. Ht 18·5 cm.
Photo: British Museum
B] Seated woman. From Tarentum. Mid fifth century B.C. Paris, Louvre Museum. Cat. no. C 247. Ht. 19·5 cm.
Photo: Chuzeville

C] Standing man. From Paestum. About 400 B.C. Paris, Louvre Museum. Cat. no. C 574. Ht 24 cm.
Photo: Chuzeville
D] Standing woman. From Paestum. Late fifth century B.C. Paris, Louvre Museum. Cat. no. C 571. Ht 28·5 cm.
Photo: Chuzeville
E] Seated goddess (Hera). Paestum. Unknown provenance. About 400 B.C. British Museum. Reg. no. 1956. 7–19.2. Ht 22 cm.
Photo: British Museum
F] Hera Eilithyia. Excavated Foce del Sele, near Paestum. About 350 B.C. Paestum Museum. Ht 16·9 cm.
Photo: Paestum Museum

41. ATTICA, 330–200 B.C. *pages 99–101*
A] Seated girl. From Tanagra. British Museum. Cat. no. C 270. Ht 15 cm.
Photo: British Museum
B] Eros. From Athens. Late fourth century B.C. British Museum. Cat. no. C 22. Ht 55 cm.
Photo: British Museum
C] Seated boy. From Athens. British Museum. Cat. no. C 24. Ht 12·5 cm.
Photo: British Museum
D] Standing boy. Unknown provenance. British Museum. Reg. no. 1906. 10–19.1. Ht 15·5 cm.
Photo: British Museum
E] Standing woman. From Athens, Acropolis. Acropolis Museum. Cat. no. 1451. Ht 16·5 cm.
Photo: Alison Frantz
F] Standing woman. From Athens, Acropolis. Acropolis Museum. Cat. no. 1459. Ht 14 cm.
Photo: Alison Frantz

42. BOEOTIA, 330–200 B.C. *page 102*
A, B] Woman in outdoor dress. From Tanagra. British Museum. Cat. no. C 312. Ht 19 cm.
Photos: British Museum

43. BOEOTIA 330–200 B.C. *pages 101–103*
A] Woman seated (base restored). Unknown provenance. British Museum. Reg. no. 1940. 6–10.9. Ht 19 cm.
Photo: British Museum
B] Aphrodite seated on a rock. From Tanagra. British Museum. Cat. no. C 272. Ht 15·5 cm.
Photo: British Museum
C] Woman standing. From Tanagra. British Museum. Cat. no. C 305. Ht 15 cm.
Photo: British Museum
D] Woman standing. From Tanagra. British Museum. Cat. no. C 303. Ht 19·5 cm.
Photo: British Museum

E] Woman standing. From Tanagra. British Museum. Cat. no. C 304. Ht 17 cm.
Photo: British Museum

44. BOEOTIA, 330–200 B.C. *pages 101–103*

A] Woman playing knucklebones. From Tanagra. British Museum. Reg. no. 1909. 7–11.1. Ht 15 cm.
Photo: British Museum

B] Old nurse with child. From Tanagra. British Museum. Cat. no. C 279. Ht 11 cm.
Photo: British Museum

C] Woman standing, with fillet. From Tanagra. British Museum. Cat. no. C 311. Ht 20 cm.
Photo: British Museum

D] Grotesque fat woman. From Tanagra. British Museum. Cat. no. C 233. Ht 19 cm.
Photo: British Museum

E] Woman standing. From Tanagra. British Museum. Cat. no. C 255. Ht 30 cm.
Photo: British Museum

45. BOEOTIA, 330–200 B.C. *pages 101–103*

A] Boy standing. From Tanagra. British Museum. Cat. no. C 334. Ht 12 cm.
Photo: British Museum

B] Boy seated on a rock. From Tanagra. British Museum. Cat. no. C 274. Ht 20 cm.
Photo: British Museum

C] Boy standing. From Tanagra. British Museum. Reg. no. 1903. 5–18.2. Ht 13·5 cm.
Photo: British Museum

D] Boy standing. Unknown provenance. British Museum. Reg. no. 1920. 4–14.6. Ht 24 cm.
Photo: British Museum

E] Boy in petasos and himation. From Tanagra. British Museum. Cat. no. C 273. Ht 27 cm.
Photo: British Museum

F] Boy standing. From Tanagra. Boston, Museum of Fine Arts. No. 01.7816. Ht 29 cm.
Photo: Museum of Fine Arts

46. EUBOEA, THIRD CENTURY B.C. *pages 102–103*

A] Woman leaning against a pillar. From a tomb at Eretria. 275–250 B.C. Boston, Museum of Fine Arts. No. 98.893. Ht 39·4 cm.
Photo: Museum of Fine Arts

B, C] Four Erotes. From the same tomb as pl. 46A. 250–225 B.C. Boston, Museum of Fine Arts. Nos. 97.301, 304, 312, and 313. Hts 11, 9·8, 9·5, 9·7 cm.
Photos: Museum of Fine Arts

47. CORINTH, HELLENISTIC *page 104*

A] Man reclining. Excavated Corinth. Third century B.C. Corinth Museum. *Corinth*, xii, pl. 24, no. 293. Ht 7·6 cm.
Photo: Corinth Excavations

B] Thetis riding on a sea-monster. Unknown provenance. Late fourth century B.C. British Museum. Reg. no. 1907. 5–17.1. Ht 9 cm.
Photo: British Museum
C] Woman standing. From Corinth. Third century B.C. British Museum. Cat. no. C 7. Ht 26 cm.
Photo: British Museum
D] Boy riding. Excavated Corinth. Third century B.C. Corinth Museum. *Corinth*, xii, pl. 28, no. 315. Ht 7·7 cm.
Photo: Corinth Excavations
E] Boy riding. Excavated Corinth. Third century B.C. Corinth Museum. *Corinth*, xii, pl. 27, no. 314. Ht 8·2 cm.
Photo: Corinth Excavations
F] Girl with flower. Excavated Corinth. About 250 B.C. Corinth Museum. *Corinth*, xii, pl. 20, no. 239. Ht 13·8 cm.
Photo: Corinth Excavations

48. NORTH GREECE AND ISLANDS, HELLENISTIC *pages 104–107*
A] Boy. From Aegina. Third century B.C. British Museum. Cat. no. C 34. Ht 16·5 cm.
Photo: British Museum
B] Eros. From Samothrace. About 200 B.C. Samothrace Museum: *Archaeology*, xii (1959), 167, fig. 6. Ht 16·5 cm.
Photo: Samothrace Excavations
C] Asclepius. From Corcyra. First century A.D. British Museum. Cat. no. C 52. Ht 21 cm.
Photo: British Museum
D] Girl standing. From Aegina. Third century B.C. British Museum. Cat. no. C 36. Ht 11·5 cm.
Photo: British Museum
E] Eros and Adonis. From Samothrace. About 100 B.C. Samothrace Museum. *Archaeology*, xii (1959), 167, fig. 7. Ht 10·5 cm.
Photo: Alison Frantz
F] Attis seated on a rock. From Amphipolis. Second century B.C. British Museum. Cat. no. C 400. Ht 11·5 cm.
Photo: British Museum

49. CNIDUS AND ISLANDS, HELLENISTIC *pages 108–110*
A] Papposilenus. Excavated Cnidus. Late fourth century B.C. British Museum. Cat. no. C 473. Ht 10·5 cm.
Photo: British Museum
B] Woman dancing. Cretan (Knossian). Unknown provenance. Late fourth century B.C. British Museum. Cat. no. C 60. Ht 14·5 cm.
Photo: British Museum

C] Woman standing. From Knossos. Third century B.C. Heraclion Museum. Ht 17·5 cm.
Photo: British School at Athens

D] Pitcher-bearer. Excavated Cnidus. About 330 B.C. British Museum. Cat. no. C 422. Ht 19 cm.
Photo: British Museum

E] Standing woman. From Camirus, Rhodes. 330–200 B.C. British Museum. Cat. no. C 482. Ht 12·5 cm.
Photo: British Museum

F] Girl with hare. Cretan (made at Gortyn). Unknown provenance. Late fourth century B.C. British Museum. Reg. no. 1956. 2–14.1. Ht 26 cm.
Photo: British Museum

50. DELOS, EARLY FIRST CENTURY B.C. *pages 107–108*

A] Seated goddess. Excavated Delos. Delos Museum. *Délos*, xxiii, no. 382. Ht 44 cm.
Photo: French School at Athens

B] Seated goddess (or votary), naked. Excavated Rheneia. Mykonos Museum. Inv. no. 157 B. *Délos*, xxiii, no. 426. Ht 17·2 cm.
Photo: French School at Athens

C] Eros in Oriental costume. Excavated Delos. Delos Museum. *Délos*, xxiii, no. 364. Ht 25 cm.
Photo: French School at Athens

D] Standing woman. Excavated Delos. Delos Museum. *Délos*, xxiii, no. 615. Ht 35 cm.
Photo: French School at Athens

E] Standing woman. Excavated Delos. Delos Museum. *Délos*, xxiii, no. 301. Ht 40 cm.
Photo: French School at Athens

F] Aphrodite taking off her sandal. Excavated Delos. Delos Museum. *Délos*, xxiii, no. 472. Ht 35 cm.
Photo: French School at Athens

51. SMYRNA, 100 B.C.–A.D. 100 *pages 110–112*

A] Head of Zeus. Unknown provenance. British Museum. Reg. no. 1907. 5–19.10. Ht 8 cm.
Photo: British Museum

B] Head of Heracles. Unknown provenance. British Museum. Reg. no. 1907. 5–19.11. Ht 6 cm.
Photo: British Museum

C] Head of Doryphoros. From Smyrna. Copenhagen, Ny Carlsberg Glyptotek. Cat. no. 63. Ht 8·5 cm.
Photo: Ny Carlsberg Glyptotek

D] Zeus. From Smyrna. Paris, Louvre Museum. Ht 41·5 cm.
Photo: Chuzeville

E] Copy of Diadumenos. From Smyrna. New York, Metropolitan Museum of Art, Fletcher Fund, 1932. Acc. no. 32.11.2. Ht 29·2 cm.
Photo: Metropolitan Museum

52. SMYRNA, 100 B.C.–A.D. 100 *pages 110–112*

A] Head of Heracles. Unknown provenance. British Museum. Reg. no. 1907. 5–19.30. Ht 6 cm.
Photo: British Museum

B] Female head. Unknown provenance. British Museum. Reg. no. 1907. 5–19.42. Ht 5·5 cm.
Photo: British Museum

C] Female head. Unknown provenance. Late first century A.D. British Museum. Reg. no. 1907. 5–19.45. Ht 6 cm.
Photo: British Museum

D, E] Grotesque male figure. From Smyrna. Copenhagen, Ny Carlsberg Glyptotek. Cat. no. 55. Ht 24 cm.
Photos: Ny Carlsberg Glyptotek

F] Athlete (foot and base restored). From Asia Minor. British Museum. Cat. no. C 455. Total ht 33·5 cm.
Photo: British Museum

53. MYRINA, HELLENISTIC *pages 114–118*

A] Woman standing. Excavated Myrina. 100–50 B.C. Paris, Louvre Museum. Cat. (vol. ii), pl. 24e. MYR 29. Ht 49·5 cm.
Photo: Chuzeville

B] Woman standing. Excavated Myrina. 250–200 B.C. Paris, Louvre Museum. Cat. (vol. ii), pl. 124b. MYR 230. Ht 28 cm.
Photo: Chuzeville

C] Muse, playing a lyre. From Myrina. Early first century A.D. Boston, Museum of Fine Arts. No. 87, 380. Burr, *Boston Myrinas*, no. 106. Ht 32 cm.
Photo: Museum of Fine Arts

D] Aphrodite leaning against a statue. Signed by Aglaophon. From Myrina. Mid second century B.C. Boston, Museum of Fine Arts. No. 01.7751. Burr, *Boston Myrinas*, no. 10. Ht. 33·6 cm.
Photo: Museum of Fine Arts

E] Aphrodite crowning a herm of Dionysus. From Myrina. 125–100 B.C. British Museum. Cat. no. C 528. Ht 22·5 cm.
Photo: British Museum

54. MYRINA, HELLENISTIC *pages 114–118*

A] Man and woman on couch. Excavated Myrina. 150–100 B.C. Paris, Louvre Museum. Cat. (vol. ii), pl. 153d. MYR 268. Ht. 28 cm.
Photo: Chuzeville

B] Aphrodite, 'Venus Genitrix' type. From workshop of Diphilos. Excavated Myrina. Early first century A.D. Paris, Louvre Museum. Cat. (vol. ii), pl. 12a. MYR 28. Ht 29 cm.
Photo: Chuzeville

c] Flying Victory. From Myrina. Early second century B.C. Boston, Museum of Fine Arts, No. 01.7691. Burr, *Boston Myrinas*, no. 66. Ht 27·3 cm.
Photo: Museum of Fine Arts

D] Aphrodite putting on her necklace. Unknown provenance. Early first century A.D. British Museum. Reg. no. 1907. 3–10.1. Ht 27·5 cm.
Photo: British Museum

55. MYRINA, HELLENISTIC *pages 114–118*

A] Flying Eros. Excavated Myrina. 200–150 B.C. Paris, Louvre Museum. Cat. (vol. ii), pl. 47e. MYR 86. Ht 36 cm.
Photo: Chuzeville

B] Flying Eros. From Myrina. Mid second century B.C. Boston, Museum of Fine Arts. No. 01.7693. Burr, *Boston Myrinas*, no. 49. Ht 29·5 cm.
Photo: Museum of Fine Arts

c] Eros and Psyche. From Myrina, Early first century B.C. Boston, Museum of Fine Arts. No. 01.7700. Burr, *Boston Myrinas*, no. 15. Ht 32 cm.
Photo: Museum of Fine Arts

D] Eros with cornucopia. From Myrina. Mid first century B.C. Boston, Museum of Fine Arts. No. 00.322. Burr, *Boston Myrinas*, no. 18. Ht 37 cm.
Photo: Museum of Fine Arts

56. MYRINA, HELLENISTIC *pages 114–118*

A] 'Oriental Aphrodite', seated (left leg missing). From Myrina. First century B.C. British Museum. Cat. no. C 521. Ht 29 cm.
Photo: British Museum

B] Boy standing, with dog. Signed by Diphilos. From Myrina. Late first century B.C. British Museum. Cat. no. C 534. Ht 18·5 cm.
Photo: British Museum

c] Comic actor. Excavated Myrina. 50–1 B.C. Paris, Louvre Museum. Cat. (vol. ii), pl. 172d. MYR 320. Ht 16·5 cm.
Photo: Chuzeville

D] Dionysus. From Myrina. First century A.D. Boston, Museum of Fine Arts. No. 87.392. Burr, *Boston Myrinas*, no. 14. Ht 36·8 cm.
Photo: Museum of Fine Arts

E] Boy standing, with quiver. Signed by Diphilos. From Myrina. Early first century A.D. British Museum. Cat. no. C 537. Ht 23·5 cm.
Photo: British Museum

57. PRIENE, HELLENISTIC *pages 118–120*

A] Girl standing. Excavated Sanctuary of Demeter and Kore. Third century B.C. Berlin, Staatliche Museen. No. 8598. *Priene*, fig. 141. Ht 10·5 cm.
Photo: Staatliche Museen

B] Woman standing. Excavated Sanctuary of Demeter and Kore. Third century B.C. Berlin, Staatliche Museen. No. 8588. *Priene*, fig. 130. Ht 17 cm.
Photo: Staatliche Museen

C] Woman standing (head now missing). Excavated House 29. Mid second century B.C. Berlin, Staatliche Museen. No. 8553. *Priene*, fig. 416. Ht 44 cm.
Photo: Staatliche Museen

D] Woman standing. From Temple of Athena Polias. First century B.C. British Museum. Cat. no. C 451. Ht 48 cm.
Photo: British Museum

E] Woman standing. Excavated House 33E. First century B.C. Berlin, Staatliche Museen. No. 8624. *Priene*, fig. 420. Ht 17 cm.
Photo: Staatliche Museen

F] Woman standing. Signed by Gerasimos. Excavated House 16. First century B.C. Berlin, Staatliche Museen. No. 8625. *Priene*, fig. 370. Ht 20 cm.
Photo: Staatliche Museen

58. PRIENE, AMISOS AND EPHESUS, HELLENISTIC *pages 118–122*

A] Boy extracting thorn from foot. Excavated Priene, House 33E. First century B.C. Berlin, Staatliche Museen. No. 8626. *Priene*, fig. 434. Ht 17 cm.
Photo: Staatliche Museen

B] Centaur. Excavated Priene, House 13. Mid second century B.C. Berlin, Staatliche Museen. No. 8628. *Priene*, fig. 406. Ht 16·5 cm.
Photo: Staatliche Museen

C] Girl dancing. Signed by Theodotos. Excavated Priene, House 16. First century B.C. Berlin, Staatliche Museen. No. 8631. *Priene*, fig. 411. Ht 22 cm.
Photo: Staatliche Museen

D] Muse. From Amisos. Second century B.C. Paris, Louvre Museum. No. CA 1834. Ht 21·5 cm.
Photo: Chuzeville

E] The Ephesian Artemis. From Ephesus (?). First century B.C. or A.D. British Museum. Cat. no. C 452. Ht 23·5 cm.
Photo: British Museum

59. SICILY, SECOND AND FIRST CENTURIES B.C. *pages 124–125*

A] Plaque: Eros. From Centorbi. Second century B.C. British Museum. Cat. no. D 3. Ht 27 cm.
Photo: British Museum

B] Woman dancing. From Centorbi. Second century B.C. British Museum. Cat. no. D 11. Ht 28·5 cm.
Photo: British Museum

C] Aphrodite. From Centorbi. Second century B.C. British Museum. Cat. no. D 18. Ht 29 cm.
Photo: British Museum
D] Aphrodite carrying Eros. From Centorbi. Second century B.C. British Museum. Cat. no. D 21. Ht. 33·5 cm.
Photo: British Museum
E] Aphrodite removing her sandal. From near Palermo. Early first century B.C. British Museum. Reg. no. 1908. 4–11.1. Ht 26 cm.
Photo: British Museum

60. SOUTH ITALY, HELLENISTIC *pages 126–129*
A] Aphrodite Anadyomene. Unknown provenance. Second century B.C. British Museum. Reg. no. 47. 8–6.75. Ht 13·5 cm.
Photo: British Museum
B] Woman standing. From Canosa. Third century B.C. British Museum. Cat. no. D 109. Ht 23 cm.
Photo: British Museum
C] Woman dancing. From Canosa. Second century B.C. British Museum. Cat. no. D 120. Ht 34 cm.
Photo: British Museum
D] Woman seated. Unknown provenance. Second century B.C. British Museum. Cat. no. D 338. Ht 27 cm.
Photo: British Museum

61. SOUTH ITALY, HELLENISTIC *pages 126–129*
A] Woman playing knucklebones. From Capua. Later fourth century B.C. British Museum. Cat. no. D 161. Greatest ht 14 cm.
Photo: British Museum
B] Women leaning against pillar. From Capua. Third century B.C. British Museum. Cat. no. D 317. Ht 26·5 cm.
Photo: British Museum
C] Woman seated on a rock. From Ruvo. 330–200 B.C. British Museum. Cat. no. D 134. Ht 15 cm.
Photo: British Museum

62. EGYPT, 330–200 B.C. *pages 130–132*
A] Girl standing. From Cyrenaica. 330–300 B.C. British Museum. Cat. no. C 812. Ht 16 cm.
Photo: British Museum
B] Boy standing. Excavated Alexandria (Hadra Cemetery). Third century B.C. Alexandria, Graeco-Roman Museum. No. 21446. Cat. no. 109. Ht 16 cm.
Photo: Graeco-Roman Museum
C] Girl standing. Excavated Alexandria (Hadra Cemetery). 330–300 B.C. Alexandria, Graeco-Roman Museum. No. 21965. Cat. no. 121. Ht 12·5 cm.
Photo: Graeco-Roman Museum

D] Woman standing. Excavated Alexandria (Hadra Cemetery). 330–200 B.C. Alexandria, Graeco-Roman Museum. No. 9051. Cat. no. 21. Ht 27 cm.
Photo: Graeco-Roman Museum

E] Woman standing. Excavated Alexandria (Chatby Cemetery). 330–200 B.C. Alexandria, Graeco-Roman Museum. No. 17967. Cat. no. 23. Ht 18 cm.
Photo: Graeco-Roman Museum

F] Muse standing, playing a lute. Excavated Alexandria (Ibrahimieh Cemetery). 330-200 B.C. Alexandria, Graeco-Roman Museum. No. 9033. Cat. no. 83. Ht 24 cm.
Photo: Graeco-Roman Museum

63. EGYPT, 200 B.C.–A.D. 100 *page 132*

A] Bes. From Alexandria. First century A.D. British Museum. Cat. no. C 592. Ht 17 cm.
Photo: British Museum

B] Baubo. From the Fayoum. British Museum. Reg. no. 1926. 9–30.62. Ht 14·8 cm.
Photo: British Museum

C] Harpocrates on a ram. From Egypt. British Museum. Reg. no. 1928. 6–12.1. Ht 15 cm.
Photo: British Museum

D] Heracles. From the Fayoum. British Museum. Cat. no. C 587. Ht 32 cm.
Photo: British Museum

E] Aphrodite. From Naucratis. British Museum. Cat. no. C 574. Ht 38 cm.
Photo: British Museum

F] Isis. Unknown provenance. British Museum. Reg. no. 1936. 9–3.3. Ht 22 cm.
Photo: British Museum

64. CYRENAICA, HELLENISTIC *page 133*

A] Woman standing. From Benghazi. 330–200 B.C. British Museum. Cat. no. C 790. Ht 20 cm.
Photo: British Museum

B] Woman standing. From Cyrenaica. 330–200 B.C. British Museum. Cat. no. C 767. Ht 20 cm.
Photo: British Museum

C] Girl seated, writing. From Benghazi. 330–300 B.C. British Museum. Cat. no. C 718. Ht 16 cm.
Photo: British Museum

D] Woman dancing. From Benghazi. Second century B.C. British Museum. Cat. no. C 809. Ht 19 cm.
Photo: British Museum

E] Woman standing. From Cyrenaica. Second century B.C. British Museum. Cat. no. C 786. Ht 30·5 cm.
Photo: British Museum

F] Aphrodite leaning against a pillar. From Cyrenaica. Second century B.C. British Museum. Cat. no. C 797. Ht 30·5 cm.
Photo: British Museum

Acknowledgements

I should like to express my gratitude to Mrs Dorothy Burr Thompson for help at all stages of the book, and especially for reading the typescript of Chapter 8; to Mr Nicolas Coldstream for constant help in matters Geometric; to my colleagues Mr Denys Haynes and Dr Donald Strong for assistance on many doubtful points; and to my wife for her patience and forbearance at all times.

I am also grateful to heads of institutions for permission to publish photographs; acknowledgements are made individually in the list of plates. Many other people have helped me with information and with the provision of photographs. In particular I should like to thank:

Dr S. Alexiou, Mr D. M. Bailey, Mr Hollis Baker, Mr W. R. Biers, Prof. C. W. Blegen, Mr John Boardman, Prof. J. L. Caskey, Dr H. W. Catling, Prof. R. M. Cook, Prof. G. Daux, Mrs Poly Demoulini, Dr Erika Diehl, Mrs Elsbeth Dusenbery, Dr G. Foti, Miss Alison Frantz, Dr U. Gehrig, Dr Emilie Haspels, Dr M. Hirmer, Prof. A. Laumonier, Mme Simone Mollard-Besques, Dr L. Morricone, Dr G. Neumann, Dr R. Noll, Mr A. Oliver, Dr C. Pietrangeli, Dr H. Riad, Mrs Helle Salskov Roberts, Mrs G. Schneider-Herrmann, Miss Barbara Smith, Mr R. Stroud, Lord William Taylour, Dr V. Tusa, Dr N. Verdelis, Dr C. C. Vermeule, Dr K. Vierneisel, Dr Paola Zancani-Montuoro, Mlle Simone Weill, and Dr C. Zervos.

The text figures have been drawn by Miss Aldine Leith, for whose skill and understanding I am extremely grateful; the map of the Greek World was drawn by Peter Turner.

Abbreviations

AA: *Archäologischer Anzeiger*. Supplement to *JdI*.
Acc.: Accession.
Acrop. Mus. Cat. ii: S. Casson, and others, *Catalogue of the Acropolis Museum*, ii (Cambridge, 1921).
ADelt: *'Αρχαιολογικὸν Δελτίον*.
AE: *'Αρχαιολογικὴ 'Εφημερίς*.
Aegean and Near East: S. S. Weinberg (ed.), *The Aegean and the Near East. Studies Presented to Hetty Goldman* (New York, 1956).
AJA: *American Journal of Archaeology*.
AM: *Mitteilungen des Deutschen Archäologischen Instituts; Athenische Abteilung*.
Ann.: *Annuario d. R. Scuola Archeologica di Atene*.
Antike Plastik: *Antike Plastik. Walther Amelung zum sechzigsten Geburtstag* (Berlin, Leipzig, 1928).
Arch. Rep.: *Archaeological Reports*. Supplement to *JHS* (from 1955).
Atti Magna Grecia: *Atti e memorie della Società Magna Grecia*.

BCH: *Bulletin de Correspondance Hellénique*.
Blegen, *Prosymna*: C. W. Blegen, *Prosymna* (Cambridge, 1937).
Blegen, *Zygouries*: C. W. Blegen, *Zygouries* (Cambridge, Mass., 1928).
BMC (1903): H. B. Walters, *Catalogue of the Terracottas in the Dept. of Greek and Roman Antiquities, British Museum* (London, 1903).
BMC i, ii: R. A. Higgins, *Catalogue of the Terracottas in the Dept. of Greek and Roman Antiquities, British Museum*, i, ii (London, 1954, 1959).
B. Metr. Mus.: *Bulletin of the Metropolitan Museum of Art, New York*.
BMQ: *British Museum Quarterly*.
Boardman, *Cretan Collection*: J. Boardman, *The Cretan Collection in Oxford. The Dictaean Cave and Iron Age Crete* (Oxford, 1961).
Boll. d'Arte: *Bolletino d'Arte*.

BSA: *Annual of the British School at Athens.*
Bull. Ant. Besch.: *Bulletin van de Vereeniging tot Bevordering der Kennis van de Antieke Beschaving.*
Burr, *Boston Myrinas*: D. Burr, *Terracottas from Myrina in the Museum of Fine Arts, Boston* (Vienna, 1934).
Buschor, *Altsam. Standbild.*: E. Buscher, *Altsamische Standbilder* (Berlin, 1934–60).

Cl. Rh.: *Clara Rhodos. Studi e Materiali pubblicati a cura dell' Istituto Storico-archeologico di Rodi.*
Corinth: *Corinth. Results of Excavations Conducted by the American School of Classical Studies at Athens* (in progress).

Dawkins, Artemis Orthia: R. M. Dawkins and others, *The Sanctuary of Artemis Orthia at Sparta* (*JHS* Suppl. Paper no. 5).
Délos, xxiii: École française d'Athènes, *Exploration archéologique de Délos*, xxiii. H. A. Laumonier, *Les figurines de terre cuite* (Paris, 1956).

Ergon: *Τὸ ἔργον τῆς ἀρχαιολογικῆς ἑταιρείας.*
Evans, *Palace*: A. Evans, *The Palace of Minos at Knossos*, i–iv (London, 1921–35).

Furtwängler, *Aegina*: A. Furtwängler and others, *Aegina, das Heiligtum der Aphaia* (Munich, 1906).

Grace, *Arch. Sc. Boeo.*: F. R. Grace, *Archaic Sculpture in Boeotia* (Cambridge, Mass., 1939).

Hogarth, *Ephesus*: D. G. Hogarth and others, *Excavations at Ephesus. The Archaic Artemisia* (London, 1908).

ILN: *The Illustrated London News.*
Ist. Mitt.: *Istanbuler Mitteilungen.*

JdI: *Jahrbuch des deutschen archäologischen Instituts.*
Jenkins, *Dedalica*: R. J. H. Jenkins, *Dedalica. A Study of Dorian Plastic Art in the Seventh Century B.C.* (Cambridge, 1936).
JHS: *Journal of Hellenic Studies.*

Karo, *An Attic Cemetery*: G. Karo, *An Attic Cemetery. Excavations in the Kerameikos at Athens* (Philadelphia, 1943).
Kerameikos: *Kerameikos. Ergebnisse der Ausgrabungen* (Berlin, in progress).
Kleiner, *Tanagrafiguren*: G. Kleiner, *Tanagrafiguren* (15tes Ergänzungsheft, *JdI*, Berlin, 1942).
Knoblauch: P. Knoblauch, *Studien zur archaisch-griechischen Tonbildnerei in Kreta, Rhodos, Athen, u. Boeotien* (Bleicherode, 1937).
Kr. Chr.: *Κρητικὰ Χρονικά.*

Langlotz and Hirmer: E. Langlotz, M. Hirmer, *The Art of Magna Graecia* (London, 1965).
Laumonier, *Madrid Tc*: A. Laumonier, *Catalogue de terres cuites du Musée Archéologique de Madrid* (Bordeaux, Paris, 1921).
Lawrence, *Classical Sculpture*: A. W. Lawrence, *Classical Sculpture* (London, 1929).
Levi, *Tc Napoli*: A. Levi, *Le terrecotte figurate del Mus. Naz. di Napoli* (Florence, 1926).
Lindos: C. Blinkenberg, *Lindos, Fouilles de l'Acropole*, 1902–14, *i*, *Les petits objets* (Berlin, 1931).
Louvre Cat.: S. Mollard-Besques, *Musée National du Louvre: Catalogue raisonné des figurines et reliefs en terre cuite grecs, étrusques et romains*, i (Paris, 1954), ii (Paris, 1963).

MA: *Monumenti antichi pubblicati per cura della Reale Accademia dei Lincei.*
Marinatos and Hirmer: S. Marinatos, M. Hirmer, *Crete and Mycenae* (London, 1960).
Maximova, *Vases plastiques*: M. I. Maximova, *Les vases plastiques dans l'antiquité* (Paris, 1927).
Mendel: G. Mendel, *Catalogue des figurines grecques de terre cuite, Musées impériaux ottomans* (Constantinople, 1908).
Minns, *Scythians and Greeks*: E. H. Minns, *Scythians and Greeks* (Cambridge, 1913).
MMS: *Metropolitan Museum Studies.*
Mollard-Besques, *Tc grecques*: S. Mollard-Besques, *Les terres cuites grecques* (Paris, 1963).
Mon. Piot: *Fondation Piot, monuments et mémoires.*

Neutsch, *Studien*: B. Neutsch, *Studien zur vortanagraisch-attischen Koroplastik* (Berlin, 1952).
Nilssen, *MMR*: M. P. Nilssen, *The Minoan-Mycenaean Religion and its Survival in Greek Religion* (Lund, 1950).
NS: *Notizie degli scavi di antichità communicate alla Reale Accademia dei Lincei.*

Olynthus: *Excavations at Olynthus* (Baltimore, in progress).

PAE: *Πρακτικὰ τῆς Ἀρχαιολογικῆς Ἑταιρείας.*
Palaikastro: R. C. Bosanquet, R. M. Dawkins, *The Unpublished Objects from the Palaikastro Excavations, 1902–1906*) (British School at Athens, Suppl. Paper no. 1, London, 1923).
Pendlebury, *AC*: J. D. S. Pendlebury, *The Archaeology of Crete* (London, 1939).
Perachora, i: H. G. G. Payne and others, *Perachora, The Sanctuaries of Hera Akraia and Limenia* (Oxford, 1940).
Poulsen, *Strenge Stil*: V. H. Poulsen, *Der Strenge Stil* (Acta Archaeologica, viii, 1937).
Priene: T. Wiegand, H. Schrader, *Priene, Ergebnisse der Ausgrabungen u. Untersuchungen in den Iahren 1895–1898* (Berlin, 1904).

RA: *Revue Archéologique.*
RE: Pauly, Wissowa, Kroll, *Realencyclopädie der classischen Altertumswissenschaft* (Stuttgart, in progress).
Reg.: Registration.

Richter, *Furniture*: G. M. A. Richter, *The Furniture of the Greeks, Etruscans and Romans*, 2nd ed. (London, 1966).
RM: *Mitteilungen des deutschen archäologischen Instituts: Römische Abteilung.*

Sieveking, *Samml. Loeb*: J. Sieveking, *Die Terrakotten der Sammlung Loeb*, i, ii (Munich, 1916).

Tarsus: H. Goldman, *Excavations at Gözlü Kule, Tarsus*, i (Princeton, 1950).
Thera: H. von Gaertringen (ed.), *Thera: Untersuchungen, Vermessungen u. Ausgrabungen* (Berlin, 1899–1909).
Thompson, *Troy Tcs*: D. B. Thompson, *Troy. Supplementary Monograph 3: The Terracotta figurines of the Hellenistic Period* (Princeton, 1963).
Tsountas, *Dimini and Sesklo*: C. Tsountas, *Αἱ προιστορικαὶ ἀκροπόλεις Διμηνίου καὶ Σέσκλου* (Athens, 1908).
Ure, *Aryballoi*: P. N. Ure, *Aryballoi and Figurines from Rhitsona in Boeotia* (Cambridge, 1934).

Wace, *Chamber Tombs*: A. J. B. Wace, *Chamber Tombs of Mycenae* (*Archaeologia*, lxxxii, 1932).
Waldstein, *Argive Heraeum*: C. Waldstein, *The Argive Heraeum* (Boston, New York, 1902–5).
Winter: F. Winter, *Die Typen der figürlichen Terrakotten* (*Die antiken Terrakotten*, iii, Berlin, Stuttgart, 1903).

Zanotti-Bianco: U. Zanotti-Bianco, *La Magna Grecia* (Genoa, 1964).
Zervos, *Crète*: C. Zervos, *L'Art de la Crète Néolithique et Minoenne* (Paris, 1956).

Note on Orthography

The rendering of Greek proper nouns is based on the system recommended in *JHS* lxvii (1947), pp. xix f., and *BSA* xliv (1949), 330 f. Where a recognized Latin form exists, I have used it; in other cases I have used the Greek form; in yet others (where the ancient name is not known), I have used the modern place-name. Consistency, however, is not seldom sacrificed to familiarity or euphony.

Introduction

DEFINITION

The term terracotta is confined in this survey principally to statuettes or figurines (the words are used synonymously) and small reliefs of fired clay. Statues and architectural decoration in this medium, being substantially different both in conception and in execution, have not been included. Plastic vases have been considered only in cases where they appear to have had a direct bearing on the development of figurines proper; in general, their utilitarian purpose puts them in the category of pottery rather than figurines.

USE

Our sources of information for the use of terracottas in antiquity are fourfold: ancient texts; representations in ancient works of art; the circumstances in which terracottas have been found; and the evidence of the objects themselves.

A] We learn from ancient sources that the maker of terracottas was known as a *koroplathos* or *koroplastes*, a term rendered in English as *coroplast*; he was held in low esteem, and his wares were used principally as playthings for children. Plato also tells us that statuettes, of unspecified material, were offered to the nymphs in rustic shrines.

B] The evidence from works of art is equally scanty; indeed, before the fifth century B.C. it is non-existent. In the later fifth century girls and young women are represented on tombstones as holding dolls very like surviving examples in terracotta, and in a vase-painting of about 400 B.C. figurines, apparently of terracotta, are shown offered to the attendant nymphs of a fountain.

C] The evidence from find-spots, comprising tombs, sanctuaries, houses, and factory-sites, is more plentiful. The best preserved of surviving terracottas come from tombs, but their precise function in the tomb is seldom clear, since personal possessions of any kind were considered suitable for burial with the dead. Certain figures of mourners and genre pieces are however exceptional in suggesting a specifically funerary purpose. An analysis of the contents of nearly 600 tombs at Olynthus, of the fifth and fourth centuries B.C., is informative. Terracottas were present in only 62 of the tombs. They were slightly more common in children's than in adults' tombs; when present in children's tombs, were often present in large numbers.

Terracottas were dedicated as votive offerings in sanctuaries and when they became too numerous, were taken out, broken (in most cases) to prevent re-use, and buried in trenches nearby. Frequently the needs of the sanctuary were satisfied from a factory on the spot. One such has been discovered at Acragas by the temple, and the presence of others may be deduced elsewhere, as for example at Halicarnassus, from the uniform (and sometimes unique) character of the offerings.

On the rare occasions when houses have been excavated, terracottas have often been discovered in plenty, and it has been plausibly suggested that they had occupied domestic shrines.

Factory-sites, although informative in other respects, can tell us nothing about the use of terracottas in the ancient world.

D] Internal evidence can to a limited extent supplement the rather sketchy picture obtained by other means. The purpose of some terracottas is clear; they were scent-bottles, incense burners, dolls, toys, or decorative reliefs. But what of the pure figurine? A study of the favourite types, in order of popularity, may help to supply an answer.

Young women come first, followed by girls, men and boys, animals, birds and fruit. In early times we would probably be right in seeing a religious significance in all these figures, but from the seventh century B.C. onwards we increasingly meet male and female figures which appear all too human, side by side with others of whose divine or religious nature there can be no doubt. Among the former we may number such human documents as the gossiping women of the Frontispiece, and also a specialized class of mourning figures and genre scenes (e.g. pls. 11D and 32), whose purpose must have been, like Egyptian *ushabti* figures, to do some symbolic service to the dead.

It is not possible to find a formula which will account for every kind of figurine, and the search would probably be unnecessary. The ancient Greeks were probably no more rational or consistent in their religious and social customs than we are today.

METHODS OF CLASSIFICATION

A] *Chronology*. Terracottas can usually be dated when found with vases; securely, when in tombs or houses, less securely in votive deposits or wells. Sometimes a *terminus post quem* is provided by the known foundation-date of a city (such as Alexandria in 331 B.C.) or a sanctuary; a *terminus ante quem* by a known destruction-date, such as that of Athens in 480 B.C., of Olynthus in 348 B.C., of Corinth in 146 B.C., and of Pompeii in A.D. 79.

Finally they may be dated on internal evidence. Coroplasts' signatures, first found in the Hellenistic period, can be helpful, but in some cases refer to a firm rather than to an individual craftsman. Styles of hairdressing are very useful in the first century A.D.; and other terracottas, sculptures, vase-paintings and coins are all helpful criteria.

So far as absolute chronology is concerned, dates are very approximate before about 700 B.C., and it is often preferable for the early periods to use sequence-dating in place of absolute chronology. The correlation of archaeological with real dates would be somewhat as follows:

CRETE

Neolithic	6000–3000 B.C.
Early Minoan I	3000–2500 B.C.
II	2500–2200 B.C.
III	2200–2000 B.C.
Middle Minoan I	2000–1900 or 1700 B.C.
II (Palaces only)	1900–1700 B.C.
III	1700–1550 B.C.
Late Minoan I A	1550–1500 B.C.
B	1500–1450 B.C.
II (Knossos only)	1450–1400 B.C.
III A	1400–1300 B.C.
B	1300–1200 B.C.
C	1200–1100 B.C.
Subminoan	1100–1000 B.C.

Then as for Mainland Greece

MAINLAND GREECE

Neolithic	7000–3000 B.C.
Early Helladic	3000–2000 B.C.
Middle Helladic	2000–1550 B.C.
Late Helladic (or Mycenaean) I	1550–1500 B.C.
II	1500–1400 B.C.
III A	1400–1300 B.C.
B	1300–1200 B.C.
C	1200–1050 B.C.[1]
Protogeometric	1050 – 900 B.C.
Geometric	900 – 700 B.C.

[1] Including, in some districts, Submycenaean (1100–1050 B.C.).

CYCLADES

Early Cycladic	3000–2000 B.C.
Middle Cycladic	2000–1550 B.C.

Then as for Mainland Greece

B] *Attribution.* Regional studies have made it clear that most terracottas were made not far from where they were found. Find-spots are thus the principal means of attribution. Another aid is clay, which was (and is) so common in Greece that virtually every major community could count on possessing suitable supplies within its boundaries. Thus, when a local fabric has been identified, by whatever means, it is frequently possible to add to this nucleus other pieces, of unknown origin, from the character of the clay of which they are made. Sometimes, too, the clay of terracottas corresponds with that of the vases of the same region; Corinth provides a noteworthy example of such a correspondence.

Although it is extremely difficult to communicate in print a description of the colour and texture of the various terracotta fabrics, the attempt has been made in this volume. It will usually be found when a fabric is first mentioned, and will not be given in subsequent chapters unless, as sometimes happens, the character of the clay differs in different periods.

Style may also be a criterion of origin. The distinctive wares of Boeotia, Sicily or Tarentum in the Classical period are easily identified in this way: but in periods of cultural uniformity, such as the Mycenaean and Hellenistic ages, this criterion breaks down.

Certain technical tricks may also betray the origin of a terracotta, such as the absence of a back in Cretan work: the enormously large vents on Boeotian fifth and fourth century work and conversely, the absence of a vent on most Rhodian work; or the predilection for solid pieces in Corinth in the fifth and fourth centuries B.C.

Coroplasts' signatures provide another means of attribution.

NOTE ON DRESS

A] *The Bronze Age*

Women. Minoan and Mycenaean women wore a short-sleeved jacket cut so low in front as to leave the breasts exposed, and an ankle-length skirt decorated with flounces.

Men. Minoan men wore a loin-cloth with a frontal sheath, or a kilt, and high boots. Mycenaean men wore a simple tunic of wool or linen with short sleeves and a flaring skirt.

B] *The Iron Age*

After the Bronze Age, Greek garments were no longer tailored, but consisted of rectangular pieces of cloth draped to the figure and held in place with pins or brooches.

Women. The basic female garment was either the *peplos* or the *chiton*. The peplos (sometimes known as the Doric chiton) was a woollen garment pinned on both shoulders (fig. 1). The upper edge was folded over to form an *overfall* reaching to just above the

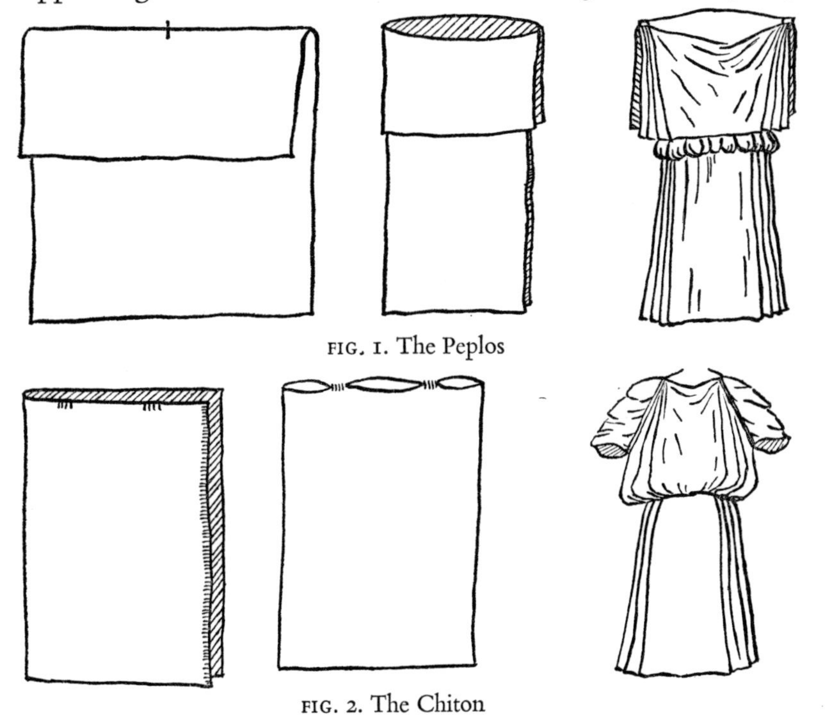

FIG. 1. The Peplos

FIG. 2. The Chiton

waist. Occasionally the garment was girdled and a fold of cloth drawn over the girdle to form the so-called *pouch* protruding below the overfall. A variation with a longer overfall, girdled outside, is known as the 'peplos of Athena'.

The chiton (sometimes known as the *Ionic chiton*) is a linen garment with sleeves (fig. 2). It was worn long by grown women, short by children.

As an outdoor garment the *himation* was worn over the chiton, less commonly over the peplos. It was usually draped over one shoulder, but there were other ways of wearing it.

When worn as on pl. 30D, it is referred to as a *transverse himation*.

The commonest form of headgear was the *sakkos*, a length of material wound several times round the head, and sometimes secured with tape. In the Hellenistic period an alternative was the sun-hat, a broad-brimmed straw hat much like that worn by Chinese coolies today. The *polos* was a cylindrical headdress worn in works of art by certain goddesses.

Men. The principal male garment was the *himation*, worn either long or short, and draped over one shoulder. It was usually the only garment. Another kind of cloak, worn by young men, warriors and horsemen, is the *chlamys*. It was fastened on the right shoulder with a brooch, and left the right side and most of the front of the body uncovered.

Men usually went bareheaded, but the *pilos*, a conical felt cap, was worn by soldiers and travellers. An alternative was the *petasos*, a floppy felt hat with a broad brim. A third kind of hat, the *kausia*, of Macedonian origin, was introduced into Greece in the later fourth century B.C. and was worn by young men and boys. In appearance it resembled a beret.

FORGERIES

It is not proposed to explain how forgeries of terracotta figurines are detected, since such a course would merely facilitate the task of future forgers. Suffice it to say that there are plenty of forgeries in this field, especially of Tanagra figures. There is also a whole class of elaborate mythological scenes which had a great vogue towards the end of last century as coming from Asia Minor, none of which are ancient.

In addition to outright forgeries, the collector must beware of defective pieces, made up with alien fragments or with plaster and heavily overpainted.

MUSEUMS

Most of the classes of figurines mentioned in this survey are well represented in the major Western European museums, such as the British Museum, the Louvre, and the Berlin Museums (East and West). In America, the Metropolitan Museum of Art, New York, and the Museum of Fine Arts, Boston, have good collections.

In Greece, the National Museum in Athens contains figurines excavated throughout Greece and the Islands, with the exception of Crete. That island is catered for principally by the Archaeological Museum at Heraclion, which (with the Ashmolean Museum in Oxford) houses almost all surviving Minoan material. Local museums in Greece and the Islands contain the results of local excavations, especially those of recent date.

In Italy, the National Museum at Naples contains figurines from throughout Southern Italy. Local museums in Southern Italy also house locally excavated material; Taranto and Reggio are particularly rich in figurines. In Sicily, good collections of figurines from sites on that island exist at Syracuse, Gela, Palermo, and elsewhere.

In Egypt, the Graeco-Roman Museum at Alexandria houses an excellent collection of Graeco-Egyptian and Romano-Egyptian figurines.

When reference is made in the text to the present whereabouts of certain classes of figurines the museum concerned is usually indicated by a reference merely to the city or town in which it is situated. Thus *London* means the British Museum; *Naples*, the National Museum at Naples, and so on.

These references to museums are usually given only when a particular fabric is first mentioned. They are not given in subsequent chapters unless there is a good reason.

CHAPTER I

Technical Processes

PRELIMINARIES

The getting and preparation of the clay, processes substantially unchanged to this day, have been frequently described in handbooks of pottery, and require little comment. Clay, to be workable, must be plastic; it must however contain sufficient inert matter to hold up the shrinkage in drying and firing, which in pure clay may be as much as 10 per cent; it must also be porous, to enable the moisture to evaporate, and vitreous, to harden in firing. As such diverse qualities are not always found in the products of one clay-bed, it may be necessary to mix different clays, or to add sand or grog (ground-up fragments of fired clay) to hold up the shrinkage.

FASHIONING

Several different methods were employed in antiquity for making terracottas: modelling by hand, throwing on the wheel, or moulding. Needless to say, these methods were used both singly and in combination.

A] Modelling by hand is the most primitive method. It was almost universal down to 700 B.C. and did not completely die out for another four centuries thereafter. Although objects of real merit can be (and occasionally were) produced by this means (an example may be seen on pl. 2C–D) the majority of ancient hand-made terracottas are crude in the extreme.

B] The potter's wheel was sometimes used, especially in the early period, to make certain basic shapes, such as the skirt of a draped woman (pl. 5D), or the body of an animal (pl. 5B–C). Details were then added by hand or with the aid of a mould. The principal advantage of this method is that it produces a hollow figure, which needs less clay than a solid one and is easier to fire.

C] The use of the mould requires somewhat fuller consideration. It was apparently used in Crete to a limited extent in the fifteenth century B.C. (see pl. 5A), but its regular use is not attested in Greek lands before the seventh century B.C. The first requirement is normally an archetype (sometimes called a patrix), from which any number of moulds may be taken. If the type were well established, an existing figurine could serve, but for a new variety, the archetype would have to be specially made. A few ancient archetypes, of hand-made terracotta, have been identified, but their very scarcity suggests that more perishable materials such as raw clay or wax or perhaps plaster were also used. Moulds could also be taken, and on occasion were taken, from existing objects of any other material, such as stone, wood, metal, or ivory.

One of the few surviving archetypes of terracotta is shown on pl. 1A–C. It was found in Athens, on the West Slope of the Acropolis, and is dated to the second half of the fourth century B.C. The figure, possible part of a group, belongs to the so-called Hygieia type of standing woman.

Although hand-made, it has been hollowed out for greater safety in firing. This was done by bisecting the figure lengthwise, hollowing out the two halves, and joining them together again with liquid clay. It will be seen that the head and arms are omitted. They would have been made separately and attached before firing, as was customary when a figurine of any complexity was envisaged.

Moulds were made of fired clay or, less commonly, of plaster. To make a clay mould, the craftsman presses wet clay over the archetype, layer by layer, until the required thickness is reached. If only a frontal mould is wanted, it can easily be lifted off when dry, but if both sides of the archetype are to be moulded, the enveloping clay must be cut and removed in two sections. After removal from the archetype, the mould is touched up with a modelling tool to remove blemishes and possibly to add further detail and, after firing, is ready for use.

Some very simple moulds were perhaps made without an archetype, by cutting direct into the clay, as a gem-engraver makes a seal, but this method would have been so exceptional that it can safely be ignored.

Another material employed in antiquity for moulds is plaster, a more popular medium today than clay. There are few such moulds extant, as plaster seldom survives in Greek soil, but figurines made in this way are recognizable by blisters on the surface caused by bubbles in the plaster. Plaster moulds were used occasionally in the second and first centuries B.C., and perhaps earlier, but did not become common till Roman Imperial times. An example, probably of Roman date, is shown on pl. 1E.

To make a figurine, the craftsman presses wet clay into the mould, layer by layer, and leaves it to dry. When the excess moisture has either evaporated or soaked into the porous body of the mould, the impression, which has shrunk slightly in drying, is easily removed. It is then further dried out.

The simplest kind of figurine, a solid piece with a moulded front and a flat back, is made by completely filling the mould with clay and smoothing down the exposed surface. This method was used not only for self-contained figurines but also (in the Archaic period) for heads to be attached to hand-made or wheel-made bodies.

To make a double-moulded solid figurine, two moulds (usually for front and back) are filled with clay and fastened together, the exact alignment being assured by means of incised guiding-lines on the sides of the moulds. When the clay has dried out, the moulds are removed. This process, which was evidently preferred to the separate moulding of front and back, is as near to piece-moulding as is practicable in clay.

So much for solid figurines. But most moulded terracottas were not solid but hollow. To make a hollow figurine, the mould is lined with a thin layer of wet clay. Sometimes, as with solid pieces, two moulds were used in combination; more often the back was composed of an unworked strip of clay. In either case the join between front and back was concealed externally by skilful retouching, and (if practicable or necessary) was also reinforced internally.

Hollow figurines were generally kept as open as possible, so that during firing the hot air could escape as it expanded, and the risk of bursting was considerably reduced. Many figurines were not only open underneath, but were equipped with a large vent in the back. Neither of these devices was absolutely necessary, since terracottas exist with nothing but a pin-hole or a knife-thrust by way of a vent, and some have no vent at all, and must have relied entirely on the natural porosity of the clay. But it was evidently considered safer by most coroplasts to leave as generous an opening as possible.

Sometimes a figurine was complete at this stage, but frequently it was necessary to repair blemishes and to touch up details. Frequently, too, parts were attached, either moulded separately or made by hand, such as bases, heads, arms, wings, or minor additions like earrings, headdresses, or objects held in the hands. An archetype for a torso needing such additions is shown on pl. 1A–C.

One method employed today in the making of terracottas has not been mentioned because there is no evidence that it was used in antiquity. In this method, known as slip-casting, liquid clay, mixed with lime, is poured into a mould and allowed to harden.

DECORATION AND FIRING

Some terracottas were decorated before firing with the characteristic black, red or brown 'glaze' of Greek vases. This form of decoration is not, technically speaking, a true glaze, but the term has the sanction of usage amongst archaeologists, and, for lack of a better, will be so employed in this survey. On the rare occasions when refeernce is made to a true vitreous glaze, it will be designated as *true glaze*. The Greek glaze was used on vases in Greek lands from the Early Bronze Age down to the fourth century A.D. It then died out, to be rediscovered in our own day. In terracottas, it was used from earliest times down to the fifth century B.C., and was universal down to about 700 B.C.

The glaze is basically an iron-rich clay, highly refined, which was mixed with water and painted on the unfired figure. This essentially monochrome decoration could be diversified by the addition of a purplish-red colour, made by mixing the 'glaze' mixture with red ochre; by the addition of white clay, or by incision; i.e. cutting back through the glaze into the underlying clay body.

One single firing served to 'bake' the figure and to develop the glaze from a colourless wash to the rich black, red or brown of the finished product. But it was in fact a three-stage process. In the first stage (necessary to fire the terracotta) an oxidizing atmosphere is maintained in the kiln (i.e. air is allowed to enter), and a temperature of 750° to 950° Centigrade is reached.

In the second stage, the atmosphere is changed from oxidizing to reducing by the introduction of green wood or damp sawdust and by the exclusion of air. This action produces carbon monoxide gas, which converts the red ferric oxide of the clay into black ferrous oxide or magnetic oxide of iron. The clay body and the glaze are now both black.

In the third stage air is readmitted to convert the black ferrous oxide or magnetic oxide to red ferric oxide. In time this process would redden both figure and glaze, but the body of the figure, being more porous than the glaze, is converted more quickly, and the craftsman, by choosing the right moment to damp down the fire, produces a batch of figures with a reddish body and a black glaze.

The perfect glaze is a deep lustrous black, but this effect was by no means always achieved. Imperfect final reduction or too thin an application of glaze result in the frequent phenomenon, a reddish or brownish or unevenly coloured glaze.

A true vitreous glaze was occasionally used. A lead glaze, either yellow or green in colour, such as was used on pottery and lamps in the first century B.C. and the first century A.D., is occasionally found on terracotta figurines of the same date made in Asia Minor. Examples are recorded from Smyrna, Cyme and Tarsus.

A third method of decoration was first employed in the seventh century B.C. and was universal from about the fifth century B.C. onwards. The entire figure, or more often only the front, was first painted with a slip of white clay, and it was then fired. The firing process was simpler than for glazed terracottas, since only one, oxidizing, stage was required. After firing, tempera colours were brushed over the white slip. The binding-medium for these colours has long since perished in surviving examples, a fact which accounts for the very fugitive nature of the colours; it may well have been white of egg, a material employed today in tempera-painting.

The pigments, which were chiefly earth-colours, have been identified by analysis. The red is red ochre or (less commonly) cinnabar. The pink is a mixture of red ochre and white, or (from the Hellenistic period) rose madder. The yellow is yellow ochre. The blue is blue frit (i.e. ground-up blue glass). The green is malachite. The black is soot or charcoal, and the white is chalk or gypsum.

A fourth method, gilding, was occasionally used in the Hellenistic period. At Smyrna, in particular, in the first centuries B.C. and A.D., figurines (especially those copying famous sculptures) were completely or partially gilt.

ANCIENT WORKSHOPS

The sites of ancient terracotta factories have been identified, from the presence of moulds and (less commonly) blocks of pigment, at a number of localities, notably in the Athenian Agora, and at Corinth, Olynthus, Acragas and Tarentum. No kilns specifically for the firing of terracottas have as yet been identified, but they were doubtless similar to those used for pottery. Indeed, the same kilns may well have been used for firing both kinds of wares.

It seems reasonable to suppose that in general the necessary moulds were made in the factories producing the terracottas. When a foreign type was to be copied, it was doubtless easier to make a mould from an imported figurine than to import the mould; but moulds were evidently on occasion imported, as one signed by Sosibios, a coroplast of Myrina, was found at Delos.

CHAPTER 2

The Earliest Terracottas, 7000-2000 B.C.

CRETE

The earliest Cretan terracottas have been found in Middle and Late Neolithic levels, especially at Knossos. The series runs from about 5000 to about 3000 B.C.

To the Middle Neolithic belong human figures of three kinds: crude males (very rare); flat stylized females, which are peculiar to this period in Crete, but which may be forerunners of the Cycladic marble figures (pl. 2A); and stumpy steatopygous figurines of a kind common throughout the Aegean basin at this period, particularly in Anatolia. The latter (found also at Phaestos) occur in two main varieties: squatting, with the legs bent under the body (pl. 2B), and seated, with the knees drawn up in front. Birds and animals are also found, especially doves, bulls, goats and dogs. There is no paint on any of these figures, the decoration being restricted to incised patterns.

Both types of steatopygous female figures continued into the Late Neolithic period, but the flat figurines did not outlast the Middle Neolithic.

The Early Minoan period (3000–2000) is poorly represented. A crude female figure from Palaikastro is attributed to Early Minoan II (2500–2200). It is unpainted, with a columnar body and stumps for arms; of the features, only eyes and nose are indicated.

FIG. 3. Bear drinking from a bowl. From Syros. Early Cycladic, about 2500 B.C.

THE CYCLADES

No terracotta figurines, in the strict sense of the word, have been recorded from the Cycladic Islands in the period under review. The nearest approximations are a plastic vase in the shape of a bear drinking from a bowl (fig. 3), which is dated about 2500 B.C., and a class of objects looking remarkably like frying-pans, which were probably in fact models of wombs.

MAINLAND GREECE

A recently discovered site at Nea Nikomedia in Macedonia has produced figurines of steatopygous fertility-goddesses exhibiting connections with Anatolia, which are probably as early as the seventh millennium B.C. They were made of sun-dried clay and consequently do not qualify, strictly speaking, as terracottas; but they deserve a passing mention in view of their high antiquity. The example in fig. 4 was made in four sections – head, trunk, and legs – which were subsequently pegged together.

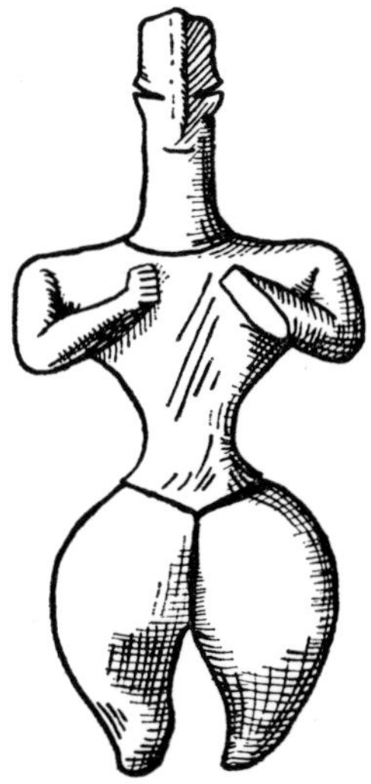

Towards the end of the long Neolithic period figurines, this time of true terracotta, became relatively common. Grossly steatopygous female figures are again the most popular varieties (fig. 5). On pl. 2E is a less usual conception, a seated woman with a baby, from Sesklo in Thessaly.

Occasionally, however, the Late Neolithic potter showed that he could produce figurines of considerably finer quality. That illustrated on pl. 2C and D, from Lerna, could rank as a work of art by any standards. Found in one of the later (but not the latest) of the Neolithic levels, it may be dated in the fourth millennium B.C. Her head and the lower part of her right leg are missing, but she is otherwise in good condition. The subject is again a naked woman, but how different from her humbler sisters. She stands in a graceful pose, her arms bent across her body, below the breasts. The contours of the female body are treated with sympathetic understanding and the concentration on the sexual parts, so frequent at this date, is completely missing. She has been aptly named the Aphrodite of Lerna.

FIG. 4. Goddess. From Nea Nikomedia in Macedonia. Early Neolithic, 7000–6000 B.C.

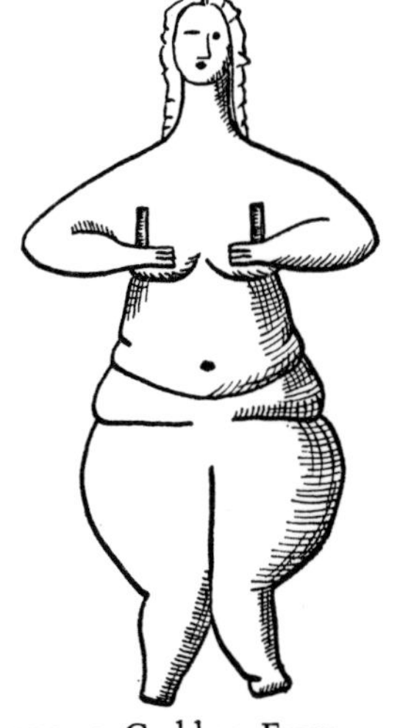

FIG. 5. Goddess. From Sesklo (drawn from fragments). Neolithic, 4000–3000 B.C.

Fragments of figures which may well have been similar have been found at Eutresis in Boeotia and at Tiryns.

The Early Helladic period (3000–2000 B.C.) is sparsely represented so far as terracottas are concerned. A few primitive female figures have however been found; in general they are finer than the typical Neolithic variety, but considerably less fine than the

Aphrodite of Lerna. We may cite as representative a figure from Zygouries from the middle part of this period, and one from Lerna from the end of it.

Mention should also be made of a widespread but puzzling class of figures resembling (and possibly representing) anchors. Examples from stratified deposits at Lerna serve to date the type to Early Helladic III (2300–2000).

CHAPTER 3

The Middle Bronze Age, 2000-1550 B.C.

CRETE

Terracottas became comparatively common in Crete in Middle Minoan times, and present a remarkably uniform appearance whenever found. Most are votive figures, from mountain sanctuaries such as Petsofa (near Palaikastro) and Piskokephalo; others come from a house (or perhaps a sanctuary) at Chamaizi, and from various other sources. A few figurines were also found in the communal tombs of the Mesara Plain in the south.

These figures are small and hand-made. They represent for the most part human beings (or deities), animals, and parts of the human body, and although simply made, are not without a certain style. The examples from Petsofa are made of a pinkish, lightly fired clay, and are decorated with red glaze and white paint. In accordance with an ancient tradition, possibly learnt from Egypt, male flesh is coloured red, female flesh white. When one compares these figures with contemporary masterpieces of gem-engraving, it is apparent that we are dealing not with art, but with the humble offerings of the poor. Most of the Middle Minoan figures are dated to the Middle Minoan I period, which, outside the palatial centres, runs from 2000 to 1700 B.C.

The human figures, male and female, are mostly standing, but we may note an exceptional seated female on a detachable stool from Trapeza. The men wear a codpiece (possibly of Libyan origin), a belt, and a dagger, and some also have on a loin-cloth (pl. 3C). The women wear an elaborate headdress and a low-cut dress, leaving the breasts exposed, with a flounced skirt (pl. 3D–E). The animals include goats, ibex, dogs, stoats and tortoises. The human limbs may be interpreted, by analogy with historical examples, as thank offerings for recovery from sickness.

From Phaestos come figures of bulls painted, in the Kamares style of 1900–1700 B.C., with white and other colours on a black glaze (pl. 3B).

Finally a few figures and rhytons were found in communal tombs in the Mesara in South Crete. From the associated finds they could be either Early or Middle Minoan; the later date is the more probable in view of the scarcity of Early Minoan terracottas and their popularity in Middle Minoan times elsewhere in Crete. We may cite as representative a figure of a deer (pl. 3A) and hand-made rhytons in the shape of bulls, some with acrobats.

THE CYCLADES

No Middle Cycladic terracottas have as yet been recorded.

MAINLAND GREECE

No figurines in the strict sense of the word have been found in any Middle Helladic context. Two rhytons in the shape of bulls (?) were however found at Eleusis in the Middle Helladic portion of a disturbed tomb. The excavators reasonably suggest a Cretan origin for the type, but the objects themselves are probably locally made. Other fragments of modelled terracotta have been found in a few Middle Helladic tombs, but all are probably from vases.

CHAPTER 4

The Late Bronze Age, 1550-1050 B.C.

CRETE

The typical Late Minoan figurine is the so-called Household Goddess. The basic shape is a hollow wheel-made cylinder, which forms at the same time a flaring skirt for a standing goddess and a support for a figurine which may be as tall as 70 cm. or more. Her arms are usually raised in a gesture apparently denoting her divinity.

These figures of goddesses were found almost exclusively in palatial or domestic shrines, a fact which has associated them in the eyes of archaeologists with the special care of the household. Although claims have been made for a considerably higher antiquity, in a masterly study Alexiou has established that most were made between 1300 and 1000 B.C.

The earliest dated examples come from the Shrine of the Double Axes at Knossos, of about the thirteenth century B.C. Five were found at a shrine at Gazi near Knossos of about 1250–1150, and nine at a refugee-settlement at Karphi (in the Lasithi Plain), of about the eleventh century B.C. These latter are really post-Minoan, but are mentioned here for the sake of convenience.

Connecting links between the Middle Minoan figurines and the Household Goddesses are few, but one such exists in a female figurine with a flaring skirt found in a fifteenth-century deposit in the palace at Phaestos.

On pl. 5D is illustrated one of the finest of the Household Goddesses, the so-called Poppy Goddess from Gazi. Marinatos has observed that the poppies of her headdress have been slit in the way in which such flowers are treated today to obtain opium. He therefore suggests that opium-induced trances were part of Minoan religion; and he may well be right.

Small solid hand-made figures in the Middle Minoan tradition are also known. With the Household Goddesses in the Shrine of the Double Axes at Knossos was found such a male figure, rather more naturalistic, which has usually been identified as a votary.

A small female statuette of about 1400 B.C. from the cemetery at Hagia Triada was half-sitting and was bored for the insertion of a rod or a cord; the decoration was in red glaze on a white slip. Nearby were found two terracotta posts topped by figures of doves. The group (fig. 6) has been plausibly restored as a woman, or possibly a goddess, seated in a swing hanging from the two posts.

Mention should also be made of a group of dancing women from Palaikastro, which come from a domestic shrine of the fourteenth century B.C., and of three models of cult-scenes from a tomb at Kamilari, near Phaestos, of about the same date. In one, votaries place offerings on altars in a shrine; in another, women squat on the ground kneading dough; and in the third, four men dance a round dance, their arms linked.

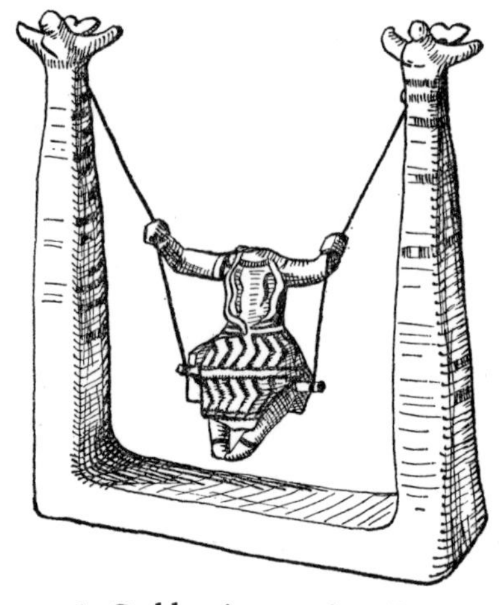

FIG. 6. Goddess in a swing. From Hagia Triada. Late Minoan, *c.* 1400 B.C.

Two rhytons in the shape of bulls are recorded from Pseira. Although, strictly, vases rather than figurines, they are noteworthy for technical reasons as well as for their attractive appearance. One comes from a house of LM IA date (1550–1500); the other (pl. 5A), more naturalistically rendered, from one of LM IB date (1500–1450). Both were believed by their excavator to be hollow-moulded and, to judge from external appearances, he was right. This view is strengthened by the existence of a number of fragments identical with the earlier type, also from Pseira, which hint at the sort of mass-production for which a mould is particularly suitable. No moulds certainly for the manufacture of terracotta figurines have as yet come to light in deposits as early as Late Minoan, but certain clay moulds for animals, animal-heads, flowers and shells from Gournia were clearly intended for objects of faience or clay, and may provide the missing evidence.[1]

If this is indeed so, we have here the first recorded use of the mould in Crete for such a purpose; a practice which was discontinued after the fifteenth century for some seven hundred years.

Although from 1400 B.C. to the end of the Bronze Age, Crete was an integral part of the Mycenaean *koine*, the Cretans, for reasons which must have been largely religious, never accepted the typical Mycenaean terracottas. Very few indeed of these figures have been found in Crete, and those few are almost certainly imports from some other part of the Mycenaean world.

There was however one type of figurine common to Crete and the Mycenaean world,

[1] H. B. Hawes, *et al.*, *Gournia, Vasiliki, etc.* (Philadelphia, 1908), 35, figs. 13–14 and pl. XI, 19A. Zervos, *Crète*, figs. 516–17. I am indebted to Dr S. Alexiou for drawing my attention to these moulds.

the large wheel-made animals which are more fully described below (see p. 16). It is represented by two good Cretan examples, a bull (pl. 5C) and a donkey carrying two jars, pannier-wise. The type probably evolved in Crete out of plastic rhytons in animal form, such as the bull-vases from Pseira mentioned above (pl. 5A). As however this variety of figurine was made throughout the Aegean world, it is more logically regarded as a Mycenaean type, and is discussed below.

THE GREEK MAINLAND AND THE ISLANDS

In the Late Helladic, or Mycenaean, period, we know of no terracottas from mainland Greece or the islands (apart from Crete) before about 1420 B.C. Then, for some three centuries small hand-made figures, chiefly of women and animals, became extremely popular. In the fourteenth and thirteenth centuries (LH IIIA and B), like the contemporary pottery from whose workshops they doubtless emanated, these figures achieved a remarkable uniformity throughout the length and breadth of the Mycenaean world, from Sicily in the west to Cyprus and Syria in the east. The only exception to their almost universal popularity was the island of Crete, where very few have been found, and those few evidently brought by Mycenaean settlers or visitors. Larger wheel-made figures are also occasionally found in this period.

In the twelfth century the established types of hand-made figures continued in a coarser and less stereotyped form, as witness those found in a shrine at Asine. At the same time wheel-made animal figures achieved a vogue, which continued into the eleventh century.

Mycenaean terracottas are extremely plentiful and occur in tombs (especially those of children), in shrines, and in houses. Considerable work has been done on their typology and significance. Wace, Blegen, and above all Furumark have worked out a chronological framework, based on tomb-evidence, while Mylonas and Nilssen have undertaken the more difficult task of examining their functions. Mylonas's view that these figurines were the Mycenaean counterparts of the Egyptian *ushabtis*, intended for the journey to the nether world, while tenable in certain instances, is hard to square with all the facts. In most cases they would appear to represent divinities, sacred animals, and the like.

The clay is that of contemporary Mycenaean pottery, very similar at all places; pinkish in colour, with a cream surface, and fired hard. The glaze fires either red, brown or black, variations in colour being frequently observed on the same piece.

A] *Solid, hand-made figures*

These are made simply, but not crudely, in a kind of artistic shorthand, and in a restricted range of subjects.

1. *Standing Goddesses.* The three varieties have been conveniently named by Furumark

after the Greek characters ϕ, ψ, and τ, which they happen to resemble. The origin of these distinctive types is unknown, but it would appear in the light of our present knowledge that the ϕ type was a Mycenaean invention of about 1420 B.C. and that the other two types evolved from it.

a) The ϕ type (pl. 4F) depicts a woman standing with her arms folded across her breast. She wears a two-piece garment, apparently consisting of a jacket and a tight skirt. Her head is sometimes bare, sometimes decorated with a shallow crown-like headdress, through which a plait of hair emerges, to fall down her back. Occasionally she holds a baby against her breast with crudely indicated hands. The forerunner of this type comes from an interment of about 1420–1400 B.C. in a tholos tomb at Pylos (pl. 4B). The somewhat crude treatment of the figure indicates that the canonical proportions had not yet been worked out. The type died out soon after 1300 B.C.

A rare variation has two seated goddesses with a child between them, possibly the same 'two goddesses' of certain linear B tablets from Pylos. Another variation shows a woman, apparently of this type, engaged in making bread. This figure, which strangely anticipates Boeotian genre pieces of the fifth century B.C. (p. 77), can scarcely be divine, and must be a sort of *ushabti*.

b) The τ type (pl. 4G) is almost, if not quite, as early as the ϕ. It had a considerably longer life, however, for it lasted in a pure form from 1400 to 1200 B.C., and in a degenerate form for another century, to 1100 B.C. It differs little from the ϕ type, but the arms are folded rigidly across the breast, to give a more angular outline. Goddesses of this class always wear a stephane.

c) The ψ type (pl. 4H) is really the ϕ type with the arms raised. It started about 1300, the time when the ϕ variety was on the way out, and continued in a pure form till 1200, and in a degenerate form till 1100 B.C.

One variation of the twelfth century found at Perati in Attica and on Naxos, has the arms touching the head in the age-old gesture of a mourner. These variations would suggest the representation of human beings rather than goddesses in these particular instances.

2. *Seated goddesses*. A draped, or more rarely, naked goddess is sometimes represented seated on a throne (pl. 4A). Occasionally the throne is empty and was evidently occupied by a separately made figure of a goddess of clay or of some other material (pl. 4C).

3. *Sacred Marriage*. A group in Budapest (fig. 7) depicts a man and a woman lying on a couch, and evidently represents a Sacred Marriage. An empty couch from the Argive Heraeum may have served the same purpose with separately made figures.

4. *Chariot-groups*. Chariot-groups are fairly common in the fourteenth and thirteenth centuries (pl. 4E). From the hind-quarters of two horses set side by side emerges a rudimentary chariot, occupied by two men, the charioteer and his passenger. A thick

ribbon of clay running from the chariot to the horses' heads could represent either the pole, or the reins, or perhaps both.

5. *Ploughing scenes.* Ploughing scenes are also occasionally found (fig. 8). They resemble

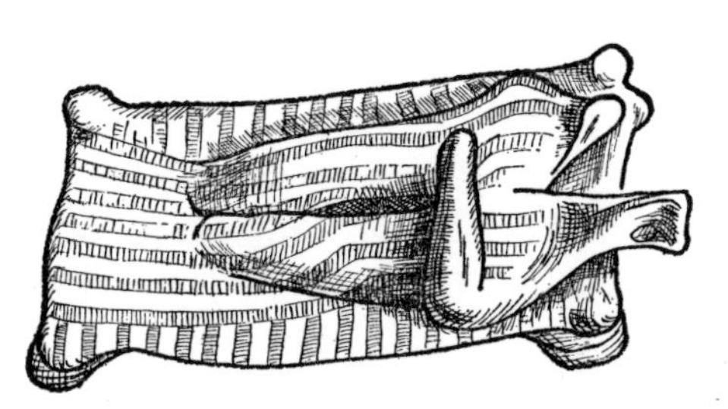

FIG. 7. Sacred Marriage (?). Mycenaean, 1400–1200 B.C.

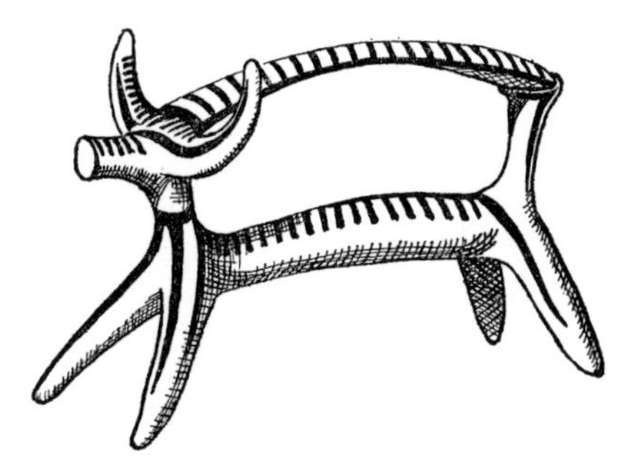

FIG. 8. Ploughing group. From the Argive Heraeum. Mycenaean, 1400–1200 B.C.

the chariot-groups, but with the difference that the animals are single oxen and there is only one man behind, indicated in a very summary fashion indeed.

6. *Horse and rider.* A figure of a horse and rider was discovered at Mycenae, and remains of a similar piece at the Argive Heraeum. These pieces have been hailed as establishing the existence of the riding of horses very much earlier than had been previously believed. It may however be a god – and gods could ride almost any animals at almost any time. In this connection we should note a figure whose authenticity has been doubted, but probably unjustly, in which a ψ type goddess rides on a horse.

7. *Bull-jumper.* Another very rare type clearly of Cretan inspiration, is a bull-jumping group.

8. *Animals.* Animals by themselves are also known. Bulls (pl. 4D) are common in contexts of the fourteenth and thirteenth centuries; a deer comes from a tomb at Perati in Attica of the twelfth century, and there are other unpublished figures of animals from houses at Mycenae.

9. *Altars(?).* Objects which are either altars or tripod basins are also occasionally found.

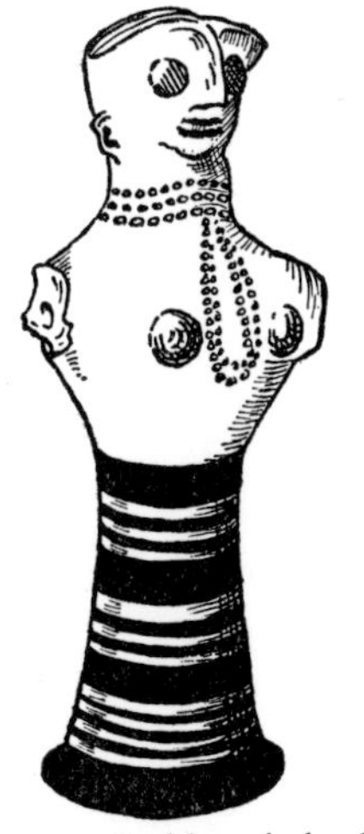

FIG. 9. Goddess (wheel made). From Mycenae. Mycenaean, 1400–1200 B.C.

B] *Wheel-made figures*

1. *Women.* Female figures with flaring skirts, composed basically of a truncated cone thrown on the wheel, with the head and arms roughly modelled by hand, are occasionally found (fig. 9). Several examples are recorded from Mycenae and one from Pylos.

These figures, averaging some 18 cm. in height, are larger than most of the solid varieties. The technique, but not the style, is Cretan (cf. pl. 5D).

2. *Animals.* Large statuettes of bulls, horses and donkeys, some 15 to 40 cm. high, with wheel-made cylindrical bodies and hand-made legs, heads and other attachments, made their first appearance about 1200 B.C. and lasted for more than a century.

The date of these animals is roughly fixed by the occurrence of one in a twelfth-century tomb at Ialysus, and by the association of another with Protogeometric pottery at Amyclae. Decoration, in glaze, is either in the elegant Close Style of the twelfth century or in a sort of Submycenaean usually dated in the first half of the eleventh century.

They were widespread throughout Greece and the islands. Unlike the solid Mycenaean terracottas, which were virtually unknown in Crete, and the Household Goddesses, which were confined to Crete, these figures were popular in both Minoan and Mycenaean spheres. We may for convenience classify them as Mycenaean because of their universality in the Mycenaean *koine*, and because most surviving examples are of Mycenaean make, but the type was almost certainly invented in Crete, where hollow figures of animals had a long history (see p. 10).

This class seems to have died out in most centres by the middle of the eleventh century, but probably survived in Crete, to be re-introduced into the Greek world towards the end of the Dark Ages.

Bulls are commonest. A fine example from Phaestos (pl. 5C) is decorated in a characteristically Cretan pattern of the twelfth century B.C. It stands squarely on four sturdy legs, its trumpet-mouth and projecting tongue giving it a strangely appealing expression. A deposit at Amyclae near Sparta has yielded similar animals (bulls and horses), but decorated in a simpler way, like Submycenaean vases of the first half of the eleventh century B.C. A donkey carrying jars pannier-wise comes from a tomb at Ialysus of the twelfth century (pl. 5B); another comes from Phaestos.

CHAPTER 5

The Dark Ages, 1100-700 B.C.

INTRODUCTION

Except in Crete, where there was probably a continuous development throughout the Dark Ages, the manufacture of terracottas in the Aegean area seems to have come to a halt soon after 1100 B.C., and to have been resumed in the ninth century. By the mid eighth century the output was quite considerable, and for some fifty years somewhat uncouth figures, decorated in the style of the contemporary Geometric pottery, were produced in many areas, especially Attica. Then, soon after 700, the introduction of the mould completely transformed the coroplast's craft.

CRETE

The tenth-century (Subminoan) Household Goddesses from Karphi have already been considered. To the same period belong a hand-made sphinx and a model shrine, a simpler version of that on pl. 6c, from a sacred spring at Knossos.

Other sources of Dark Age figurines are votive deposits from a sanctuary at Hagia Triada and from the Dictaean Cave, and objects from the settlement at Vrokastro. Hand- and wheel-made animals from these deposits may well extend from the eleventh to the eighth centuries, but the evidence is inconclusive. The next securely dated evidence consists of a female figurine from a house at Phaestos (fig. 10), which is dated from its context between 850 and 825 B.C. It is a clumsy, stumpy object with a roughly cylindrical body, rudimentary breasts and a large head.

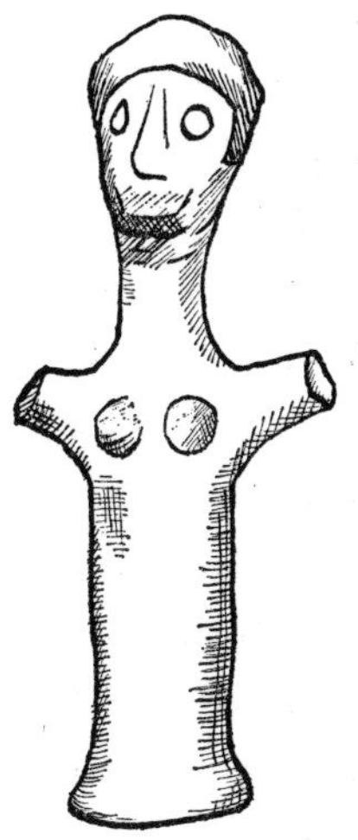

FIG. 10. Goddess. From Phaestos. 850–825 B.C.

A model of a shrine, said to have been found at Archanes, near Knossos, is illustrated on pl. 6c. It can be dated from the style of its decoration (Protogeometric B) to the second half of the ninth century. The shrine is circular with a detachable door, behind which is a seated female figure possibly representing a cult-statue, her arms raised in the characteristic Minoan gesture of divinity. A model of a somewhat similar, but rectangular, building from Khaniale Tekke, continues the tradition into the eighth century.

Many sites, such as Gortyn, Arkades, Lato and Anavlochos, have produced hand-made human figures which, by comparison with dated examples from Samos (below), should probably be placed in the eighth century. It would thus appear that by this date Cretan terracottas were again in step with the rest of the Greek world, or perhaps that the Greek world had at last caught up with Crete in this respect.

IONIA

A] *Samos*

Terracottas of the ninth to the sixth century B.C. have been found on the site of the Heraeum at Samos, some in contexts which admit of fairly close dating.

The principal types in the period under review are human and animal figures, some hand-made, some wheel-made. The decoration is in a poor brownish glaze, sometimes over a cream slip. The clay varies in colour between orange, pale orange, and brown. It contains mica, frequently in large amounts, and often also brown, grey or white inclusions. The texture is rather coarse. The only external influence which has been identified is Cypriot, which is first felt in the late eighth century.

THE PRINCIPAL TYPES

1. *Animals.* Bulls and, less frequently, horses, with hollow wheel-made bodies and hand-made heads and limbs, are the commonest figurines in the early stages. They apparently started as early as the ninth century, but are not attested in quantities before the eighth, when they flourished until after 700 B.C. Their origin is not known. It does not apparently lie in imported Cypriot pieces, for these are not found here till the type is fully established. It may be that there is a link between these animals and those of the Late Bronze Age discussed on p. 16, by way of Crete, where it appears that the tradition lived on longer than elsewhere.

Small solid hand-made animals are also found in the eighth century, becoming commoner in the second half. In contrast with the wheel-made varieties, they comprise principally horses sometimes ridden, and (less commonly) bulls and rams.

2. *Human figures.* Clumsy hand-made figures of both sexes were made throughout the eighth century, but were not really plentiful before about 720.

Towards the end of the eighth century, a new type of figure evolved under strong

Cypriot influence. It has a hollow wheel-made body, conical in shape, and a hand-made head and arms; a typical example is shown on pl. 6F. The features are coarse but expressive, and the heads are thrown so far back that the unbroken line of forehead and nose is frequently horizontal.

B] *Miletus*

Little is known of terracottas from Miletus at this date, but two pieces of the Geometric period have come to light, both probably representing the same type, and both of local clay.

Near the Temple of Athena, on the site of a spring, associated with Geometric pottery of the eighth century, was found a fragment of a rider. His head, his arms and his mount are unfortunately missing, but enough is preserved to show that he had long hair and was sitting upright, with his arms in front of him. The decoration, partly schematic and partly naturalistic, indicates that he was wearing a himation draped round his hips. On another part of the site was found the neck of a horse (?), done in much the same style, which could well come from a similar figure. The clay has a pale micaceous slip, and the decoration is in a brownish-black glaze.

RHODES

A few terracottas have been found in Rhodian tombs of Geometric date, and a number from votive deposits which cannot be closely dated should also, from their style, be placed in this category. Rhodian clay from the Geometric period to the seventh century is coarse in texture and brown or pale orange in colour. It contains little or no mica, and is fired at a high temperature. There is a secondary kind which is finer in texture and paler in colour.

THE PRINCIPAL TYPES

1] A bell-shaped doll with a hollow wheel-made body and hand-made head and arms comes from a tomb at Ialysus of the ninth century B.C. It is decorated in the same way as contemporary Geometric pottery. This, the earliest recorded Rhodian terracotta after the Mycenaean period, may perhaps derive from Attic pieces such as that illustrated on pl. 7C. Eighth century developments of this type are recorded from the neighbouring island of Cos (see p. 20).

2] Solid hand-made human figures, with the head characteristically thrown back so that the long nose is often parallel to the ground, are found in a tomb at Ialysus of the late eighth century, and a votive deposit at Camirus. A figure of a rider from Lindus is very much in the same tradition, but may be as late as the early seventh century from the style of the bird painted on his back, which recalls the seventh century 'bird bowls'. The female figure from Camirus on pl. 6D is completely Geometric in style, with its block-like body and raised head.

3] Wheel-made female figures with hand-made heads and other additions, like the Samian piece on pl. 6F, occur in a votive deposit at Lindus, and should probably be dated in the late eighth century.

COS

1] The earliest recorded Coan terracotta, shown on pl. 6A–B, comes from a tenth century tomb on Cos. A plastic vase in the form of a centaur, it is probably the earliest surviving representation of this mythical creature.

2] Hollow wheel-made dolls with holes for detachable legs have been found in eighth century tombs of the Seraglio Cemetery at Cos (pl. 6E). These dolls, made by the local potters and decorated in the same way as contemporary vases, derive from a ninth century type represented in Rhodes (see p. 19). They also bear a striking likeness to certain Boeotian dolls which may well be their contemporaries (cf. pl. 9D–E).

3] Wheel-made figures of birds, decorated in a purely schematic manner, have been found in tombs with the dolls. They resemble figures of cocks from slightly later Athenian tombs (see p. 23). Both may share a common origin in Cyprus or Phoenicia.

ATTICA

The manufacture of terracottas appears to have been resumed in Attica in the second half of the tenth century B.C. Our principal sources are Athenian tombs in the Cerameicus Cemetery and on the site of the later Agora, the model publication of both of which sites has done much to illustrate the development of this craft in the Dark Ages.

Attic Geometric terracottas were made by the men who made the vases. The decoration, for the most part in a good black glaze, is frequently identical with that on the vases, and the clay is the same: brownish in colour, fairly fine in texture, with a little mica. The material may conveniently be divided into two phases.

Phase I. 950–800 B.C.

Some time after 950 B.C., two varieties of terracotta make their appearance. One type consists of hand-made doll-like figures with bell-shaped skirts and detachable legs (pl. 7C). It occurs in two Cerameicus tombs, and in a cemetery at Nea Ionia (an Athenian suburb), in association with jars, bowls, beads and spindle-whorls of the same fabric. This ware is characterized by fine clay, unglazed but decorated throughout with incised or impressed patterns of a simple kind. Influence from the lower Danube has been suggested to account for this intrusive style, but it is not clear whether these pieces are imports or local imitations. This peculiar ware had a life in Athens of about a century, from 950 to 850 B.C., but dolls are only recorded from the first half of this period, a phenomenon which may be due to nothing more than the luck of excavation.

The other type is represented by a solitary example from the Cerameicus, of the late tenth century (pl. 7D); a deer, with hollow wheel-made body and hand-made head, legs and tail. It is decorated in a schematic manner with black glaze in exactly the same way as contemporary pottery, and it is in truth a vase (probably a scent-bottle) rather than a simple figurine. This technique looks back to the Mycenaean and Submycenaean figures discussed above (p. 16), and forward to the eighth century horses mentioned below. The gap of rather more than a century between the Mycenaean animals and the deer cannot at present be bridged in Greece, but continuity of this technique throughout the Dark Ages is certain in Cyprus[1] and probable in Crete, where the deposit from Hagia Triada (see p. 17) may well provide the necessary evidence.

3] The next class to be considered comprises hand-made figures of horses, which are comparatively plentiful in the Cerameicus, sometimes as separate figures, sometimes attached to the lids of pyxides (toilet jars). The animals are very simply made. They are

FIG. 11. Horse. From Athens, Cerameicus. Ninth century B.C.

FIG. 12. Horse. From Athens, Cerameicus. 750–725 B.C.

decorated in black glaze, which covers most of the body; some parts, usually the head and neck, are however painted with geometric patterns on the clay ground (fig. 11). By a combination of stratigraphic and stylistic analysis, the excavators of the Cerameicus have worked out the development of the terracotta horse through the ninth and eighth centuries B.C. The stylistic evaluation depends not only on the decoration of the horses themselves, but also on that of the vases whose lids some of them adorned.

[1] P. Dikaios, *Guide to the Cyprus Museum*[3] (Nicosia, 1961), 200, no. 14A (1050–950 B.C.). *Swedish Cyprus Expedition*, iv, pt 2 (Stockholm, 1948), figs. vii and xx.

Phase 2. 800–700 B.C.

The eighth century saw the introduction of a number of new types in Attica. In all cases the decoration is schematic rather than naturalistic, being done in the same way as the vases (and evidently by the same vase-painters). The modelling is primitive indeed, but there is a restraint about it which contrasts favourably with contemporary works, for example from Boeotia or Samos.

Attic terracottas of this period may be divided into two categories, those entirely hand-made, and those primarily wheel-made.

A] *Hand-made*

1. *Seated goddesses.* Enthroned female figures, probably goddesses, are occasionally found (pl. 7F–G). On pl. 7A is such a seated figure whose throne was evidently made separately and has not survived.

2. *Mourning women.* Mourning women also occur. An example from a late eighth century tomb in the Agora (or possibly two fragmentary examples restored as one) has scenes of mourning women actually painted on its breast. The enthroned goddess on pl. 7F–G incorporates a mourning figure as part of the back of the throne, and it may be that other mourning figures should be restored the same rather surprising way.

3. *Standing women.* There are also female figures with arms outstretched, whose function is not certain. One in Oxford comes from Eleusis (pl. 7E).

4. *Horses.* Horses continued much as before, both free-standing and on the lids of pyxides. A horse of 750–725 B.C. is shown in fig. 12.

5. *Chariot-groups.* Such horses were occasionally incorporated into a four-horse chariot-group, evidently a child's toy. Several examples of this type are known. One fragmentary group from a tomb in the Agora of the late eighth century serves to date the class. The example on pl. 8B is the most complete of the surviving groups. The whole group is set on a platform which runs on four large wheels. The rear wheels in a sense do duty as the chariot-wheels, but the front wheels are completely irrelevant to the chariot. The whole group however is eminently suited to being pulled or pushed about by its youthful owner.

A man wearing a pilos and carrying a Dipylon-type shield over his left arm is driving the chariot, which is drawn by four horses decorated in the usual Late Geometric manner. The hands of the charioteer and the horses' heads are pierced to take reins of cord or leather.

It is worthy of note that Greek chariots normally had one occupant, in contrast to the Mycenaean variety, which invariably carried a passenger in addition to the charioteer.

6. *Other creatures.* A centaur comes from a tomb in Athens. A dog and a bird were found in a tomb in the Agora of the late eighth century, and there is another similar bird in Oxford (pl. 7B).

B] *Wheel-made*

1. *Cocks.* Cocks, decorated in a completely schematic way with chevrons, chessboard squares, etc., are found in a tomb of 750–725 from the Cerameicus.
2. *Pomegranates.* Pomegranates, similarly decorated, are also found.
3. *Mule with amphoras.* A mule carrying a load of amphoras, equipped with four large wheels like those of the chariot-groups, made a popular child's toy. The example on pl. 8A is complete except for the wheels and for the rider's head and right arm. On a raised seat in the middle of five amphoras sits a man; he was originally holding reins (of cord or leather). Holes in his right hand and in the horse's head show how they were attached.

Other examples of this type exist; one was excavated in a tomb in the Cerameicus of the late eighth century B.C. We are reminded of the Mycenaean piece from Ialysus illustrated on pl. 5B.

BOEOTIA

The earliest post-Mycenaean Boeotian terracottas are hollow wheel-made figures of women with bell-shaped bodies, generally interpreted as dolls. They are decorated in black glaze, in a partly naturalistic, partly schematic way. Not many are known and none, as it happens, come from controlled excavations. The most highly developed examples, which are equipped with separately made legs to be attached with wires or cords (pl. 9D–E), may be dated from the scheme of their decoration to the later eighth century B.C.

Other examples, like that on pl. 9C, are typologically more primitive, and from their general resemblance to the dolls from Cos (pl. 6E), should probably be dated earlier in the eighth century. It would not be unreasonable to suggest that the type covers the entire eighth century, more or less.

Why such a distinctive kind of terracotta started in Boeotia at such a date is hard to explain. It would however appear, from a ninth century example in Rhodes (p. 19) and from eighth century examples in Cos (p. 20), that the type was developed in the Eastern Aegean, and was borrowed in Boeotia, alone of the mainland Greek communities. That it ended when it did, leaving a void of perhaps a century in the local terracotta industry, is less surprising in view of the fact that these dolls were the work of ordinary potters, not of coroplasts, and are best regarded as a special kind of pottery.

LACONIA

Laconian terracottas of the Dark Ages, which are few in number, come from the Sanctuary of Artemis Orthia at Sparta and from the Sanctuary of Apollo at Amyclae.

Crude hand-made figures of human beings and animals (mostly horses) are first recorded at Artemis Orthia in levels of about the middle of the eighth century B.C., but did not become at all common till the seventh (p. 51).

Two much-discussed heads from Amyclae (pl. 9A and B) are more important. They cannot be dated stratigraphically, but, for the reasons given below, they can safely be placed in the late eighth century.

Both heads are hand-made apparently on wheel-made necks, so that we may suppose them to come from wheel-made figures like the Samian example on pl. 6F. But they are of a far higher quality than that piece, or indeed than any other surviving terracotta heads of the Geometric period.

One head (pl. 9B) is that of a helmeted warrior with long hair, a wide brow, large eyes, a pointed nose, and a rather feeble mouth. The head is covered with a white slip; details of features and hair are indicated in black glaze and the conical helmet has a meander-pattern in added red. The other (pl. 9A) is in general similar, but wears disc-earrings and a stephane, and is evidently female; she has lost her nose, but it was presumably pointed, like that of the warrior.

Kunze has studied both heads. By comparison with statuettes of bronze and ivory he dated the male head to the early eighth century; this date has been rightly reduced by Hampe to the later eighth century. We cannot, with Kunze, date the female head in the Mycenaean period, as there are no Mycenaean parallels to it, and in any case the two heads are clearly contemporary. We are therefore left with the only possible solution, that both heads are of the later eighth century.

AEGINA

Among the votives from the Temple of Aphaea are a crude hand-made female figure and a number of heads evidently broken from similar figures. In style they somewhat resemble pieces from eighth century contexts at Samos, and that is presumably their date. They are identified by Furtwängler as local products.

A number of primitive animals from the same source are probably contemporary with the human figures.

OLYMPIA

In the lowest levels of the excavations on the Altis were found terracottas very similar in style to the early figurines from Samos, especially those attributable to the eighth century. As at Samos, they comprise men, women, horses and bulls.

CHAPTER 6

The Seventh and Sixth Centuries B.C.

INTRODUCTION

Soon after 700 B.C. the Greek terracotta industry was transformed by the introduction of the mould. Mould-made terracottas had long been in common use in the east, but, if we except their rare appearance in Late Minoan Crete (see p. 12), were hitherto unknown in Greek lands. This invention reached Greece either from Syria or from Cyprus, or from both areas simultaneously. We should probably be right in envisaging immigrant craftsmen setting up workshops in the principal Greek cities and taking on local apprentices, with the consequent hellenization of a basically oriental industry.

Several important results stemmed from the introduction of this new technique. In the first place, it was possible to mass-produce figurines of real artistic merit. In the second place a completely new figure-style accompanied the new technique. And in the third place, the arts of the potter and the coroplast began to diverge.

The new technique is discussed in detail above (see p. 2). The new style, the so-called Dedalic style, named in modern times after Daedalus, the legendary Cretan artist, has been described as 'the strong clear style of all the progressive areas in Greece in the seventh century'.[1] It obviously owes a considerable debt to Egyptian art. There is however no evidence for direct Egyptian contacts with Greece as early as the beginning of the seventh century, and the influence from that quarter evidently first reached Greece at second-hand, in the strongly Egyptianizing arts of North Syria and Phoenicia.

It is not known where in Greece the Dedalic style crystallized out of its oriental components, but it seems fairly certain that the credit for this important step should go either to some Cretan city or (less probably) to Corinth. Nor can we determine for certain the medium in which the style was developed, since it occurs early in clay, bronze, ivory and wood (but not at first in stone). Clay is however the cheapest and most ubiquitous of

[1] T. J. Dunbabin, *The Greeks and Their Eastern Neighbours* (London, 1957), 37.

materials, and is the most likely choice both for the imported models and for the local adaptations.

The Dedalic style is primarily a method of rendering the human face, and is entirely at variance with the clumsy but vigorous efforts of the Geometric artist. The typical Dedalic face, viewed from the front, is approximately triangular or trapezoidal, tapering downwards from the forehead. The hair is arranged in a short fringe across the forehead and falls in a mass on the shoulders like the Egyptian wig on which it is evidently modelled. It also bears a striking resemblance to an English judge's full-bottomed wig.

There is no longer any attempt, as in the best figurines of the previous period (pl. 9A and B), to reproduce the human face in a naturalistic manner. The profile is much too flat; the shape of the face is quite unnatural, and the eyes are set much too high. The artist has in fact taken over a set of ready-made conventions of some sophistication, designed rather to produce an aesthetically satisfying formula than to hold a mirror to nature. That such stylization was basically foreign to the Greek mentality is demonstrated by the rapidity with which in the sixth century it gave place to an almost completely naturalistic rendering of the human face.

The Dedalic face has been studied in detail by Jenkins in a series of perceptive articles. We may accept his conclusions with two reservations. The style was not, as he believed, restricted to Dorian communities, but was almost universal throughout the Greek world in the greater part of the seventh century. And secondly, in his stylistic sequence and in his absolute chronology he attempts considerably greater precision than is warranted by our knowledge of seventh century Greek art.

The Dedalic face may be studied in two ways. In the first place, there are strongly marked local peculiarities, which persist throughout the life of this style, and which have been studied particularly for Crete, Rhodes, Corinth and Laconia. In the second place, cutting across local difference, is a regular stylistic development, from a thin triangular face with a pointed chin to a fat trapezoidal face with a square chin.

Jenkins's stylistic phases, with his dates, are as follows: Protodedalic, 680–670: Early Dedalic, 670–655; Middle Dedalic (with three sub-phases), 655–630; Late Dedalic, 630–620; Subdedalic, 620–600.

What of the bodies which went with the Dedalic heads? Sometimes they were moulded in one piece with the head to make a Dedalic plaque, a local adaptation of the Syrian Astarte Plaque[1] (pls. 10, 11, 15). These plaques are solid, with a fully moulded front and a flat back, and portray a frontal female figure. In some examples she stands out in relief against a background; in others the surrounding clay has been cut away, to give the effect rather of a flat figurine.

Like her Syrian prototype, she can be either naked or draped; but, except in Crete, the

[1] See *Berytus*, ix (1949), 69 ff.

draped version found considerably more favour in Greek eyes. Whether naked or draped, she usually has both arms by her sides, but the naked variety sometimes presses both hands to her breasts, or one hand to her breast and the other to her womb, in the typical guise of the oriental fertility-goddess from whom the type is ultimately derived.

Dedalic heads were also employed on shapeless hand-made or wheel-made bodies. In Ionia the bodies tended to be wheel-made and cylindrical; in Rhodes hand-made and cylindrical; on the Greek mainland hand-made and completely flat.

The above remarks apply roughly to the seventh century. In the sixth century the development of terracottas took one course in Eastern Greece, another on the Greek mainland. In the former area plastic vases and figurines of the Gorgoneion and Aphrodite Groups reigned almost supreme; they are discussed below (p. 30). In mainland Greece, development of seventh century figures continued almost to the end of the sixth century. The bodies, generally hand-made and flat, were if anything more uninspired than their predecessors. The heads followed, from a considerable distance, the developments initiated by the sculptors of the period. In addition to the moulded, or partly moulded, varieties just mentioned, purely hand-made figurines of inferior quality continued to flourish throughout the seventh and sixth centuries, and even beyond.

In the west we find evidence both of the Eastern and the Mainland Greek developments.

CRETE

The seventh century saw a substantial output of terracottas in Crete; indeed, as has been remarked above, it seems probable that the Dedalic style originated there. After the beginning of the sixth century there was a considerable drop in the output not only of terracottas, but indeed of every artistic product.

Material of this period has been found in many places, in particular at Praisos, Lato, Siteia, Knossos, Anavlochos, Axos, Gortyn and Arkades. There is little evidence for export outside Crete, but isolated pieces probably of Cretan origin have been found at Perachora, the Argive Heraeum, and Tarentum.

The commonest varieties are Dedalic plaques and other kinds of reliefs, but free-standing human figures are also found. Decoration is in matt paint. It is rare elsewhere to find terracottas decorated so early in this medium, but is hardly surprising in Crete, in view of the popularity of vases in this technique at a date quite as early.

The clay of Eastern Crete is powdery and lightly fired. It is usually pale orange in colour and frequently has a brown or cream surface. That of Gortyn is somewhat similar, but paler; that of Axos rather coarser. The clay of Knossos varies somewhat; it is described below on p. 59, in connection with the more abundant material of the fifth and fourth centuries.

THE PRINCIPAL TYPES

1] Dedalic plaques are commoner in Crete than elsewhere, a fact which suggests that it was here that the Syrian Astarte Plaque evolved into the Greek Dedalic plaque. The evolution may be traced from Protodedalic, through Early, Middle and Late Dedalic to the Subdedalic of about 600. The naked type with hands to sides (pl. 10E) is most popular, but the other varieties, naked and draped, are also found. A high polos is generally worn. Pl. 10D shows a simple draped variety; pl. 10E one with unusually elaborate drapery; and pl. 10A a later version, of about 600 B.C., perhaps representing Cybele.

2] Reliefs of a man in profile with Dedalic hair, wearing a long chiton, are common at Praisos (pl. 10C). The type has frequently been discussed, and is assigned to the first half of the seventh century. The man is perhaps a charioteer, a function which would explain the long chiton, and the position of the arms.

3] Reliefs of warriors in the style of Late Geometric vase-painting are also common at Praisos. Boardman has argued convincingly that these reliefs are no earlier than the early seventh century.

4] Rectangular relief-plaques with sphinxes and griffins were made throughout the seventh century, and have been found at many sites (pl. 10B). The faces on the sphinxes are usually frontal, and cover the Early, Middle and Late Dedalic phases. Sometimes the relief is converted to a cut-out by the removal of the background clay. The same moulds were evidently used for these plaques and for relief-decoration on clay storage-jars.

5] A rarer type of plaque has a winged man, sometimes called a demon. His head and chest face the front, while his legs stride to the right. In his hands he holds the tendrils of a plant, which makes an artistic frame to the lower part of the plaque. Identical versions of this type have been found at Perachora and at the Argive Heraeum. The style of the head is without doubt Cretan, and it seems probable that we have here two Cretan imports, rather than local copies, as has been alleged.

6] Narrative reliefs are another Cretan speciality of the seventh century. The story of Theseus and Ariadne is told on plaques from Tarentum, from Gortyn and Perachora, and the murder of Agamemnon is portrayed on another plaque from Gortyn.

7] Dedalic heads on wheel-made bodies occur rarely. An Athena from Gortyn is a particularly fine example of this type of figurine.

8] Dedalic heads on hand-made bodies, flat or cylindrical, are also found at Gortyn, but are rare. From Gortyn too come hand-made pseudo-Dedalic heads on hand-made bodies.

RHODES

Rhodes has yielded a rich harvest of terracottas of the seventh and sixth centuries B.C. The principal sources are tombs at Camirus and Ialysus and votive deposits at Camirus,

Ialysus and Lindus. The characteristic products of the seventh and of the sixth centuries differ so greatly that the two centuries are best considered separately.

A] *The seventh century*

Quantities of imported Cypriot pieces indicate the direction from which the Rhodian coroplasts of the seventh century drew their inspiration. Apart from a few old-fashioned survivals of the Geometric style, the characteristic figurines of the seventh century are in the very different Dedalic manner; some completely moulded as plaques, most with hand-made bodies and moulded heads.

Decoration is generally absent; when present it is in a poorish black glaze. The clay is the same as in the previous period (see p. 19).

THE PRINCIPAL TYPES

1] Some crude hand-made pieces in the style of the eighth century continued into the seventh. An example is a mourning woman from Camirus.

2] Fully moulded Dedalic plaques, probably copied from Cretan models, were made in Rhodes, but were never popular. The favoured variety is the naked woman with arms at her sides (pl. 11A); it seems to have been discarded after the Early Dedalic period. These plaques are unusual in having a substantial base, which enables them to stand upright.

3] The characteristic Rhodian terracotta of the seventh century is a standing woman with a moulded head and a hand-made cylindrical body, nearly always solid. The only modelling on the body consists of stumpy arms and blobs of clay for the breasts. The bodies are clearly copied from contemporary Cypriot figures, many of which have been found in Rhodes, but the heads are purely Greek in style. They run the whole gamut from Protodedalic, through Early, Middle and Late Dedalic, to Subdedalic.

An Early Dedalic figure in pl. 11D reaches a somewhat higher standard than usual. It represents a mourner tearing her hair; scratches, filled with red, on breast and cheeks indicate that she has already drawn blood from those areas. A typical Middle Dedalic piece, with its broader face, is shown on pl. 11B.

Our series continues with the Late Dedalic face of pl. 11C with its almost square jowl; and ends with pl. 11E, where the Dedalic canon is dissolving in an attempt at greater realism.

4] A few crude hand-made animal figures were also produced in the seventh century.

B] *The sixth century*

The sixth century is represented in Rhodes chiefly by plastic vases and figurines of the so-called Gorgoneion and Aphrodite Groups (see below). If the suggestion made below is correct, the former were made locally, the latter imported, but certainty is still far away in this field.

THE GORGONEION AND APHRODITE GROUPS

Towards the end of the seventh century B.C. a group of plastic vases (the Gorgoneion Group) originated somewhere in the Eastern Greek world and rapidly attained such popularity that in many East Greek centres local production of figurines virtually ceased in favour of these minor masterpieces. In the course of the sixth century a related group, the Aphrodite Group, evolved from it and became even more popular. Then, around 500 B.C., this second group was succeeded by a third, the Post-Aphrodite Group.

The origin of these groups is as yet unknown. The two last-mentioned have so much in common that a common origin may be regarded as certain. Whether the Gorgoneion Group was made in the same centre is less certain. The two strongest candidates for all groups are Rhodes and Samos, where the majority have been found. To judge from the clay, it is possible that the Gorgoneion Group was made in Rhodes, the other two at some South Ionian centre, whether that centre be Samos, Miletus, or elsewhere in that neighbourhood. So far as style is concerned, the Gorgoneion Group has all too little to tell us, but the other two have strong stylistic ties with the sculptures of Samos and Miletus. It may then be accepted as a working hypothesis, but no more, that the Gorgoneion Group is Rhodian, the Aphrodite and Post-Aphrodite Samian or Milesian.[1]

A] *Gorgoneion Group*

This group, named after one of the subjects represented, originated in the late seventh century, and lasted for rather more than fifty years. It was evidently extremely popular, for representatives of it have been found in considerable numbers in the ancient Greek world and beyond. Most have been found in Samos and Rhodes. They also occur in the Islands, Western Asia Minor, and the Greek colonies in South Russia; in Sicily, Magna Graecia and Etruria. Surprisingly few have been found on the Greek mainland, which was perhaps a Corinthian preserve for traffic of this kind; and Corinthian plastic vases were in every way as attractive as these (see p. 47). About the middle of the sixth century this group was succeeded by the Aphrodite Group (p. 32), with which it had been in competition for some little time.

The Gorgoneion Group comprises scent-bottles rather than true figurines, a fact which may help to explain their wide distribution. They were evidently exported full of scent, and were bought as much for their contents as for themselves: but we can assume that, once acquired, they were retained, to be refilled when necessary.

They are all hollow-moulded by means of two moulds, generally for the front and back

[1] This is not the opinion I held in *BMC* i and ii. I am grateful to J. Boardman and to Erika Diehl (*AA* 1964, 493) for helping me to change my mind. For comparable Ionian sculptures, see Buschor, *Altsam. Standbild.*, passim; also C. Blümel, *Die archaisch-griechischen Skulpturen der staatlichen Museen* (Berlin, 1963), passim.

respectively. The vase-mouth is wheel-made and was attached after moulding, usually to the top of the piece, in the form of a shallow cylinder with a flanged top. These pieces were alwayscare fully touched-up after moulding. The style is simple, with little detail, except in the case of the late type of pl. 12C. The rendering of the human face is hard and unsympathetic. The clay is fairly fine in texture, with a finer surface. It is generally pale orange or brown, occasionally almost white. Mica is seldom present in any quantity. The fabric is light in weight, with thin walls.

The decoration consists of a glaze, at its best dead black, with a metallic sheen, but too often misfired to a dull brown. It is helped out with applied red, dark purple (a mixture of red and black) and white, and with incised lines.

Similar clay and decoration is found in certain cups, from Rhodes and elsewhere in Eastern Greece, of about 600 B.C. They must surely come from the same centre as the Gorgoneion Group. That centre has not as yet been identified for certain, but Rhodes is certainly a strong probability.[1]

THE PRINCIPAL GORGONEION TYPES

1. *Female busts.* Female busts comprise one of the commonest varieties. The earliest surviving version is shown on pl. 12A. The wig-like coiffure is in the Dedalic tradition, but the modelling of the face is in the Postdedalic style of 620–600 B.C.

The canonical type is shown on pl. 12B. The face, though coarse-featured, is considerably more lifelike than pl. 12A, and the Dedalic coiffure has been abandoned in favour of a more naturalistic arrangement. The whites of the eyes are indicated in brilliant paint; the brows, lids and irises are marked with dark purple. She wears a red chiton, a black transverse himation, a necklace and disc-earrings. The type had a long life; it is dated by tomb-groups from about 610 to 570 B.C.

A third version, dated about 570 B.C., is illustrated on pl. 12C. It exhibits a remarkable increase in realism and sensitivity. The costume is basically the same, but the treatment is different. The fleshy slant-eyed face and the crinkly folds of the drapery are characteristic of East Greek sculpture of this period, and the bust breathes the spirit of some lost masterpiece.

2. *Male busts.* Male busts are occasionally found. They differ little from the earlier type of female bust of pl. 12B, but for the addition of a moustache.

3. *Gorgoneion bust.* A Gorgon bust also occurs. Although the type is rare, it has given its name to the group.

4. *Female figures.* Complete female figures in this group are represented by one surviving example (pl. 12D), and a possible second (see p. 38). The upper part is a replica of the standard female bust of this group shown on pl. 12B; the lower part consists of a cylindrical

[1] K. F. Kinch, *Vroulia* (Berlin, 1914), pl. 8:2.

body. The himation arches over her stomach, the right side extending lower than the left. Her right arm is stiffly at her side; her left is raised to her breast. This is a clumsy and probably an earlier version of the Samian sculptural type known best in the so-called Hera of Cheramyes in Paris.[1] This type is probably copied from a vanished marble predecessor of the Hera. By analogy with the busts, it should be dated in the late seventh or early sixth century.

The top of this piece is damaged, and it is not clear whether it was originally a plastic vase or a simple figurine. Detailed examination has however revealed possible traces of the vase-mouth, and it would be unreasonable to regard this as a pure figurine, the only one in the whole surviving Gorgoneion Group.[2]

5. *Sirens.* Sirens figure occasionally in the Gorgoneion Group repertoire; they were probably a late addition. They are important as they lead on directly to the popular Aphrodite Group siren.

Other types of plastic vase, less relevant to the development of figurines, include heads of warriors and various animals, and complete figures of animals, birds and cockleshells.

B] *Aphrodite Group*

The Gorgoneion Group died out about 550 B.C. leaving the field clear for the Aphrodite Group. This group evolved about 575 B.C. from the Gorgoneion Group and for some twenty-five years coexisted with it. By the middle of the sixth century the canonical Aphrodite types were established, many of them to persist with little change for half a century.

Terracottas of this new group were made as plentifully as their predecessors, and exported even more widely. The difference between the two are fourfold.

1. *Decoration.* The glaze decoration of the Gorgoneion Group is replaced by the more attractive polychrome matt paint. During the period of competition pieces of the same type occasionally recur in both techniques, but the matt-painted varieties soon completely won the field. It is sometimes hard today to see the reason for this change, because the matt paint is fugitive, and seldom survives burial in the soil. Consequently, while we see the Gorgoneion pieces in virtually their original condition, the Aphrodite Group seldom preserves more than a faint echo of its once brilliant colours.

2. *Clay.* The characteristic clay is unlike that of the Gorgoneion Group. It varies in colour between pale brown and pale orange and is extremely micaceous. The surface has a waxy feel. Similar clay is found in figurines of various dates from Ephesus and Priene. The characteristic clay of Samian figurines is somewhat different, but this clay would not be impossible for Samian if it were refined more than was usual for figurines.

[1] R. Lullies and M. Hirmer, *Greek Sculpture* (London, 1957), pls. 30–31.

[2] Dr Pietrangeli was so kind as to examine this piece for me.

B. Woman holding a hare. See pl. 12F. British Museum

3. *Style.* Old types were brought up to date, and new types were devised. Busts, whether human or animal, give place to complete figures, and there is a corresponding increase in size. The style is richer and more voluptuous; faces are fuller and softer, and folds and creases of drapery are rendered with loving precision.

4. *Function.* Whereas the Gorgoneion Group was apparently composed entirely of plastic vases, this group comprises both plastic vases and figurines proper, the only material difference between the two classes being the presence or absence of the familiar vase-mouth.

Technically, there is little difference between the two groups, apart from the method of decoration. Where the piece is a figurine and not a vase, there is a knife-thrust or pin-hole in the underside. Careful retouching was again the rule.

It is possible that all the human figures in this group are copied from contemporary works of sculpture. Some possible models have survived, from Samos, Miletus and other Ionian cities (see note 1, p. 30).

The principal subjects comprise human figures in various poses; human busts; mythological creatures; animals; animals' heads; birds. This group flourished from about 575 B.C. and was exported not only to the areas to which the Gorgoneion Group had penetrated, but also in quantities to the Greek mainland. The Aphrodite Group was also imitated in many places, especially Thasos, Sicily and Locri.

The group ceased to exist about 500 B.C. to be succeeded by the less popular Post-Aphrodite Group (see p. 64). The reason for this abrupt change is not clear, but it must in some way have been connected with the Ionian Revolt, from the effects of which the East Greek cities did not recover for many years.

THE PRINCIPAL APHRODITE TYPES

In the absence of any statement to the contrary, all the types described below were made both as vases and as figurines.

1. *Standing women.* Several principal varieties may be noted.

a) A rare type, always a scent-bottle (pl. 12E). This is one of the earliest types of this class of standing woman. It evolved from the type shown on pl. 12D, in the second quarter of the sixth century. She wears a chiton and a transverse himation going over her right shoulder, arching over her stomach and falling lower down the right side than down the left. Her right arm is stiffly by her side; with her left hand she is apparently holding some object, not indicated, against her breast. Her hair is tightly curled over her head, and falls on her shoulders. Her face is full, with almond-shaped eyes.

b) The position of the arms is reversed, with a more balanced effect (pl. 12F, Colour Plate B). In addition, she grasps the central panel of the chiton and pulls it to the side. In her right hand she holds a young hare to her breast. Her full face has rather a frigid smile, and her eyes bulge. This version (found only as a vase) also belongs in the second quarter of the sixth century.

c) The type from which the group is named evolved about 550 and proved extremely popular, being widely exported and imitated. It is the first human type in this group to be made both as a plastic vase (pl. 13D–E), and as a figurine (pl. 13F). She stands with the left foot forward, wearing a headband, chiton and transverse himation. With her left hand she holds a dove to her breast, and with her right she draws to the side the central panel of the chiton, a motive already found in the foregoing type. This motive was apparently invented in Ionia and was to become extremely popular in sculpture and in the minor arts in the second half of the sixth century B.C.

The effective way in which the himation arches over the top of the buttocks recalls an Attic statue, the so-called Aphrodite of Lyons.[1] On the evidence of tomb-groups, this type may be dated to the third quarter of the sixth century. It is by no means certain that Aphrodite herself, and not a votary, is represented; but the name will serve to give a descriptive title to the group. Occasionally she is equipped with crude hand-made wings, attached after moulding.

d) Like type *c*, but with the position and function of the arms reversed (pl. 14C). This type also evolved around 550 B.C., but had a longer life than the other, for examples have been found in contexts as late as the end of the sixth century. In these later examples the features and the drapery are more naturalistically rendered.

e) A rare variant of types *c* and *d* has both arms raised symmetrically to the breast.

f) The figure is janiform, with two frontal aspects, and no back, often incorporating two different types.

g) In some examples the standard Aphrodite figure has been cut off at the waist, leaving a bust of the same order as the Gorgoneion vases. This type is always a vase.

h) A rare and late type has a face modelled closely on the seated type of pl. 13A, but a body approaching the Post-Aphrodite style of pl. 24A. An example from Sicily is shown on pl. 14E. The body is like type *d*, but the naturalism is carried a stage further. It is clearly transitional between the Aphrodite and the Post-Aphrodite phases. From its occurrence in the west it should be placed in the former rather than in the latter category, and should be dated at the very end of the sixth century.

2. *Seated women. a*) On pl. 13A is the simplest form of seated woman. She sits stiffly on a throne with a footstool, hands on knees, wearing a low stephane, headband, chiton, and symmetrical himation covering her head, back and sides hanging in folds from the knees. She has a plump and smiling face with almond-shaped eyes. The fleshy face and the block-like treatment of the seated body have many parallels in surviving East Greek

[1] H. Payne and G. M. Young, *Archaic Marble Sculpture from the Acropolis* (London, 1936), pl. 22.

sculptures of the sixth century. Evidence from tomb-groups suggests the origin of this type in terracotta about 550; it lasted till about 500. The normal pieces, about 15 cm. tall, were made both as vases and as figurines, but there are also a few much larger and more ornate examples, which are always figurines and never vases.

b) Another common seated woman of this fabric (pl. 13B) differs from the foregoing in that she wears a tall polos and the figure is never a plastic vase. The time span is the same as for the foregoing class. The polos suggests a goddess, in particular Hera, but the absence of attributes generally, and the different character of two attributes occasionally found (a dove and a child), suggests that her identity was not irrevocably fixed.

3. *Sirens.* Sirens were also popular (pl. 14A). The siren of the Aphrodite Group derives directly from a later Gorgoneion type (see p. 32). On the evidence of recently published tombs at Corinth and Tarentum, the type evolved as early as 575 B.C. and persisted for about three-quarters of a century. The body is that of a bird, with spreading tail and folded wings. The head, turned sideways to face the spectator, is that of the standard Aphrodite Group figure.

4. *Standing men.* A heavily draped man (pl. 14D) stands with his left leg slightly advanced, arms stiffly at sides, wearing a long chiton and a transverse himation pinned on his left shoulder. The type, usually a figurine proper but occasionally a vase, owes much to a sculptural type represented at Samos.[1] The evidence of tomb-groups indicates that it had a long life throughout the second half of the sixth century.

5. *Seated men.* Seated men are occasionally found. They resemble the first class of seated women (pl. 13A), but with a male head, bearded.

6. *Seated pair.* Occasionally we find a composite piece composed of a man and woman seated side by side.

7. *Reclining men.* A half-draped man reclines on his left elbow. In his left hand he holds a bowl, or more commonly, a rhyton.

8. *Kneeling figures.* Naked men and, occasionally, satyrs are presented in a kneeling position (pl. 13C). The type has strong Egyptian affinities. There is a contemporary Attic version (pl. 16).

9. *Crouching dwarfs.* Crouching dwarfs are very common. A naked dwarf stands with his knees bent, hands clasped over his stomach (pl. 14B). His face is fat and smiling, and his stomach and buttocks protrude. The type is found in two sizes, about 15 cm. and 7 cm. tall respectively. The larger variety is generally made as a vase, the smaller never. Additions to the figure, frequently of a grotesque nature, are not uncommon. Blinkenberg discusses this class at length; in his view we have here a derivation of the Egyptian Ptah-Sokhar-Osiris comparable with the Phoenician Pataikos.

10. *Other types.* Other types of the Aphrodite Group, always made as vases, are modifi-

[1] Buschor, *Altsam. Standbild.*, figs. 160–162.

cations of established Gorgoneion types. They comprise figures of animals, animal-heads and birds and are of less importance than the others for the study of terracottas.

IONIA

A] *Samos*

Samian terracottas of the seventh and sixth centuries come principally, as before, from the Samian Heraeum; a few, in addition, were found in tombs nearby. The Aphrodite Group, whose Samian origin is possible, but not certain, has been considered separately.

The first half of the seventh century is characterized by wheel-made human and hand-made animal figures. The great advance over the eighth century lies in the occasional use of the mould, probably introduced from Cyprus, and virtually restricted at this stage to human heads on wheel-made bodies, although fully moulded Dedalic plaques are occasionally found. The heads are sometimes in the canonical Dedalic style, but more frequently in a less elegant but more vigorous local idiom.

In the second half of the seventh century local wares are scarce, their place being largely taken by imported Cypriot terracottas and by figurines in other materials, such as bronze, ivory and wood.

At the end of the seventh century the Samian coroplasts were again active. Their characteristic product of the late seventh and the first half of the sixth century is a hollow-moulded figurine. This is apparently the earliest instance of the use of this technique for figurines. This period is also richly represented by the technically related Gorgoneion Group of plastic vases, probably of Rhodian origin (see p. 30).

The second half of the sixth century was dominated in Samos, as at many sites, by plastic vases and figurines of the Aphrodite Group, which was possibly made in Samos or nearby.

Throughout the seventh century, the development was strongly affected by Cypriot figurines, which were imported in small quantities in the first half of the century and in large numbers from the mid seventh to the early sixth. As stated above, it seems likely that the technique of moulding was learnt from Cyprus, for moulded Cypriot figurines are found in Samos made in this way as early as the beginning of the seventh century.

The clay is the same as in the previous period (see p. 18). The decoration is more varied, white, added red and violet being employed in addition to the standard black glaze.

THE PRINCIPAL TYPES

1] In the early seventh century solid hand-made human figures are found, in the same technique as the crude eighth century figures, but generally better made.

2] Draped human figures (female more often than male) with hollow wheel-made bodies continued throughout the seventh century. Generally, an attempt is now made to give the body a more naturalistic effect than before, by pinching in the waist. The heads now take several forms. They can be modelled by hand; they can be thrown on the wheel with the body and subsequently modelled by hand; or they can be moulded. The moulded heads, which may be either solid or hollow, are in the Dedalic style, or in a less elegant local style. Pl. 15B shows a true Dedalic head, of about 650 B.C.

3] Solid Dedalic plaques also occur in the seventh century (pl. 15A), but were never common.

4] Hollow-moulded female figures make an early appearance at Samos, in the late seventh century; so early that the home of this technique may well be located here.

In a fairly common type, which originated in the late seventh century and lasted into the early sixth, a woman in long drapery stands with both hands on her stomach (pl. 15G). Her hair is arranged in tight curls across her forehead and falls in an unkempt mass on her shoulders. Front and back are both moulded. The type, though technically advanced, is less so aesthetically. The hideous face, the enormous hands and feet and the ungainly pose, are remarkable even for this early period.

A second type is represented by a fragmentary standing figure of the late seventh century, also hollow-moulded back and front. This figure bears a close resemblance to the Gorgoneion type shown on pl. 12D, except that the arms were at the sides, and should perhaps be classed with that group. The base was attached separately and completely closed the figure underneath, so that the piece may well have been not a figurine but a plastic vase. Folds in the drapery were added with a modelling tool.

5] Hand-made and wheel-made figures of animals continued without much change from the eighth century for at least another fifty years.

6] Finally, satyr-masks, probably reproducing in clay the masks (of linen) actually used in satyr-plays, were found at Samos, and are surely of local workmanship, as none similar have been found elsewhere. On stylistic grounds, they may be dated in the second half of the sixth century.

B] *Ephesus*

Another Ionian city in which terracottas were produced is Ephesus, where examples have been found on the site of the Artemision. The amount of extant material is not great, but the general development would appear to correspond partially at least to that of Samos. The full seventh century is represented by Dedalic plaques; the late seventh and early sixth by wheel-made female figures; and the second half of the sixth by plastic vases and figurines of the Aphrodite Group.

Ephesian clay is orange in colour, very micaceous, rather coarse in texture, with a finer surface, and usually lightly fired. Decoration is in glaze (firing black or red) sometimes over a white slip.

THE PRINCIPAL TYPES

1] There is an example in London of a clumsy hand-made statuette of a standing woman, of about 600 B.C.

2] Figurines with hollow wheel-made bodies are also found. The body of one example has a pinched-in waist, like Samian examples of the late seventh century. No heads survive, and their nature is consequently unknown.

3] Dedalic plaques occur in the Early, Middle and Late styles. The Early Dedalic variety (pl. 15E) is naked, with hands by the sides. The Middle and Late Dedalic pieces are draped, with the hands clasped over the abdomen, an unusual pose for this type of plaque (pl. 15F).

c] *Miletus*

The only evidence at present available from Miletus is a very fine Dedalic head, in the Middle or perhaps the Late Dedalic style, from the Temple of Athena. It is probably not a figurine in the strict sense of the word, but an archetype for the making of a mould.

COS

After the dolls of the eighth century, there is no recorded evidence of a Coan terracotta industry before the second half of the sixth century, when we find local imitations of Aphrodite Group figures. These pieces, which come from the Asklepeion and from a shrine of Demeter, are readily distinguishable from their models by certain technical differences and by the clay.

Technically they are inferior to the genuine Aphrodite pieces, being thick-walled and unduly thick from front to back, with a tendency to come apart at the joins. The clay is pink to red in colour, generally fine in texture, and hard.

AEOLIS

The site of Larisa on the Hermus, excavated first by the Swedes and later by the Germans, between 1902 and 1934, has produced a number of figurines of the seventh and sixth centuries B.C.

A few hand-made pieces in the Late Geometric style have been found in seventh century levels. The clay of some is the grey *bucchero* of Aeolic pottery; of others, a coarse, friable, reddish-brown variety, rich in mica, which was generally used in subsequent periods.

The sixth century is represented by a few poor imitations of Aphrodite Group figurines.

THE CYCLADES

Our knowledge of Cycladic terracottas is at present too fragmentary for a systematic study, but the available evidence may be summarized as follows.

A] *Thera*

There is evidence of a terracotta industry on this island from quite early times. Local products are readily identifiable by the coarse, red, volcanic clay of which they are made.

1] A group of crude hand-made figures of naked, or nearly naked, women, and a horse, should be dated in the late eighth or the early seventh century.

2] Three female figures are more worthy of consideration. The heads are moulded in the Middle Dedalic style of the mid seventh century. Not unnaturally, considering the geographical position of Thera, there is evidence of strong Cretan influence. Only one piece is complete; it has a hollow wheel-made body. The woman is a mourner, who tears the left side of her head with her left hand, her left cheek with her right (pl. 15H). She wears a long chiton with short sleeves, tightly belted. A figurine from Lato indicates the Cretan origin of this type.

The second and third figures have almost completely lost their bodies. One was tearing her hair with both hands, and is clearly a mourner like the first example; the other was apparently holding her arms forward from the elbows. The decoration, which is well preserved, is in matt paint, another indication of Cretan influence.

In the sixth century the needs of the Theran population seem to have been satisfied principally with imported pieces of the Aphrodite Group, of which considerable numbers have been found on the island. The only local piece hitherto identified is a coarse, apparently hand-made, figure of a standing woman, without a head, which may perhaps date about 600.

B] *Siphnos*

Two large figures of draped women, their heads missing, come from a votive deposit on Siphnos. They are decorated in the style of Cycladic vases of the first half of the seventh century; but it is not certain on which particular Cycladic island the figurines, or the vases, were made. The complete pieces were wheel-made like the seventh century Theran examples mentioned above.

C] *Paros*

About 200 figurines (local products and imports) were found at the Delion at Paros. The local clay is normally of various shades of brown, but occasionally brick-red, and contains mica. Two varieties were noted, one fine in texture, the other coarser, with white particles.

A few of the terracottas are hand-made or moulded solid; the majority are hollow, and double-moulded.

The repertoire is composed almost entirely of copies of the Aphrodite Group, which was also imported in quantity.

D] *Naxos*

A head from a Dedalic plaque, in the style of about 650 B.C., is recorded from Naxos. A brief excavation-report refers to 'many archaic idols', evidently of terracotta, but these are not illustrated or further described.

E] *Delos*

Delos has no natural clay and there is no evidence for local production from imported clay before the Hellenistic period. Numbers of terracottas of the sixth century were found on the island, but all are imports, most, it would appear, from Ionia and Cyprus. The principal sources are the Sanctuary of Hera and the Purification Trench on Rheneia.

THASOS

Thanks to its mines, Thasos was a rich island, where the arts flourished. Our sources for early terracottas are two deposits at the Artemision.

The seventh century is represented by the lower part of a wheel-made female figurine decorated in the Orientalizing style.

The sixth century is represented chiefly by imitations of the Aphrodite Group, but there was one popular indigenous type, a seated goddess wearing a chiton, a symmetrical himation and a polos (pl. 15D). Her forearms, attached separately, were stretched forwards. The face indicates a date in the first half of the sixth century B.C. These pieces, which are completely moulded in front, probably betray the influence of the Corinthian terracotta tradition, but are, nevertheless, a genuine local creation.

The clay is brick-red and very micaceous.

LEMNOS

Lemnos was always somewhat on the periphery of the Greek world, and seems to have preferred to look eastwards to Asia Minor. A number of terracotta types however deserve mention.

1] Draped female figures with moulded heads and wheel-made bodies, their arms raised, come from a votive deposit dated by the excavators in the eighth century, but more probably to be assigned to the seventh.

2] Flat figures, moulded in front, of a winged goddess and a siren, both wearing earrings and a spreading polos, are another characteristic Lemnian creation. The heads are in the style of the late seventh or early sixth century.

3] Another variety, which can be dated stylistically about the second half of the sixth century, consists of flat cut-out figures, about 1 cm. thick, with considerably less modelling than the foregoing. Details are lightly incised, and were formerly indicated in colour, which has now largely perished. The types include a man with a lyre, a reclining woman, and a man with a dog (pl. 15c).

ATTICA

The production of terracottas in Attica continued unabated throughout the seventh and sixth centuries. In Athens itself, figurines have been found on the Acropolis (where they were buried after the Persian sack of 480 B.C.); on the Pnyx; in the Agora; and in the Cerameicus cemetery. Sources outside Attica include Eleusis, Brauron and Menidi. Of these sites, the Agora and the Cerameicus provide valuable chronological evidence. Final publication of both sites is still awaited, but much useful information is available in the preliminary reports.

Most figures of the seventh and sixth centuries are hand-made. Moulds were occasionally used for heads, but for little else. The subjects are virtually restricted to standing and seated women, warriors, horses (with or without riders) and chariots. Complete figurines, generally depicting mourners, were often attached to funerary vases, by which they can be dated. The fully moulded female figures which appeared in the late sixth century are discussed in a later chapter (p. 72).

The usual clay is the pale brown colour of contemporary Attic vases, fine in texture, and generally slightly micaceous.

For decoration, glaze was still employed, but as an increasingly popular alternative, matt paint is now found, sometimes resting on the clay, at others laid over a white slip. The inference to be drawn from this innovation is that the craft of the potter and the coroplast were now beginning to diverge.

THE PRINCIPAL TYPES

1] Hand-made female figures with columnar bodies, and rudimentary arms, are widespread. They occur in deposits in the Agora and on the North Slope of the Acropolis dating between 650 and the early fifth century, and also on the Acropolis itself, on the Pnyx, and at Eleusis.

2] Hand-made figures of warriors were found in a shrine in the Agora of 700–650 B.C. (pl. 17c).

3] Horses, with and without riders, are very common (pl. 17A). They occur in deposits in the Agora and on the North Slope of the Acropolis between 700 and the early fifth century, and also on the Acropolis and at Eleusis.

4] Chariot groups continued from the eighth into the seventh century, but in an inferior form. They occur in a votive deposit and a well in the Agora of 700–650 and in undated contexts at Menidi and Eleusis.

5] A funeral group in Athens from Vari, usually dated about 600 B.C., may be regarded as an elaborate version of the primitive class. It consists of a wagon carrying a corpse, which is covered with a cloth. Round the corpse stand four female mourners. A horseman escorts the wagon.

6] Figurines with flat hand-made bodies and moulded heads have been found on the Acropolis, in the Cerameicus, and elsewhere. The series may have started in the seventh century, since a number of Dedalic heads, possibly broken from such figurines, have survived (pl. 17B). For the sixth century the evidence is more plentiful; in Attica these figurines were more often seated than standing.

Figures of this kind were often attached to vases. A series from the Cerameicus on vases by the Cerameicus Painter are securely dated to the early sixth century. Other vases of the seventh and sixth centuries from this cemetery have attached figures, in nearly all cases representing mourners. They must have been made specially for burial with the dead.

Pl. 17E shows a free-standing example from a tomb in the Cerameicus of 540–530 B.C. A goddess is seated on a throne with ornamental arms. She wears a peplos secured on the shoulders by large circular-headed pins, earrings, and apparently some sort of diadem. An ornamental chain hangs loosely between the pins securing her drapery.

The fleshy and somewhat amorphous face betrays the influence of East Greek art, which was making its presence felt in the sculptures of this period.

7] The typically East Greek variety with a moulded head and a wheel-made body occurs at Brauron and is imitated in four exquisite figures of mourners (attached to a base), from a tomb in the Cerameicus (pl. 17D), but here the bodies are hand-made. The style of the faces would suggest a date contemporary with the Cerameicus Painter's attached figurines, i.e. the early sixth century. The decoration is in glaze.

8] A painted plaque of a goddess comes from a seventh century shrine in the Agora. She stands with her arms raised in an attitude reminiscent of the Minoan Household Goddess of pl. 5D. On each side of her is a snake, another feature whose origin goes back to the Bronze Age. The plaque is gaily coloured in red, green, yellow and white. The head, in the Dedalic style, is moulded in relief, and attached to the plaque.

9] An exquisite scent-bottle from the Agora in the form of a kneeling boy athlete (pl. 16) cannot go unnoticed, although it is the work of a potter rather than a coroplast, and has not the justification of the East Greek plastic vases, to have influenced the course of subsequent terracottas.

It was found in association with pottery of 540–530 B.C., and its date in that decade is thus reasonably certain. He is depicted binding a fillet (which was supplied in some other material) round his brow in token of an athletic victory, probably at the newly inaugurated Panathenaic Games. The face and the whole figure clearly owe much to the contemporary Aphrodite Group (see p. 32), but the clay leaves no doubt of its Attic origin, and the face and the body have a muscularity at variance with the less athletic East Greek youths.

10] Protomes ranging in date from the early to the late sixth century have been found at a number of sites. For the most part they are made in the form of a flat figurine cut off at breast level.

The oldest of these, of about 600 B.C., come from Brauron, and are among the earliest

FIG. 13. Female Protome. From Brauron. About 600 B.C.

FIG. 14. Female Protome. Attic type. About 550 B.C.

Greek protomes (fig. 13). They were perhaps taken from Phoenician originals, for it would appear that Phoenicia was the home of this type of abbreviated figurine.[1] In these we see the remains of the hieratic quality of the Dedalic style. Another type, of the mid sixth century (fig. 14), has a rayed headdress and a splayed body; a third has a nondescript head and a rectangular body.

[1] D. Harden, *The Phoenicians* (London, 1962), pl. 77, and figs. 60–61.

MEGARA

A number of terracottas in London and Paris were found at Megara and were presumably made there. They have plank-like bodies and coarse moulded heads in the style of the earlier sixth century. As might be expected from their place of origin, these pieces stand stylistically halfway between Athens and Corinth.

BOEOTIA

Although terracottas were produced in Boeotia in the eighth century (see p. 23), it seems that very few were made in the seventh. There is no well-dated source for this period, nor is there much undated material which could belong to that century. For the sixth century, however, there is a wealth of material, the key to which is provided by the cemetery of Rhitsona (the ancient Mycalessus), an exceptionally well-excavated and well-published site. Grace's detailed study of Boeotian sixth century sculpture has also done much to explain the development of contemporary terracottas.

The tombs at Tanagra, excavated belatedly by the Greek Archaeological Society after the robbers had done their worst, produced numerous terracottas of this period, but no details of the excavation have been published.

The most popular subjects are female figures, either entirely hand-made or with moulded heads and hand-made, or (less commonly) wheel-made bodies, and hand-made animals.

The clay is fairly fine in texture, usually micaceous, and varying in colour between yellow ochre, pale orange and brown. It is generally lightly fired.

From 600 to 550 B.C. two systems of decoration were employed; black glaze with added red, and matt paint (only in black and red) over a white slip. From 550 to 500 only matt paint was used, and yellow was added to the earlier repertoire.

THE PRINCIPAL TYPES

1] Hand-made female figures with cylindrical bodies, rudimentary arms, long necks and virtually no heads are recorded from tombs at Rhitsona of the early sixth century. A related type is found in Attica as early as 650 B.C. (see p. 42) and it was probably introduced into Boeotia from that quarter.

2] Hand-made female figures with a flat body, a long neck and a mouse-like head crowned by a low polos with a large volute (pl. 18A–B) were common at Tanagra, but are not recorded at Rhitsona, and cannot therefore be dated stratigraphically. The women usually stand, but occasionally sit. The decoration is in glaze. Grace dates the type tentatively, but with a fair degree of probability, to the early sixth century, with a possible origin in the seventh.

3] Figures somewhat similar to the foregoing are also common at Tanagra, and have been found in addition in mid sixth century tombs at Rhitsona. They differ in their smaller size, shorter necks, and more bird-like faces, and in their matt-painted system of decoration (pl. 18C–D).

4] Female figures with completely flat bodies and fully modelled heads, nearly always moulded, are the sixth century Boeotian figurines *par excellence*. The bodies either stand or are made to sit by being bent at hips and knees with some sort of support behind (see pl. 19A). The heads, in contrast to the bodies, are naturalistically rendered and are often made with great care, even when modelled by hand.

These figures started about 600 B.C. and continued throughout the sixth century. The women usually wear a tall polos, which suggests that a goddess is indicated, and a pomegranate necklace, which argues for Demeter or Persephone.

There are two stages of development. From 600 to 550 the heads are of particularly high quality and the figures are mostly decorated with black glaze and added red. As this variety is not represented at Rhitsona, it can only be dated by the style of the heads. These, however, since they frequently resemble heads attached to Corinthian vases, are susceptible to a fairly close dating. The seated figure on pl. 19A–B, with a hand-made head, can be dated by this means to the early part of the century; the standing figure, with a moulded head, on pl. 18E, is dated about 575 B.C., and that on pl. 18G falls into the second quarter of the sixth century.

From 550 to 500 decoration is in matt paint, and the faces are flatter and less carefully made. A standing example is shown on pl. 19C, and a seated example on pl. 18F. The Corinthianizing style of the earlier group is replaced by one strongly influenced by the Aphrodite Group. The latter figures, which occur in dated tombs at Rhitsona, were mass-produced to a much greater extent than their predecessors. Their much greater numbers are partly due to the fact that they also took the place of the completely hand-made female figures, which were no longer made after the middle of the century.

5] Female figures after the East Greek model, with moulded heads and wheel-made bodies, were made in small quantities in the first half of the sixth century B.C. (pl. 19F). The decoration is in glaze. Most of the surviving examples are said (probably correctly) to come from Tanagra. As none have been recorded from Rhitsona they can only be dated by the style of the heads.

6] Hand-made figures of horses, sometimes ridden, are recorded from Rhitsona throughout the sixth century B.C., and may have originated in the seventh. Many varieties are found, some decorated with glaze, others with matt paint. The commonest variety is the zebra-striped creature with its legless and feature-less rider shown on pl. 19E.

7] Various other hand-made creatures are found; a bird, a dog with a hare in its mouth, and a squatting monkey (pl. 19D).

8] A few forerunners of the popular genre-figures of the early fifth century (see p. 77) were produced in the sixth. A ploughing scene should probably be dated to the beginning of the century, and a chariot-group to the middle years. A woman seated in front of a table set with loaves of bread may be dated by the style of her head to the second half of the century.

CORINTH

Few terracottas appear to have been made in Corinth in the four centuries between the end of the Mycenaean period and about 700 B.C. The seventh century, however, saw a renaissance in the art of the Corinthian coroplast, which was to flourish for many centuries. For the seventh and the greater part of the sixth century there is a wealth of material, from two sanctuaries of Hera at Perachora, from various deposits in Corinth itself, which include the workshops in the Potters' Quarter, where a quantity of moulds have been discovered, and from a recently discovered sanctuary of Demeter and Kore on Acrocorinth. A votive deposit at Solygeia, near Corinth, has produced a few figurines of this period, and there was considerable export to Ithaca.

The material has been exhaustively studied by Jenkins, Gladys Weinberg and Agnes Stilwell with the result that we have an unusually detailed picture of the Corinthian terracotta industry at this period.

Next to Crete, Corinth has claims to be considered the cradle of the Dedalic style. The discovery at Corinth of an imported Astarte Plaque[1] and a mould made locally from a Syrian model are weighty arguments, but the Prededalic and Early Dedalic material from Corinth is not great as compared with the Cretan material, and the claims of Crete should probably be preferred.

Although made in considerable quantities, Corinthian terracottas were seldom exported far from home before the late sixth century. A few early pieces have, however, been recorded from Rhodes and the west.

The standard of workmanship was not high, a somewhat surprising fact in view of the excellence of contemporary Corinthian plastic vases, made between 620 and 550, in the form of sphinxes, squatting men, lions, hares, rams, etc. These vases are not directly considered in this survey as, unlike the contemporary Gorgoneion Group, they seem to have exerted no influence whatever on the local terracotta industry. The reason for this discrepancy is doubtless that in Corinth the plastic vases were made by the potters, whose wares had for long been of the highest quality, while the figurines were made by the coroplasts, a separate and inferior class. Their products were mass-produced, and, apart from occasional heads of good quality, seldom amounted to anything more than decorated strips of clay.

[1] See p. 26.

Corinthian clay is by far the finest in texture of any used in antiquity for terracottas. It contains little or no mica and is always pale in colour, varying between cream and green and, occasionally, pale orange. Recent investigations have demonstrated that its characteristic qualities are due to the presence of calcium, which counteracts the effect of iron during the firing.

Decoration in the seventh century was in black glaze with added red. In the sixth century matt paint was used as an alternative system, usually applied direct to the clay, less commonly laid over a white slip. Colour was used more generously in the hand-made than in the mould-made pieces.

THE PRINCIPAL TYPES

1] Hand-made female figures of extreme simplicity were made in vast numbers in this period. They generally stand, but are occasionally bent into a seated position and supported behind. Between 700 and 550 the bodies are more often cylindrical than flat, the faces are raised, and the features, if represented at all, are markedly angular. From 550 to 500 the bodies are more often flat, the faces are rounded, and occasionally some attempt is made to model the features. Elaborately applied and painted decoration now becomes common.

2] Hand-made naked standing male figures are also found in the seventh and sixth centuries, but were never popular.

3] Hand-made animals are also found. Horses, with or without riders, are fairly common, and a few hand-made dogs and rams occur in the sixth century.

4] Female figures with moulded heads and flat hand-made bodies were common throughout this period. The characteristic seventh century variety stands with her arms raised in a religious gesture of high antiquity (see p. 11). The heads, in the Dedalic style, are well moulded, and run the gamut from Prededalic to Postdedalic (see pl. 20A, C, E).

A more elaborate type, on pl. 20B, said to come from Thebes, depicts two goddesses, probably Demeter and Persephone, each wearing a low polos and a peplos, seated side by side in a country cart; their faces are in the Late Dedalic style. The pole and wheels of the cart, which are missing, were made separately, possibly of wood, and attached.

The characteristic body of the sixth century is bent at the hips and knees into a sitting position, and supported behind by two struts. Elaborate applied decoration in the shape of earrings, dress-pins, necklaces and pectoral bands is frequently found, but never to the same degree of elaboration as at Argos. The arms are indicated by pinched-out stumps. The heads, influenced, however indirectly, by sixth century sculpture, show an advance in style, if not in workmanship, over the seventh century. Fine sixth century examples, unusually complete, have recently been found at Solygeia (pl. 20D, F).

5] Males (*kouroi*) in this technique are less common, but a fine example from Perachora deserves mention. The head, in the style of the early sixth century, is moulded; the hair was added after moulding; the body is hand-made, with more modelling than is usually found on figures of this class. He stands stiffly, his right foot slightly advanced, his arms held forward from the elbows. The stocky proportions of this figure recall the Argive statues of Cleobis and Biton at Delphi.

6] Female figures with a hollow wheel-made skirt, a hand-made body above the waist, and a moulded head were made in Corinth for a short period, between 625 and 550. The real home of this technique was in the East Greek cities (see p. 37).

7] Fully moulded Dedalic plaques (generally with raised arms) were made throughout the seventh century, but were never common. In the majority of these pieces the clay surround was left on the figure when it left the mould, but on occasions the clay was pared off and a free-standing figure resulted. A type of seated figure of the second quarter of the seventh century was so made. This process was commonest in the last quarter of the seventh century, when standing figures were no longer rendered with raised arms, and it was consequently as easy to make a figurine as a relief.

AEGINA

The island of Aegina is most conveniently considered at this point, since in the period under review it was artistically in the Corinthian orbit.

A head at much the same stage of development as the Laconian head on pl. 21A was found at Aegina. It is uncertain whether it is of local manufacture, or, as Jenkins believes, an Argive import.

The only other terracottas of any importance for the seventh century are four Dedalic plaques from the same mould depicting a draped woman grasping her breasts with both hands. The best preserved example is shown in fig. 15. They are pierced at the top for suspension. Two come from the Temple of Aphaia, two from the Temple of Apollo (at one time miscalled the Temple of Aphrodite).

FIG. 15. Dedalic plaque. From Aegina. About 660 B.C.

These plaques were thought by Jenkins to be Rhodian imports, but the clay is not Rhodian, and the existence of the type in four separate examples here, and nowhere else, is in itself strong presumptive evidence of local origin. The style of the heads is Early Dedalic, and the date about 660 B.C.

In the sixth century, local needs were evidently satisfied by imported figurines and plastic vases of the Gorgoneion and Aphrodite Groups.

ARGOS

As in Boeotia, so in the Argolid, the output of terracottas was apparently slight in the seventh century, but considerable in the sixth. The material comes mostly from Argos, the Argive Heraeum, Tiryns and Perachora. There was little regular export beyond the Corinthia, but isolated specimens have been recorded from Arcadia, Sparta and Boeotia.

The figurines of the seventh and sixth centuries have flat hand-made bodies; the heads are either hand-made and very primitive, or moulded, and more naturalistic. The decoration is predominantly in matt paint, in contrast with the glaze of most contemporary Corinthian pieces. The clay is fairly fine and slightly micaceous, with clear colours, ranging from orange to yellow ochre. The core is frequently grey, a sign both of light firing and of the imperfect combustion of the organic matter present in the clay.

THE PRINCIPAL TYPES

1] Completely hand-made human figures with flat featureless bodies, bent into a seated position and supported behind by two struts, were made throughout the seventh and sixth centuries. The heads are pellets of clay, pinched out in front and equipped with smaller pellets for the eyes. From the start, these pieces were diversified by applied blobs and strips of clay for headdresses, pins, necklaces and pectoral chains. Towards the middle of the sixth century this system of ornamentation ran riot, and the figurines were smothered in a welter of applied decoration. The almost universal presence of a low polos suggests a connection with Hera, as might be expected at Argos.

2] A less common standing type has a stouter rectangular body and a more robust, but scarcely more naturalistic head. An example in London, of unknown provenance, is decorated in glaze paint.

3] Pieces like the common variety described above, but with moulded heads, started towards the end of the seventh century with heads in a Postdedalic style, and continued throughout the sixth. The style of the heads was influenced by Corinthian art, but a distinctive local flavour is always apparent. From 550 onwards, like their counterparts with hand-made heads, these figurines become increasingly overloaded with applied ornament. One of the rare examples of the type to survive in anything like a complete state is shown on pl. 21F. Less commonly, female figures with moulded heads were made in a standing position.

4] Large masks, somewhat resembling gorgons, were found at Tiryns in a votive deposit together with pottery of about 700 B.C. These masks, which are quite different from the better-known masks from Sparta (see p. 52), are probably copies in clay of masks used in some religious ceremony.

TEGEA

The terracottas from Tegea in Arcadia are in most respects like those of Argos, differing only in the style of the heads, which is closer to Corinthian, and in the clay, which is darker in colour than Argive, and frequently contains white particles.

LACONIA

Laconian terracottas of the seventh and sixth centuries come from the neighbourhood of Sparta; the Sanctuary of Artemis Orthia, the Sanctuary of Athena Chalkioikos on the Acropolis, and the Shrine of Helen and Menelaus (the Menelaion) nearby. Amyclae, a fruitful source of earlier pieces, has little material to show for this period.

Laconian clay is fairly fine, usually micaceous, and powdery; it varies in colour between yellow ochre, orange and brown. It is lightly fired. Decoration is in black glaze; occasionally a light red wash, probably a dilute glaze, is also found. It has been observed that the moulded Dedalic faces are either picked out with black glaze over a cream slip, or with red wash applied direct to the clay.

The bases of our knowledge are the recorded stratification of the Orthia Sanctuary and a penetrating analysis by Jenkins of the Dedalic style in Laconia.

THE PRINCIPAL TYPES

1] Crude hand-made figures of men, women and animals continued from the eighth century (p. 23), and in greater quantities. These are of no artistic and little chronological significance.

2] Fully moulded Dedalic plaques, sometimes (a Laconian speciality) cut off at waist-level, were popular throughout the seventh century and debased versions of them continued into the early sixth. The goddess is usually draped, with her hands by her sides, but is occasionally naked, with hands either by her sides, or one to her breast, the other to her womb. The characteristic Laconian face is easily recognized, less easily described. On pl. 21C and D are typical half-plaques in the Early and Middle Dedalic styles, and on pl. 21B is the upper part of a solid type of plaque of transitional Early–Middle Dedalic date, wearing a feather headdress. Pl. 21G shows the naked variety. An elaboration of the Dedalic plaque shows a goddess, evidently Artemis Orthia, holding in front of her a lion rampant. The style of the head places this type in the late seventh century (pl. 21E).

3] An early Laconian moulded head is shown on pl. 21A. The bottom edge is broken, and it is uncertain whether it came from a figurine or a vase. This head, which comes from the Acropolis, combines the aggressively extended chin of the Geometric fashion with the flat, triangular Dedalic face. The mould was evidently made by a coroplast acquainted with the beginning of the Dedalic style, but more at home in the Geometric idiom. A date about 680–670 is possible. The decoration, in glaze, is carried out with meticulous attention to detail.

4] Naked male figures (*kouroi*) with Dedalic heads, and sixth century derivations are occasionally found. They are completely moulded in front, with flat backs.

5] Female figures with moulded heads and hand-made bodies, so common at Corinth, are occasionally found, but were never really popular.

6] A fully moulded type, related to the Dedalic plaques, shows a woman's head, flanked by horses' heads. This motive, represented also at Sparta in ivory and lead, and at Luristan in bronze, is probably of Persian origin. It probably reached Sparta by way of Phoenician art, although Phoenician objects of this nature have yet to be discovered.

7] Votive masks, starting in the seventh century and continuing through the sixth, are a peculiar Laconian feature, and were found in vast quantities at the Orthia Sanctuary. The types, which include old women, youths, warriors and grotesques, are probably copies of masks worn on some ceremonial occasions, perhaps at the Spartan dances in honour of Artemis, for which there is literary evidence. There is little doubt that such masks are ultimately of Phoenician inspiration, since similar ones have been found at Carthage, at the Phoenician colony of Tharros in Sardinia, and at other Phoenician sites.[1]

SICILY

The production of terracottas in Sicily started in the seventh century and continued throughout the period of this chapter. Our principal sources are votive deposits and tombs at Acragas, Gela and Selinus, and also a factory-site at Acragas. The Sanctuary of Demeter Malophoros near Selinus has proved a particularly rich source of figurines. Over 12,000 in number, they range in date from the late seventh to the mid fourth century B.C.

The most popular types are Dedalic plaques and later developments from them; kouroi; and local imitations of imported figurines of the Aphrodite Group.

Contacts with some East Greek or mainland centre in the seventh century must be postulated to account for the introduction of the Dedalic style, but our present knowledge does not permit its identification. In the sixth century there were strong eastern contacts, as witnessed by the copious import of plastic vases and figurines of the Gorgoneion and Aphrodite Groups. There were also contacts with Corinth, and, nearer home, very close ties with Locri, in which the influence appears to have been reciprocal.

The appearance of the clay is described below, on p. 86, when the evidence is more plentiful.

[1] D. B. Harden, *The Phoenicians* (London, 1962), 199.

THE PRINCIPAL TYPES

1] Fully moulded Dedalic plaques in the form of a standing woman, hands at sides, are recorded from Gela and Selinus. She is most commonly draped, but naked versions are occasionally found. These plaques are very like popular Dedalic types of Greece proper, but the uncouth appearance of the face frequently betrays their provincial origin. Sometimes, as in Laconia, the figures were cut off at the neck or the waist. The draped variety continued to be made right through the sixth century with little alteration except that the heads were periodically brought up to date. Examples of these later versions come from Selinus, Acragas and Megara Hyblaea. Occasionally they were converted into seated figures by being bent at knees and hips and supported behind by a strut.

2] Figures of kouroi in the same technique are less common. A late seventh century example comes from Selinus, and one from a tomb of 550–500 B.C. from Megara Hyblaea.

3] Figures of seated women, wearing a polos and a peplos, are recorded from Selinus. These figures, which seem to be copies of a type more frequently found at Locri, were hollow-moulded and subsequently worked over by hand. They probably date from the second half of the sixth century.

4] Statuettes of the Aphrodite Group, which were imported in vast quantities, were also imitated in Sicily with varying degrees of success. That shown on pl. 22E is an unusually successful effort. There is, it is true, a certain coarsening as compared with the Ionian model (cf. pl. 13F), but, when the greatly increased scale is taken into account, it is surprising how much of the spirit of the original remains.

LOCRI

There is as yet no evidence for Locrian terracottas before the sixth century, but this apparently late start may be due merely to the chance of excavation. The principal sources for the sixth century are deposits at Locri and at the Locrian colony of Medma nearby. The material is to be found principally at Naples, Reggio and Taranto.

Crude figures of standing and seated women are common, and imported plastic vases and figurines of the Aphrodite Group were also imitated.

There are many resemblances to contemporary Sicilian terracottas. The clay is discussed below, on p. 88, when the evidence is more plentiful.

THE PRINCIPAL TYPES

1] Figures of standing women, wearing a peplos and a polos, moulded in front, and solid, were made throughout the sixth century. They may have their arms at their sides, or stretched forward from the elbow, or one hand may be raised to the breast. In certain mid sixth century examples the peplos is completely modelled, and given, rather surprisingly, a semicircular overfall (pl. 22A). These figurines measure between 15 and 20 cm. in height.

2] In the last third of the sixth century the prevailing type of standing woman is larger than the foregoing (about 45 cm. tall), is hollow, moulded in front and, in the better examples, lavishly retouched. Before retouching, the body is virtually without modelling. She, too, wears a polos and a peplos.

3] At the end of the sixth century a new standing type arose under East Greek influence, wearing a chiton and a transverse himation. It also averages about 45 cm. in height.

4] Seated versions of type 2 were also made in the later sixth century.

5] At the end of the sixth century type 4 was brought up to date. The faces show the influence of East Greek art, the hair is arranged in graceful waves, and the modelling is greatly improved.

6] Male figures are not common, but kouroi moulded in front and solid are occasionally found. A figure of Hermes Kriophoros (carrying a ram) made in this way, probably in the late sixth century, is the predecessor of a long series of such figures which were made throughout the fifth century.

7] Plastic vases and figurines of the Aphrodite Group were imported, as in Sicily, and here too were widely imitated. The types imitated include standing and seated women and sirens, the latter sometimes attaining enormous proportions.

FIG. 16. Woman with child. From Tarentum. About 600 B.C.

TARENTUM

Tarentine figurines of the seventh and sixth centuries are surprisingly rare, but the high quality of the surviving pieces suggests that there was a flourishing terracotta industry.

The chief source is a sanctuary of Persephone on the Pizzone plateau, in the south-east part of the ancient city. In the lower levels of this deposit were found a few terracottas of the late seventh and early sixth centuries B.C. There are three examples in Oxford.

1] A Dedalic figure in the form of a draped woman, her hands on her sides, is shown on pl. 22F. This, the commonest type of Dedalic figure from Old Greece, is solid, and fully moulded in front. The face, in the Late Dedalic or perhaps Postdedalic style, puts this piece in the last quarter of the seventh century. It is tempting to look for a Laconian model in this Spartan colony.

2] A kouros, standing stiffly, hands at sides, is shown on pl. 22C. The face is in the early sixth century style.

3] Another kouros has a pointed hat and rests his left hand on his hip.

A figurine in Trieste, from Tarentum, has a moulded head in the style of the late seventh century and a tubular wheel-made body; a fashion commoner at Locri than at Tarentum. She holds a child to her breast (fig. 16).

PAESTUM

Paestum, originally known as Poseidonia, was founded by colonists from Sybaris early in the seventh century B.C., and soon became a flourishing settlement.

Figurines of this period are not plentiful, but the series starts shortly before the end of the sixth century with seated women. They are solid, moulded in front, bent at waist and knees and supported behind. In one example the woman nurses a minute horse, and has in consequence been identified as Hera Hippia. All wear a peplos.

The clay, like that used for later Paestan pottery, is somewhat coarse and slightly micaceous, and varies in colour between orange and reddish brown. It was generally fired at a high temperature.

OTHER WESTERN SITES

Several other sites in South Italy have produced a few figurines attributable to this period. They may conveniently be taken together, not because they are in any sense a unity, but because the existing evidence is too scanty for individual treatment.

The sites comprise an unidentified locality near Sybaris, the temple of Hera Lakinia at Croton, and the temple of Apollo at Metapontum.

The site near Sybaris has produced a few fully moulded Dedalic plaques not unlike the example from Tarentum on pl. 22F.

From Croton comes a hand-made figurine of a woman holding both hands to her breasts in a gesture more familiar in Syria and Cyprus than in the west. The head, which is largely missing, was in the Dedalic style of the seventh century.

From Metapontum come frontally moulded figurines of men and women. The female figures are Dedalic plaques, with the hands at the sides (pl. 22B). Their farouche expressions recall contemporary Sicilian plaques. The men are naked kouros types (pl. 22D). To judge from the heads, they were made later than the female figures, in the first half of the sixth century. In some examples the left hand rests on the hip; some wear a pointed hat.

NAUCRATIS

The Greek settlers at Naucratis in Egypt, on the western branch of the Nile, started to make terracotta figurines soon after the foundation of the settlement about 615 B.C. The earliest pieces are Dedalic plaques in the Rhodian style, with an added Egyptian flavour. Later, in the course of the sixth century B.C., the Egyptian influence increases.

The clay is coarse and micaceous. Usually dark in colour, it varies between a dirty orange and a brown, frequently with a grey core. It is known to Egyptologists by the name of Nile mud.

CHAPTER 7

The Fifth and Fourth Centuries B.C.

INTRODUCTION

This chapter covers the Late Archaic and Classical periods. It runs from 500 B.C. (in some cases slightly earlier) to about 330 B.C., so that the title is convenient rather than strictly accurate.

The typical figurine of the sixth century (with the exception of the Gorgoneion and Aphrodite Groups) was a sorry object by any aesthetic standards. The use of the mould was the exception rather than the rule and the workmanship bore witness to the maker's speed rather than to his skill. Those who wanted something better would import the figurines and plastic vases of the Gorgoneion and Aphrodite Groups. At times, especially towards the end of the century, local coroplasts would try their hand at imitating and adapting these imported pieces, but it was evidently not until the supply dried up about 500 B.C. (doubtless for reasons connected with the Ionian Revolt) that it became really necessary to satisfy the needs of the more discerning public from local resources.

We therefore find that around this date almost every Greek community of any standing was beginning to produce figurines of some merit which owed a considerable debt, both technical and stylistic, to the Aphrodite Group.

The connecting link between these two systems is the Post-Aphrodite Group which, for some two generations, continued the work of its predecessor. The lead given by this group was followed first by Rhodes; soon after by Attica, Boeotia and Corinth. In the west, the Sicilian Greek communities and the South Italian colonies of Tarentum, Locri and Paestum soon followed suit.

The figurines of the first quarter of the fifth century (now regularly hollow-moulded) reflect, in their humble way, contemporary sculpture of the Late Archaic period. The favourite subject is a standing woman wearing a chiton and a transverse himation. Seated women come next in popularity.

The critical period for sculpture, about 475 B.C., when the Late Archaic style gave way to the Early Classical, was of less direct importance so far as concerned terracottas. In their case, the transition was more gradual, but by the middle of the fifth century it is clear that the rather fussy Late Archaic style has given way to the stark simplicity of the Early Classical. This new style makes its greatest impact in the sculptures of the Temple of Zeus at Olympia, especially in the treatment of female drapery. The Ionic chiton, with its elaborate folds and creases, is succeeded by the Doric peplos, with its simple lines and a strong vertical–horizontal accent.

So far as terracottas are concerned, this process is best observed in the two Attic types of pl. 30E–F. The so-called First Attic Type of pl. 30E gives the transitional stage, much commoner in terracottas than in sculpture, between the Late Archaic and the Early Classical idioms. The Second Attic Type of pl. 30F shows the process completed.

In the later years of the fifth century the influence of the Parthenon made itself felt in a richer and more voluptuous treatment (see pl. 31E–F). The fourth century saw on the one hand a tendency to re-hash old favourites, which results in a stiffness and frontality at odds with the spirit of the age; on the other, a considerable raising of standards. This latter process, particularly noticeable in Attica, involved a greater freedom of execution and a more faithful copying of sculptural models, and was to culminate in the Tanagra style of the late fourth century (see p. 97).

Although there was much interchange of ideas, local peculiarities persisted in many centres throughout this period. As examples we may cite the characteristic styles of Boeotia, Corinth, Sicily, Tarentum, Paestum and Cyrenaica, which will be discussed in detail below. Certain areas, such as Attica, Corinth, Sparta, Crete, Melos, Locri and Tarentum, also produced their own varieties of small reliefs during this period.

With certain exceptions, figurines are now hollow-moulded, with hand-made backs. Vents are rectangular and undersides are open. Decoration is normally in matt paint.

This chapter ends about 330 B.C., just before the conquests of Alexander the Great transformed the entire Greek world and, with it, Greek art.

CRETE

After a lull in the sixth century, the Cretan terracotta industry revived in the fifth and flourished for some three or four centuries. The time is not ripe for a comprehensive study of Cretan terracottas of this period, as the material is largely unpublished, but several separate schools may tentatively be identified.

In the west, figures of Pan, of the fifth and fourth centuries, were found in a sanctuary at Hyrtakina; and two votive reliefs have recently been discovered in Arkouda Cave in Akroteri, one of Apollo Citharoedus (playing a lyre), the other of Artemis. They appear to be influenced by Melian reliefs (see p. 69), and were made about 460 B.C.

In the east, where the typical clay is pale and friable, figurines are recorded from Olous and Praisos. From the former site come copies of almost every Rhodian fifth century type; from the latter site, undistinguished reliefs.

In the south, Gortyn, so fruitful a source before and after this period, has so far yielded little material of the fifth and fourth centuries.

In Central Crete, large statuettes in a coarse reddish clay have been found at Axos. They are mostly in the Severe Style of the mid fifth century, and in the richer style of the late fifth century.

In North-Central Crete, the historic site of Knossos has produced a rich and original series, of which a detailed study is being prepared. This series comes from a votive deposit on Gypsades Hill in the neighbourhood of a temple dedicated to Demeter. It is therefore possible to recognize a genuine Knossian school, to which a few pieces from old collections in London, Paris and elsewhere can now be seen to belong.

The series starts with imitations of foreign types, and from 500 to 450 or so the principal varieties are derived from Rhodian, Attic or Corinthian models. Thereafter, local types evolved and flourished until they were replaced, about 330 B.C., by the universal Tanagra style.

Knossian terracottas were made in several different ways. They could be moulded solid, with flat backs, a process reserved chiefly for the smaller pieces; they could be hollow-moulded, with flat backs; or the back could be omitted as if from a hollow-moulded piece, and the base extended backwards to form a support.

Several distinct varieties of Knossian clay are found, possibly representing different clay-beds; all varieties seem to have been used impartially at any time. One variety is fine and hard, usually pink or pale brown in colour; it could be mistaken for Corinthian, but is harder and browner. Another common variety is coarse and fairly hard, orange or yellow in colour, both shades being frequently found in the same piece. A third, and less common, variety is fairly fine, rather soft, and darkish pink in colour. Mica is seldom present in any quantity.

THE PRINCIPAL KNOSSIAN TYPES

Many types are represented at Knossos only by fragmentary examples. In consequence the pieces illustrated are in some cases without a known find-spot, but their Knossian origin is evident from the style, technique and clay.

1. *Standing women.* A Rhodian type (cf. pl. 24F) and the First and Second Attic types (cf. pl. 30E and F) of the mid fifth century were all imitated.

Pl. 23C shows a type which was common itself, and in numerous variations. A woman stands, wearing the Peplos of Athena, whose folds are attractively arranged in a somewhat formal symmetry. This kind of drapery goes back ultimately to such fifth century sculptures as the Athena Parthenos, but the closest parallel to this rendering of the folds is in a terracotta in London which must, from the style of the face, be dated around the middle of the fourth century.[1]

Another even more popular fourth century type is a woman, probably representing Demeter, who is tightly swathed in a chiton and himation and wears a low polos (pl. 23A). Her left hand rests on her hip and in her right hand she holds a phiale against her side. The pose and the arrangement of the drapery are closely paralleled in a relief in Athens which can be securely dated to the year 387–6.[2] Allowing for the delay in transmission from sculpture to terracotta, we should probably be right in dating the emergence of the type about 375 B.C. It evidently had a long life at Knossos, for minor variations are known, some showing a considerable decrease in modelling. We might put the life of this type at, say, 375–325 B.C.

Pitcher-bearers were common in the fifth century and even commoner in the fourth. The standard fifth century type echoes in a feeble way the canons of the Severe Style (pl. 23B). In the later fifth and the fourth, the rich style of the later fifth century sculptures held sway.

2. *Seated women.* A Rhodian type of two women seated, sharing a himation, in whom we should probably see Demeter and Persephone, was imitated at Knossos.

The standard Attic type of pl. 30C was imitated in several sizes and many minor variations. A local adaptation of the type is also found in countless numbers (pl. 23D). The forms have been greatly simplified, and she holds a phiale (libation-vessel) on her lap. Moulds were used again and again until the modelling was almost entirely worn away. Such over-production would suggest that the type had a very long life.

Pl. 23F shows a later type of seated woman, also extremely popular at Knossos. She sits, hands on knees, on a stool with ornamental legs, on a cushion. Her thick hair is arranged in an arch round the upper part of her face. The style of hairdressing (paralleled in the frieze from the Temple of Apollo at Bassae)[3] might indicate a date in the late fifth century, but the sweetness of the face would suggest a fourth century date. Such a popular type probably had a long life, and may well have covered the first half of the fourth century. An Attic type (pl. 31E) has many similarities, and may well have been the inspiration for this Knossian version.

A related type (pl. 23E) is equally common at Knossos. It differs in the substitution of a throne for a stool, and in the arrangement of the drapery, but the effect is much the same, and here too was probably Attic influence.

[1] *BMC* i, no. 729 bis.

[2] H. K. Süsserott, *Griechische Plastik des 4 Jahrhunderts vor Christus* (Frankfurt, 1938), pl. 2:4.

[3] Lawrence, *Classical Sculpture*, pl. 67.

3. *Standing men.* In the fifth century, naked men, feeble copies of sculptural types such as the Choiseul-Gouffier Apollo,[1] were fairly common.
4. *Miscellaneous figures.* Other foreign types imitated in the fifth century include a squatting satyr playing the pipes, a squatting boy, both probably Rhodian-derived, and a Corinthian-type doll.
5. *Protomes.* From the mid fifth century onwards, simple protomes were popular. There is no originality to them, and all are probably taken from Rhodian models.

RHODES

There was a considerable output of terracottas in Rhodes in the fifth century. In the fourth, on the basis of our existing evidence, production appears to have been considerably curtailed.

Our sources for the fifth century down to 408 B.C. are the same as for the seventh century. After the foundation in 408 B.C. of the city of Rhodes as a federal capital, the three older cities declined, and the cemeteries of Camirus and Ialysus, which had previously been so productive, were apparently deserted. Our only reliable source for the fourth century is a votive deposit at Lindus, the so-called *Petit Depôt.* This deposit was dated by Blinkenberg 'after 300 B.C.', but subsequent authorities are agreed that his chronology is too low, and that the correct date is roughly from 400 to 330 B.C.

The typical Rhodian terracotta of this period is hollow-moulded and has a flat handmade back, with no vent. The underside could be treated in several ways; it could be left open, or it could be closed and partially opened with a stick or a finger. Occasionally there is no opening whatever in the base or in the back.

The clay at Camirus and Lindus is generally a leathery brown colour; at Ialysus rather paler. It is lightly fired, and is regularly covered with a fine slip. Mica is normally (but not invariably) absent.

There are many types, but the commonest are a standing and a seated woman. Squatting boys, negroes and satyrs, reclining men, and various animals are also found. Protomes were also very popular throughout this period.

The first two-thirds of the fifth century are dominated by standing and seated women, at first in a Late Archaic style derived from the Aphrodite Group, later in the Severe Style, and animals and birds. The later years of the century are characterized by Blinkenberg's so-called *types sveltes*, a style devoted chiefly to seated women of slender proportions, with formal curls, but used occasionally for standing women and protomes.

In the fourth century deposit from Lindus there is a greater variety of types: standing

[1] Lawrence, *Classical Sculpture*, pl. 41A (left).

women, some associated with Athena and others with Artemis; seated women; women with babies; standing men. Protomes were still very common.

Types similar to Rhodian occur in the fifth century at many places; Attica, Boeotia, Crete, the west – but for two reasons it would appear that most if not all were evolved in Rhodes; it is in Rhodes that we can actually trace this evolution of numbers of these types; and Rhodian imports have been found on some of these other sites side by side with what must be local imitations.

THE PRINCIPAL TYPES

1. *Standing women.* The typical Rhodian standing woman of the early fifth century (pl. 24D) is a simplified version of the Post-Aphrodite type of pl. 24A. The heads show some advance on those of the Post-Aphrodite figures, and are probably slightly later in date. The face has lost, or is fast losing, the Archaic Smile, and the hair has acquired a central parting.

At some time in the second quarter of the century this type reflects the influence of the Severe Style by changing the drapery from the Archaic chiton and transverse himation to the First Attic type (see p. 73), with the peplos open down the right side (pl. 24E). The right hand is still raised to the breast and holds an offering (indicated in paint). The motive had a long life. In the later fifth century we find it associated with the *svelte* style of face, and it continued throughout the first two-thirds of the fourth century, with occasional modifications of the face to suit the changing fashions in sculpture.

A version of the Second Attic type, with the peplos closed, and a stronger vertical–horizontal accent, was introduced into Rhodes about the middle of the fifth century, but was never popular, and was soon dropped.

Another mid fifth century type, probably a Rhodian invention, (pl. 24F) wears a chiton, and over it a himation worn with very strong vertical–horizontal emphasis.

In the fourth century the himation is worn diagonally, and is rendered in a naturalistic way, and the figures grow more and more naturalistic, and point the way to the Tanagra style of the late fourth century.

In the early fifth century a standing woman of Post-Aphrodite style has a child by her right side and another on her left shoulder (see p. 65). In the fourth century Rhodian variety, she has one child, who rests on her left shoulder (pl. 25D). The development of this type could well be continuous, with the lacunae still to be filled by future discoveries.

Other standing types are found in the fourth century; an Athena; a pitcher-bearer; a woman holding a basket on her head with both hands (pl. 25B); a woman with a piglet hanging from her right hand; or with a torch on her right shoulder.

2. *Dancing women.* A graceful figure of a woman performing a stately dance is represented in the fourth century deposit at Lindus (pl. 25E).

3. *Seated women.* The characteristic seated figure of the fifth century (pl. 24B) has a body like that of the Aphrodite Group (cf. pl. 13A), but the head, like those of the standing figures, bears witness to the later date.

Towards the middle of the century an Early Classical type of head, as on contemporary standing figures, replaces the Archaic head.

About the same time the Attic type of seated woman (cf. pl. 30C) was introduced into Rhodes and was copied there.

Towards the end of the century the typical seated female figure belonged to Blinkenberg's *types sveltes*, referred to above. An example is shown on pl. 24C. The head is like that of the standing variety; she wears a chiton and a himation going over her head. The slender proportions are in marked contrast with the plump figures of the earlier periods.

The seated woman of the fourth century, although still frontal, is considerably freer in style and more relaxed in appearance than in the fifth century.

A seated woman with a child, counterpart of the standing type, starts early in the fifth century and can be traced right through till about 330 B.C.

4. *Squatting women.* A woman squatting, playing knucklebones, a type probably of Attic origin, occurs in the fourth century deposit at Lindus.

5. *Standing men.* They are rare in the fifth century, but one type of the mid fifth century shows a young man wearing a himation round his hips.

In the fourth century we find two types of standing men; both bearded, and both possibly representing Zeus. One stands straight but not stiffly, wearing a low polos (pl. 25F), the other, of a less regal appearance, adopts a more relaxed stance.

6. *Reclining men.* A reclining man derives from an Aphrodite Group type. It has two versions, a Late Archaic, of the early fifth century, and an Early Classical of the middle of the century, differing chiefly in the style of the head.

7. *Children, etc.* A baby in a cradle comes from tombs of the early fifth century; a squatting infant, a squatting negro (pl. 25C) and a charming representation of a boy riding a mule (pl. 25A) from mid fifth century tombs.

8. *Satyrs.* Squatting grotesques, usually described as satyrs, are common in the early fifth century and continue into the middle years. They may be connected with the Egyptian Ptah-Sokhar-Osiris, the Aphrodite Group version of which flourished in the late sixth century. The earlier version is ithyphallic, the later not. The later version spread to Boeotia, where it was much copied.

9. *Animals and fruits.* Pigs, doves, cocks and tortoises were popular in the fifth century. All these animals had a religious significance, which doubtless explains their presence in tombs and sanctuaries; the pig belonged to Demeter; the dove and the tortoise to Aphrodite; the cock to Dionysus or Asclepius. Of fruits, the apple (for Aphrodite) and the pomegranate (for Demeter) were popular.

10. *Protomes.* Protomes of a kind were made throughout the sixth century in several Greek centres, particularly in Attica (see p. 44), but it is not till the fifth and fourth centuries that this form acquires a character of its own. Greek protomes are nearly always female.

A] The most primitive form is straight-sided, and persists right through the period covered by this chapter. The earliest examples portray a female face with slit eyes, wide cheekbones and a pointed chin (pl. 26A). It is dated by tomb-groups to about 500 B.C. An example from Delos is inscribed with a dedication to Hera, but it is by no means certain that that goddess is always represented.

From an exceptionally well-preserved specimen in Rhodes it is possible to see this type in its original colours. She wears a white chiton with horizontal stripes, alternately blue and red, secured at the neck by a brown cord with red tassels. Her hair is contained by a red band over which she wears a stephane decorated with vertical lines in red and blue. Over all this she wears a pale brown himation with stripes in a darker brown. In her ears are discs of lapis-lazuli blue.

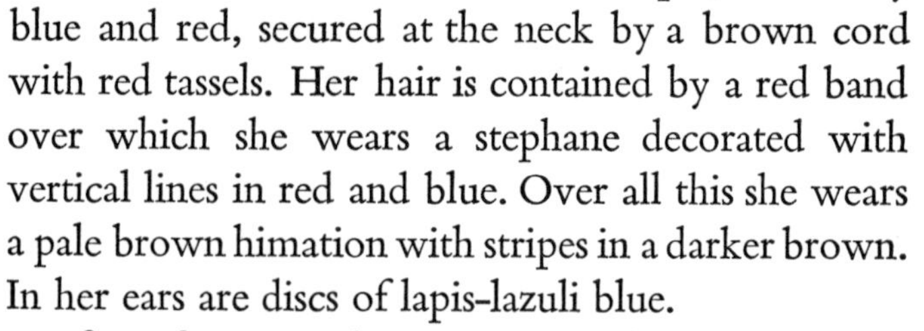

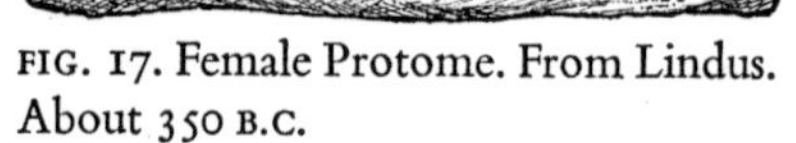

FIG. 17. Female Protome. From Lindus. About 350 B.C.

After a few years the type was modified by the substitution of a fuller face, with a less pointed chin. This variety often has three rows of stylized dog-tooth curls (pl. 26B).

In the later fifth century the head is that of the *svelte* figurine (pl. 26D) and in the fourth it corresponds with contemporary figurines.

B] A more sophisticated variety may be called the modelled protome, for the sides are no longer straight, but approximate to the head and shoulders of the human form. About 480 B.C. such a protome was produced having a chiton, with a short overfall, indicated plastically.

The middle of the century saw the creation of a type which was to last till about 330, the only alteration being in the increasingly naturalistic treatment of the faces. She wears a peplos and raises both hands to her breast in a manner recalling the figurine on pl. 24E. An example of the mid fifth century is shown on pl. 26C; one of the mid fourth in fig. 17.

POST-APHRODITE GROUP

An early first century group, evidently the product of the factory producing the figurines and plastic vases of the Aphrodite Group, consists principally of a class isolated by Blinkenberg as *types gracieux*. We may conveniently call it 'Post-Aphrodite'. The style is a modification of the Aphrodite style, with the same painstaking rendering of detail, and the same technical characteristics, but the repertoire is much poorer and no longer includes plastic vases. Backs are also moulded, as before, and the underside is regularly closed and pierced with a knife-thrust. The clay, too, is the same.

The types comprise a standing and a seated female figure, and a few other varieties. Productions of these figures ceased about 450 B.C.

THE PRINCIPAL TYPES

1. *Standing women.* The type shown on pl. 24A derives directly from the latest variety of the Aphrodite Group (pl. 14E). She wears a chiton and a transverse himation falling in elaborately stylized folds, like the later marble korai from the Athenian Acropolis. In her right hand she holds an offering, usually a flower, to her breast. The type is dated by tomb-groups to the early fifth century.

Another standing woman of this fabric has a child by her right side and another on her left shoulder.

2. *Seated women.* The seated woman of this fabric is very like the standing variety, but she sits on a circular stool with a projecting top.

IONIA

Little is known of Ionian terracottas in the fifth century, except that a few pieces in London, from Samos, echo the *gracieux* style.

Seated women with babies from Ephesus belong to the fourth century, and resemble the piece from Calymna on pl. 27C.

HALICARNASSUS, COS, etc.

Halicarnassus, the neighbouring island of Cos, and other nearby islands are here grouped together for convenience. The principal sources of figurines are deposits at Halicarnassus and Cos; subsidiary sources are Calymna and Nisyros.

Cos was a Greek settlement from early times, and figurines have been excavated at sanctuaries of Asclepius and Demeter near the ancient city and in a cave-sanctuary of Pan at Aspri Petra by Cape Kephalos. Halicarnassus was also originally a Greek settlement, but contained a strong local element of Carian stock, which was intensified in the fourth century by the famous Carian prince Mausolus. Its art, however, was always purely Greek.

Great numbers of figurines were excavated here by C. T. Newton in 1856 and are now in the British Museum. They were found in a votive deposit at a sanctuary of Demeter and Persephone, stacked in layers by types 'like articles in a shop'.[1]

Although these figurines are extremely fragmentary and badly worn, and although

[1] *BMC* i, 102.

they can only be dated by internal evidence, they are of the greatest importance for the history of Late Archaic and Classical figurines, since they provide a uniquely rich series from around 500 to about 330 B.C., the date when the city was conquered by Alexander.

So rich is the deposit that almost every type represented can be reconstructed from the numerous fragments surviving, many of them mould-brothers. Such reconstructed drawings are shown in figs. 18–23. Figurines sufficiently complete in themselves are shown in photographs on pl. 27.

In the early stages the Coan and Halicarnassian schools were extremely close to each other, but in the course of the fifth century they diverged somewhat.

The style owed much to Ionia, and at Cos at least Ionian imports in the sixth century are evidence of contacts with that quarter, but there was from the start a considerable indigenous element which is quite unmistakable.

The favourite types are standing women, some carrying a pitcher on their heads, and standing men. There are several technical characteristics in the figurines of Halicarnassus. The backs are not moulded; there is frequently an abnormal depth from front to back; the bases are open underneath; and one arm is frequently made separately and attached after moulding. In the back there is sometimes a square vent, sometimes a round one and sometimes none. The clay is rather coarse, with very large crystals of mica. It is lightly fired and very powdery, varying in colour between orange, pale orange, green, cream and a purplish brown. The clay of the Coan pieces sometimes approaches that of Halicarnassus, but in other examples is finer and harder.

THE PRINCIPAL TYPES

The types described below come more often from Halicarnassus than from the other sites, since the Halicarnassus material is very much more plentiful, and unless the contrary is stated, they may be assumed to come from Halicarnassus. The women, who mostly come from Halicarnassus, represent Demeter or Persephone. The men should represent Asclepius at Cos, Dionysus at Halicarnassus.

1. *Standing women.* In the early fifth century there are a number of types of standing women, in chiton and himation, all showing the influence of Ionian terracottas. One is shown on pl. 27A; the influence of the Aphrodite Group is plain, but the face indicates a date shortly after 500 B.C.

The standing women who can be dated to the mid fifth century are few; in all probability the types developed in the previous period continued into this. The last third of the century however and the beginning of the fourth are richly represented by types reflecting the influence of the Parthenon. The women mostly wear a chiton and a himation with an ornate triangular overfall. They may hold a sheaf of poppies, a young pig, or a hare (fig. 18).

The type continued, with suitable modifications, into the early fourth century. In fig. 19 the pose has become more relaxed and the drapery more clinging. The goddess, naked to the waist, leans against a tree-trunk, holding a young pig against her breast. Her successor of the middle of the fourth century leans against a pillar in an even more relaxed pose, which reveals the influence of Praxiteles, and holds in her left hand the sacred box of Demeter and Persephone (pl. 27D).

A figure of Artemis from Nisyros of the early fourth century, now in the Louvre, is very close to a Knossian type (cf. pl. 23A), but for the torch which she carries.

FIG. 18. Demeter or Persephone. Halicarnassian type. Late fifth century B.C.

FIG. 19. Demeter or Persephone. Halicarnassian type. About 380 B.C.

2. *Pitcher-bearers.* A specialized class of standing female figures holds a pitcher on her head. She first appears in the middle of the fifth century, when she corresponds closely with the Second Attic standing type of pl. 30F. In the later fifth century and in the first two-thirds of the fourth she corresponds fairly closely with the ordinary standing women of Halicarnassus. Two unusually well-preserved examples, both of the later fifth century, are shown on pl. 27F and G. The former, in a peplos and himation, looks back to the Severe Style of the mid fifth century, while the latter, in a clinging chiton and more ornate himation, looks forward to the more relaxed treatment of the fourth century.

3. *Seated women.* Seated women are rare in this group, but mention should be made of a

mid fourth century seated woman from the Cave of Pan on Cos and a seated woman with child of the early fourth century from Calymna (pl. 27C).

4. *Standing men.* The early fifth century standing men are venerable and bearded and are swathed in a long himation (pl. 27B). In the mid fifth century they may be bearded or beardless, and they tend to wear the himation in the more usual male fashion, leaving the chest exposed (pl. 27E).

The late fifth century men are very much the counterparts of their womenfolk. They may be bearded or beardless. Two principal types are found. The first wears a himation with strong vertical–horizontal accent like certain men on the Parthenon frieze (fig. 20). The other has an elaborate overfall to the himation (pl. 27H). Both types wear a stephane decorated with rosettes.

In the early fourth century the male types of the preceding period continue with little alteration (fig. 21), but are supplemented by a standing man tightly draped in a long diagonal himation (fig. 22). The mid fourth century standing man (fig. 23) is the counterpart of the female type shown on pl. 27D.

FIG. 20. Dionysus (?). Halicarnassian type. Late fifth century B.C. FIG. 21. Dionysus (?). Halicarnassian type. Early fourth century B.C. FIG. 22. Dionysus (?). Halicarnassian type. Early fourth century B.C. FIG. 23. Dionysus (?). Halicarnassian type. About 350 B.C.

5. *Squatting boys.* Figures of fifth century squatting boys, as in Crete and Rhodes, are found on Cos. Fourth century versions occur in the Cave of Pan on that island.

6. *Pan.* A figure of Pan, seated cross-legged, was found in the Cave of Pan on Cos. It was made around the mid fourth century.

7. *Protomes.* A few protomes of the late fifth and early fourth centuries are reported from Cos and Calymna.

AEOLIS

A] *Larisa*

A few figurines and protomes of the fifth and fourth centuries were found at Larisa, in the reddish-brown clay also used earlier (see p. 39). The style and the repertoire are in the general East Greek tradition best represented at Rhodes.

B] *Assos*

The American excavations of 1881–3 produced a number of figurines covering the fifth and fourth centuries B.C. The clay is coarse in texture, and varies in colour between pinkish red and yellow.

Particularly noteworthy is a group of female figures of the early fifth century. They stand or sit, and wear the normal Late Archaic chiton and transverse himation, and in addition a conical hat. They are unusually well modelled, and rest on separately made bases.

C] *Troy*

The Troy of the Classical period is represented by three fine figurines excavated in 1890 at In-Tepe nearby and now in Istanbul. All are in the style of the mid fourth century, and show every sign of Attic influence, but the clay and the technique are local. The clay is very fine in texture, with a soapy feel, lightly fired, reddish in colour, with a black core.

The subjects of these figurines are: (1) Aphrodite and Eros standing side by side; (2) Two female dancers; (3) Aphrodite reclining, naked, with Eros behind her.

D] *Lesbos*

A few undistinguished figurines of the fifth century were excavated at Mitylene by C. T. Newton and are now in the British Museum. The clay is pink, and contains mica.

THE CYCLADES

A] *Melos*

In the fifth and fourth centuries Melos produced little in the way of terracottas apart from the celebrated Melian reliefs. These reliefs have been exhaustively studied by Jacobsthal, and his definitive work needs little modification beyond the addition of a very few new types which have come to light since its appearance. A list of the subjects of Melian reliefs, known and unknown to Jacobsthal, will be found on p. 150.

The great majority of surviving examples have been found on Melos. They were however exported to a limited extent, since isolated pieces have been recorded from other Aegean islands, the Troad, Attica, Corinth, South Italy, Sicily and possibly Egypt.

Jacobsthal dated the series between 475 and 445 B.C. In view of the date of the grave which contained the reliefs on pl. 28, this dating is perhaps a trifle high, and it would perhaps be safer to suggest a date between 465 and 435 B.C.

Melian reliefs are flat plaques, about 0·5 to 1·5 cm. thick, and about 16 cm. in height. They are moulded in front; the backs are flat, and frequently somewhat striated. The background clay is usually cut away, so that the figures stand clear, but sometimes a greater or lesser amount of the background is retained. The reliefs are pierced for attachment to some other objects, which are generally believed to have been chests or coffins. It is also possible that on occasion they were used to decorate the interiors of houses.

The reliefs were decorated with matt paint and must have looked very gay when new. The clay is unmistakable. It varies in colour between brown and orange, frequently has a cream slip, and presents an unusually dead matt appearance. Mica is occasionally present. The reliefs are fired at a higher temperature than most terracottas, for they had to withstand considerably more wear and tear.

The subjects are mostly mythological, but include a few domestic scenes. The style has been described by Jacobsthal as a provincial Ionic *koine*, which in its later stages came under the all-pervading influence of Attic art. It is not great art, and the proportions of the human body are often grotesquely distorted, but there is always a certain rather unsophisticated charm, and the arrangement of the figures seldom fails to be decorative.

On pl. 28 are two examples from a tomb at Camirus of the third quarter of the fifth century. Pl. 28B shows Eos, goddess of the dawn, carrying off the youth Kephalos. The original colouring survives to an unusual degree: the base was blue; the chiton of Eos yellow with the red stripe – her wings blue, red and black. The hair of both figures was black and the flesh of Kephalos, in accordance with the usual custom, was red.

Pl. 28A shows Peleus carrying off Thetis. The nymph occupies the centre of an almost heraldic composition. The upper part of her body faces the front, but her legs show that she is moving to the right. On the (spectator's) left Peleus grapples with her; on the other side a lion (one of the manifestations assumed by Thetis) rises up on its hind-legs to attack him.

B] *Paros*

For this fabric see p. 40 above. Parian terracottas continued into the fifth and fourth centuries, comprising chiefly provincial copies of Attic and other types.

c] *Delos*

There is no evidence for a terracotta industry on Delos in the fifth and fourth centuries, but many imports are recorded, in particular from Rhodes, Attica, Boeotia and Corinth. The so-called Katharsis Trench on Rheneia, dating from the Athenian purification of Delos of 426–425 B.C., gives an excellent *terminus ante quem* for the numerous figurines found therein.

ATTICA

Although the primitive figures of the previous chapter continued on a limited scale into the fifth century, in general Attic terracottas of the late sixth and early fifth century show a considerable advance, both technical and artistic, over their predecessors, and over many of their contemporaries. During the period with which this chapter is concerned, Attica was among the principal centres of terracotta production.

The material comes principally from Athens; in particular from the Acropolis, the Agora, the Pnyx and the Cerameicus cemetery: also from Eleusis and Brauron. Certain classes, especially the seated goddess (pl. 29), were widely exported.

The story opens with moulded, basically solid, figures of standing or (more commonly) seated women. Later we find hollow-moulded figures of women, at first derivations from Rhodian models, but subsequently genuine Attic creations.

Evidence for the end of the fifth century has recently come to light in a series of graves near Syntagma Square in Athens. For the fourth century the evidence is not as plentiful, but from what little there is, it would appear that certain types of standing and dancing women made in Boeotia and Rhodes and probably elsewhere during this period are fairly faithful copies of Attic models. From these it is apparent that a growing freedom and naturalism was preparing the ground for the Tanagra style of the late fourth century.

Three rather special classes were however plentiful in the fourth century: actors (chiefly from Comedy), dolls and plastic lekythoi, i.e. scent-bottles in the form of figurines. The latter however stand rather apart from the main stream of terracottas, and should more correctly be regarded as vases.

The clay of the fifth and fourth centuries is fairly fine, with a little mica. It is generally either yellow ochre or orange in colour: the two colours are quite distinct, and may correspond to two separate clay-beds.

THE PRINCIPAL TYPES

A] *Primitive*

An early fifth century deposit in the Agora yielded primitive human figures, horses and horsemen like those current in the seventh and sixth centuries (p. 42), and a tomb at Plato's Academy, of the same date, yielded a similar horseman.

B] *Late Archaic*

Towards the end of the sixth century, about 520 B.C., two types of figurines appeared in Athens and surpassed all others in popularity for over half a century.

The first type (pl. 29) is a woman seated on a throne with a winged back and a footstool, her hands on her knees. She wears a chiton and a symmetrical himation going over her head; in her hair is a stephane and in her ears are disc-earrings. The modelling is flat and angular.

Pieces of this type were made solid in a single mould, and have a flat, unworked back. They were made in many sizes. In the smaller examples (9–12 cm. high) a pin-hole runs up inside from under the base; in the larger (15–20 cm.) the lower part has been hollowed out after moulding.

These figurines may be dated to the period 520–450 B.C. The earliest are dated by the resemblance of the heads to plastic heads on Attic jugs by the potter Nikosthenes of about 520 B.C.[1] the latest from a Rhodian tomb-group of about 450 B.C.

These seated goddesses were found in their hundreds, buried in trenches on the Acropolis at Athens after the Persian sack of 480 B.C. The type is distributed throughout the Greek world, but is considerably more plentiful in Attica than elsewhere, and there can be no doubt that it is Attic in origin. The primitive body suggests a copy or an adaptation of a much older cult-statue; one thinks of the venerable olive-wood image of Athena which was kept in the Erechtheum and in its predecessors, but the question is much disputed.

That Athena was generally intended is probable; the example illustrated even has a painted aegis. One from the Agora, who nurses a baby, may possibly represent Athena Kourotrophos. But since a piece in Berlin is inscribed with a dedication to Hecate, in all probability the type, designed as an Athena, could if necessary serve other purposes.

The seated Athena has a standing counterpart (pl. 30D) also found chiefly on the Acropolis, and occasionally in the Agora and at Eleusis, but very rarely outside Attica. She stands stiffly with her left foot slightly advanced, wearing a stephane, a chiton and a transverse himation; in her right hand she holds a flower or a fruit to her breast. She is in fact the clay version of the marble korai also found on the Acropolis.

The offering in the hand suggests a votary, but she sometimes wears a helmet, so that we are left in some confusion as to whether she is the goddess Athena or merely one of her worshippers.

C] *Fully developed*

The fully developed terracottas of the fifth and fourth centuries are generally hollow-moulded, with a hand-made back, in which is a rectangular vent. The undersides are

[1] *B. Metr. Mus.*, v (1946–7), 256.

regularly open. Smaller pieces (especially the actors) are, however, often solid, and in the better examples the back is also moulded.

1. *Standing women.* The standard early fifth century Rhodian woman of pl. 24D was occasionally imitated in Attica, but was not common. Towards the middle of the fifth century, two new types of standing women appear, probably as local inventions. Both have a strong and full (but eminently feminine) face, with luxuriant wavy hair; a type of face seen in the sculptures from the Temple of Zeus at Olympia, and, further developed, in those of the Parthenon. The bodies merit separate consideration. Both types have been discussed in detail by Poulsen, and, with him, we may call them the first and second Attic standing types.

The first type, which evolved in the second quarter of the fifth century, is really the standard Late Archaic formula modified to suit the austerer demands of a new age. She stands somewhat stiffly, with one leg slightly advanced, wearing a peplos open down the right side. Her right hand holds a flower to her breast, while her left gently draws the drapery to that side. The pose and the stylized folds of the open side of the peplos are in the Late Archaic manner, but the strong vertical–horizontal accent of the rest of the peplos betrays the Early Classical spirit. The example on pl. 30E comes from Aegina, and was in all probability made there, but it shows the Attic type in only a very slightly provincial form.

The second type (pl. 30F) evolved somewhat later, perhaps about 450 B.C., and is completely in the Early Classical manner, as exemplified in the sculptures from the Temple of Zeus at Olympia. The peplos is now closed down the side and both hands are by her side. The vertical–horizontal accent, foreshadowed in the first type, is now carried to its logical conclusion. This type was widely imitated.

Attic standing figures in what we would expect to be the style of the later fifth century are so rare that we are forced to the conclusion that these two types, especially the second, continued in use down to the end of the century.

One new type however (pl. 31F) fulfils our expectations. A woman, clad in a peplos over a chiton, stands with her weight on her right leg, holding an object (now missing) on the top of her head with both hands. She was probably holding a sacred basket like the related Rhodian figurine on pl. 25B. She wears ear-studs and three necklaces. Her drapery is rendered with detailed attention to folds and creases, in the manner of the Caryatids of the Erechtheum. Her face has the strong, rather full lines of the same Caryatids, and her thick hair falls on her shoulders. We should therefore date this piece in the last decade of the fifth century.

Attic standing women of the fourth century are rare indeed, but four figurines in London from Melos are almost certainly of Attic origin.[1] One, shown on pl. 31D, in a

[1] Nos. 726–9.

chiton and himation, foreshadows the Tanagra style of the late fourth century, from which she differs in little but the more restful treatment of the drapery.

We may also deduce the presence of Attic models in the better figurines (sometimes remarkably alike) from Boeotia and Rhodes.

2. *Seated women.* The standard Rhodian seated woman of the early fifth century was imitated in Attica. The Attic copy is distinguished from the Rhodian original by the clay and by slight differences in the treatment of the face. On some pieces the face is in the true Late Archaic style; in others, the Archaic is in the process of giving way to the Early Classical.

Seated figures of Artemis exist in several examples. They may be dated at the transition between Late Archaic and Early Classical. Related to these are seated women, some wearing a chiton and himation, with one hand to the breast; the himation is sometimes worn in the Archaic way, sometimes in the Early Classical way (fig. 24). Others wear a peplos with no himation, and rest both hands on their knees. The faces are all in the style of the second quarter of the fifth century.

FIG. 24. Seated woman. Attic type. 475–450 B.C.

The seated version of the Second Type of standing figure (pl. 30C), also probably an Attic invention, became extremely popular, and was widely imitated.

A fine seated woman of about 400 B.C. is shown on pl. 31E. She sits on a throne with an ornamental back, turned legs and footstool, resting on a thick cushion. She wears a chiton, a symmetrical himation, shoes and a rayed stephane over her thick wavy hair. She has a necklace and disc-earrings. The colour is unusually well preserved; reddish brown on hair and shoes, black on eyes. The throne has orange panels and dark brown legs, and the cushion is yellow with white stripes.

3. *Female busts.* A female figure, armless and cut off at waist-level, in the style of the Second Attic standing type is shown on pl. 30A. These half-figures were common in Attica, and are represented in the Katharsis Trench at Rheneia (see p. 71). They are often called dolls, but they are never pierced through the thighs for the insertion of legs, nor have any suitable legs ever been found with them. Possibly they should be regarded in the same light as the Rhodian (?) half-figures of the sixth century (pl. 12).

4. *Standing men.* Naked standing youths were made in Attica around the middle of the fifth century, but were not as popular as they were in Boeotia (p. 80).

5. *Actors.* Figurines inspired directly by comedy and (rarely) Satyric Drama became extremely common in the second and third quarters of the fourth century, and are among

the most attractive of surviving Attic terracottas. They were evidently much appreciated in antiquity, since they were widely exported and imitated.

Many types are known, and ingenious attempts have been made to identify the characters. Two sets in New York from a tomb in Athens could well represent the complete casts of two plays. Unfortunately the drama represented, later than the Old Comedy of Aristophanes, but earlier than the New Comedy of Menander, is the so-called Middle Comedy, of which our knowledge is scanty.

All parts were taken by men. When males were represented they wore the traditionally indecent comic costume consisting of a grotesque mask, padded stomach and buttocks, short chiton, tights, and attached phallus. Pl. 31B shows one of the finest of the actors, from a votive deposit at Knossos. For female parts, women's clothing was put on over the grotesque male costume. Pl. 31A, from Athens, shows a comic actor playing the role of a heroine.

6. *Dolls.* Attic terracotta dolls make their first appearance about the middle of the fifth century; a typical example is shown on pl. 30B. Hollow-moulded, back and front, they portray a naked woman, cut off halfway down the thighs and at the elbows. The premature termination of the legs and arms (not pierced, as are later types, for the attachment of movable limbs), suggests that the dolls were intended to be dressed by their young owners in real clothes which contained the missing limbs. The head is in the style of the Early Classical standing and seated figures.

In the last quarter of the fifth century a more elaborate type of doll evolved, which was to persist with little change for about a century (pl. 31C). Like the earlier type, these dolls are naked, but they are moulded only as a torso, to which movable limbs, also of terracotta, were attached by cords or wires. The heads were regularly brought up to date; the earliest examples are dated by the occurrence of one of them in a tomb at Syntagma Square of the late fifth century, a dating which is confirmed by the resemblance of the heads to those of the Erechtheum Caryatids. Other heads echo the sculptural styles of the early and middle fourth century. That on pl. 31C is dated about 350 B.C.

Dolls of this kind, but solid, had been current in Corinth from about 500 B.C. and it is probable that the Attic type is derived from the Corinthian. Like their models, these dolls also represented dancers.

7. *Animals.* Doves, cicadas, pigs and tortoises are fairly common, especially in contexts of the mid fifth century.

8. *Protomes.* The pre-Persian deposits on the Athenian Acropolis produced many protomes which are merely abbreviated versions of the seated Athena type of pl. 29. A moulded head rests on an amorphous hand-made bust. After the Late Archaic period, Attic coroplasts, in contrast to their colleagues in most other regions, seem to have almost ceased production of protomes.

9. *Reliefs.* A] Acropolis Reliefs. This class of relief comes almost exclusively from the pre-Persian deposit on the Acropolis, where they served as votive offerings to Athena. The surviving examples are very fragmentary, but a complete specimen would have been about 22 cm. high by 16 cm. wide by 1 cm. thick.

They were moulded and decorated with matt paint, and may be dated stylistically to the years round 500 B.C. Athena is represented in various capacities: as *Ergane*, spinning; as *Polias*, seated and either armed, or dressed in ordinary female clothing and holding a phiale (?); or as *Promachos*, armed and mounting a chariot.

B] Another series of reliefs related in style but commemorating Artemis, has been recently discovered at Brauron. She is represented shooting an arrow; standing, holding a lyre, with a deer beside her; enthroned, with a deer beside her; or running, with a hound.

Both sets of reliefs are perforated for attachment to a background, the nature of which is not now apparent.

10. *Plastic lekythoi.* Although having more in common with vases than with figurines, Attic plastic lekythoi of the early and middle fourth century deserve a passing mention, if only for the excellence of their workmanship.

These objects are essentially figurines moulded in front and hand-made behind, and equipped on top with the lip of a vase and at the back with a handle. The front is decorated in matt paint, as a terracotta, whilst the back, the vase-mouth and the handle are decorated in glaze, as a vase.

The subjects are mostly religious, Aphrodite, Eros and the infant Dionysus being especially popular. The range of colours is larger than one would expect on a pure terracotta of this date, comprising red, a glossy pink, two shades of blue, yellow and black.

BOEOTIA

Terracottas were as common in Boeotia and neighbouring districts in the fifth and fourth centuries as they had been in the sixth. They have been found at many sites, and have been excavated both scientifically and illicitly. Those from Halae and Rhitsona have been well excavated and well published, and form the basis of our knowledge. The mass-burial (Polyandrion) at Thespiae for the dead of the Battle of Delion (424 B.C.) has yielded figurines of great importance for chronology, but unpublished. The Kabeirion at Thebes is another important but virtually unpublished source. Eutresis is a source of less important but well-published material. The cemeteries of Tanagra have yielded copious material, most of it however illicitly excavated and none of it properly published. Although produced in such large numbers, Boeotian terracottas in the period were evidently intended for home consumption, for their export was slight. A few have however been found at Delphi, and in North Greece, especially at Olynthus and Amphipolis.

Two principal categories may be noted: *a*) genre pieces and toys; *b*) developed figurines and protomes.

The decoration is now universally in matt paint. The clay is much the same as before, perhaps somewhat coarser; in addition, some examples seem to have been deliberately fired to a grey colour.

A] *Genre pieces*

These derive from sixth century prototypes, of which a few survive (see p. 44). They flourished in Boeotia from about 510 to about 470 and were imitated elsewhere, but not widely.

In contrast with the standard Boeotian terracotta of the sixth century, the genre pieces were carefully and realistically made. They are hand-made (thus providing the exception to the rule that hand-made terracottas are inferior in quality to mould-made), except in certain instances for the heads, which are sometimes moulded. Decoration is in matt paint.

The subjects, men and women engaged in their daily occupations, are treated with almost photographic realism. Popular motives are a carpenter (pl. 32F), a butcher (pl. 32B), a scribe (pl. 32A), a barber, a musician. But by far the commonest are scenes from the kitchen, in which men, women and occasionally girls participate. An exhaustive list has been compiled by Sparkes, from which it can be seen that the following specific activities are represented: grinding, kneading, baking and grilling. The woman on pl. 32C is bending over a large bowl on a stand, grinding corn. The bowl is lit by a lamp resting on its rim. On pl. 32D she is seated in front of an oven, and on pl. 32E she is holding a pan containing cakes.

The purpose of these pieces would seem to be rather different from that of most Greek terracottas, which tended at most periods to represent deities, for these are clearly human. Many (possibly all) were found in tombs, and it is hard to escape the conclusion that they were intended to serve the same purpose as the Egyptian *ushabtis* – to minister to the needs of the dead in the next world.

Contemporary with the genre pieces, and closely related to them technically, is a group of figures probably made to serve as children's toys. The following subjects are represented; a man on a horse (pl. 32G), on a goose (pl. 33B), on a dolphin, on a cock-horse (hippalectryon) (pl. 33A); and a dog, a goat, a ram and a deer.

B] *Fully developed*

This class is regularly hollow-moulded with a hand-made back in which is a very large rectangular vent. Bases are sometimes very tall and the undersides are regularly open. Smaller pieces are sometimes solid, but are in other respects similar.

Figurines of this class are rare in the first third of the fifth century (when the genre figures predominated), but are represented by a few imitations of Rhodian, Attic or Corinthian types. From about 470 onwards they are almost universal in Boeotia, and rapidly acquire a local flavour.

1. *Standing women.* The Second Attic Standing Type was closely copied in Boeotia around the middle of the fifth century. At the same time a local variant evolved, wearing a high polos with a raised back terminating in three projections. The figure stands on a high base (pl. 33C).

In the later fifth and fourth centuries the type was again altered; the high polos is replaced by a very large and elaborate arrangement of plaits on which is set a low kalathos (pl. 33D). The peplos differs slightly from earlier examples in that the lines running from the corners of the overfall to the hips are accentuated, as in the Caryatids of the Erechtheum. The peculiar form of the headdress became very popular in Boeotia on male and female figures in the last third of the fifth century and the first third of the fourth.

In a common variant of the foregoing type she holds a casket against her left shoulder. Out of the casket emerges a fillet, the other end of which she holds to her breast with her right hand. Such caskets were apparently given as wedding presents, and these figures must represent brides or bridal attendants. It is not clear whether they are human or divine.

Pitcher-bearers and women carrying pigs were common at Eutresis between 450 and 350, but not elsewhere in Boeotia. Both are probably of Attic inspiration, and both are particularly appropriate to the worship of Demeter at Eleusis.

The fourth century also sees standing female figures of more naturalistic and less peculiarly Boeotian form, which lead almost imperceptibly to the Tanagra style of the late fourth century, and which, like the 'Tanagras', are probably of Attic inspiration. The example on pl. 34F was made about 350 B.C.

On pl. 34A is a figure of Aphrodite of the early fourth century. Other Boeotian figures of this date carry a swan, and have been identified with Leda; pl. 34D shows a mid fourth century version of the type. It has additional interest in that it is a close copy of a statue attributed to the sculptor Timotheos.[1]

Dancing figures were also popular around the middle years of the fourth century. On pl. 34C a woman is performing the so-called Mantle Dance.[2] Her himation goes over her head and completely envelops her except for her eyes and nose. The swirling movement of the dance is admirably rendered.

2. *Seated women.* In the early fifth century the popular Rhodian Late Archaic seated woman of pl. 24B was imported and imitated. In the second quarter of the century the Boeotian coroplasts followed the Rhodians by bringing the face up to date. In the third quarter of the century the Attic Severe Style type of pl. 30C was imitated and on occasions

[1] Lawrence, *Classical Sculpture*, 240, n. 4. [2] *BMC* i, no. 881.

C. Protome of young Dionysus. Boeotian. From Tanagra. Early fourth century B.C. British Museum

adapted to Boeotian taste by the addition of the tall headdress of the standing figures of pl. 33C.

After the middle years of the fifth century seated women are not common in this fabric, but we may note by way of exception the charming mid fourth century Artemis of pl. 34B. She sits on an elaborate throne, holding a fawn to her breast in her left hand, and a phiale in her right hand. Even in this humble medium it is possible to see the effect on the face of the Praxitelean school of sculptors.

3. *Europa.* Another typical Boeotian piece of the mid fifth century is known in several examples. It depicts Europa on the bull. The animal moves rapidly to the (spectator's) right, carrying Europa on its back. She wears the Early Classical peplos.

4. *Standing men.* Naked male figures, recalling in a general way a sculptural type such as the Choiseul-Gouffier Apollo,[1] are fairly common, especially from the Kabeirion at Thebes. They should be dated on stylistic grounds in the second quarter of the fifth century.

A more universal type wears a symmetrical himation covering his back and sides and holds a cock in the crook of his left arm (pl. 33E). It is not clear whether any particular deity or hero is intended. Ganymede has been suggested, but he may be just a young man. Towards the end of the century the man's head and the base become larger in proportion, a development parallel to that of the female figures; some of the men even adopt the extravagant female hairdressing fashions. This process continued into the early fourth century. On pl. 34E is an unusual version of such a figure. He differs from most of his fellows in that he holds a puppy instead of a cock, and behind him stands a bitch.

5. *Other types.* Several Rhodian types were taken over in Boeotia and there achieved a greater popularity than in their original home. Such are the mid fifth century version of the squatting satyr, sometimes playing the pipes, the squatting Hermes, and the squatting infant. These types are particularly common in the Kabeirion at Thebes.

6. *Protomes.* Protomes (chiefly female) were popular in Boeotia. The earliest examples are small and are based on Attic prototypes.

In the middle of the century we find a larger protome, more fully modelled. The woman wears a peplos, and raises her hands to her breast. This type lasted into the end of the century.

A type of protome current in the early fourth century is shown on Colour Plate C. Dionysus is depicted holding various of his attributes; an egg, a cock, a kantharos. Sometimes he is clean-shaven, sometimes bearded. This and another example in London have retained their colours to an unusual extent, and present a gay, even grand effect.

[1] See p. 61, n. 1.

CORINTH

The opening of the fifth century saw in Corinth, as elsewhere in Greece, great advances in the making of terracottas. The sources of our material and of our knowledge are in general as before (see p. 47). The workshops in the Potters' Quarter remained in production, and export to Ithaca continued.

Two tendencies are noticeable in Corinthian terracottas of this period. In the first place, hand-made pieces retained their popularity for longer than elsewhere in Greece, and from the middle of the fifth century were modelled with considerable skill. Typical subjects in this technique are creatures inspired by satyr-plays, mules with loads of various kinds, and monkeys engaged in various activities. In the second place, where moulds were used, solid figures remained for long more popular than hollow, in particular for standing and seated goddesses and for dolls. Both tendencies seem to denote a somewhat old-fashioned attitude on the part of the Corinthian coroplasts.

The decoration is in matt paint, except in the case of certain hand-made figures of the early fifth century, which are glazed. The clay is much as before.

THE PRINCIPAL TYPES

A] *Moulded*

1. *Standing women.* The typical Corinthian figurine of the fifth century is a standing female figure, usually about 11–14 cm. tall, solid, with a moulded front and a flat back. Thanks to the unusual fineness of Corinthian clay, the modelling on these figures is as a general rule considerably more detailed than was customary.

Some types are Late Archaic in style, and must have arisen about 500; others, more in the Early Classical manner, evolved in the second quarter of the fourth century. All, as we know from the excavations at Corinth, persisted unchanged down to the end of the fifth century, and possibly even into the fourth.

Throughout the fifth century figurines of this class were widely exported, and examples are recorded from the Argolid, Central and Northern Greece, Corcyra, Rhodes, the Aegean islands, Cyrenaica, Sicily, Magna Graecia and South Russia. Several varieties are known.

In the commonest (pl. 35E), she holds a flower or a fruit against her body in each hand. She wears a low polos, and a chiton with a low pouch. In another popular variety (pl. 35F) she wears a low polos and a chiton and transverse himation. Her left arm is at her side, the hand holding her drapery; her right arm is bent across her body and hand holding a wreath or some other object. The drapery and the pose come from the standard Late Archaic sculptural repertoire; we are particularly reminded of the Athena from the West Pediment at Aegina.[1] In a third example she resembles the first, and commonest

[1] R. Lullies and M. Hirmer, *Greek Sculpture* (London, 1957), pl. 69.

type, but appears as Artemis, with a bow in her left hand and a fawn in her right (pl. 35D). A fourth example, also an Artemis type, wears a chiton and a himation of the typical Early Classical form, with strong vertical and horizontal lines. In her left hand she holds a bow and in her right a fawn or a cock.

There is in Paris a composite piece consisting of three women side by side, possibly representing the Three Graces. The clay and style are without a doubt Corinthian. Stylistically they are more advanced than most of the women, for they show the influence of sculpture of about 460–450.[1]

In the fourth century, standing women are surprisingly rare, except in the Sanctuary of Demeter and Kore. Among these (largely unpublished) figurines are figures of a woman with a pig and a torch like the common Sicilian type of pl. 37B.

2. *Seated women.* These are seated counterparts to the standing women, all made from a simple mould; some solid, some hollow and backless. In one variety she wears a clinging chiton and has both hands on her knees. In another she holds a dove in her right hand (pl. 35B). These seated figures, which can be dated stratigraphically from finds at Corinth to the entire fifth century, were not exported nearly as widely as the standing varieties; they are not found outside the Greek mainland and Aegina.

During the second half of the fifth century a seated woman occurs at Corinth wearing the Early Classical peplos. In spite of this innovation, her head is much as before, and she holds both hands to her breast in the Archaic manner. These pieces also show a technical advance in that they are hollow-moulded.

A popular seated type of the mid fourth century is shown on pl. 36G. It consists of a girl on a stool, holding a ball or some other object in front of her. She wears a chiton with pouch, and her wavy hair goes up to a point in front. The type is particularly popular in Cyrenaica and South Russia.

Among the seated women may be mentioned a striking group from a deposit at Corinth of the first half of the fourth century, in which two women sit in a covered cart drawn by two horses. The women are naturalistically modelled, and foreshadow the Tanagra style.[2]

3. *Standing men.* Two standing men were found at Corinth with the group described above, and so belong to the first half of the fourth century. One is bearded, the other beardless; both are wearing a long himation, and in their freedom of execution point the way to the Tanagra style.

4. *Actors.* Comic actors were made in Corinth, as in Attica, in the fourth century B.C., but not in the same quantities. Pl. 36D shows a Corinthian version of about 350 B.C.

5. *Other varieties.* A few other Corinthian types may be mentioned. They mostly occur at Corinth itself, and many are dated stratigraphically. A reclining man is fairly common,

[1] Cat. no. C 34.

[2] *Corinth*, xv, pt ii, pls. 26 and 27, no. xvii, 36.

hollow-moulded, with a flat back. A few belong to the later fifth century, most are to the fourth. Standing youths occur in deposits of the later fifth century. Squatting boys like the common Boeotian ones of the mid fifth century were also made in Corinth. Some are solid, some hollow; all are single-moulded.

6. *Dolls.* Dancing dolls were popular in Corinth from 500 B.C. onwards. The earliest variety (pl. 35C) is a variation of the canonical standing woman, being solid and moulded in front only, with a flat back. She wears a low polos, a short chiton, and shoes, and holds castanets in her hands. The arms and legs were made separately and were attached to the body with wire or cord. There is a hole in the top of the head which must have held a peg attached by a cord, by which the doll could be dangled and made to dance. The short chiton seems to be peculiar to young girls and dancers.

The mid-fifth century dancing doll is like the early variety, but with the face brought up to date. The late fifth century variety is rather different. The body is moulded down to the knees. The back is also moulded, and the doll is consequently very much thicker front to back. Unlike her predecessors, she is naked but for a sphendone in her hair, a necklace and shoes; and instead of carrying castanets, she holds a tambourine in her left hand.

The dolls of the early and middle fourth century are of the same general kind as those of the late fifth, but the heads are periodically brought up to date. They generally hold castanets rather than a tambourine (pl. 35A).

7. *Reliefs.* Cut-out reliefs of a sphinx, a gorgon (pl. 36B), a cock (pl. 36A) and (rarely) a Victory, were made in Corinth during the fifth century. They are pierced in several places and were evidently intended to be attached to furniture. The three main types are all represented in a tomb at Argos of about 470 B.C., one of their earliest recorded appearances.

8. *Protomes.* Protomes are represented in one type, basically an enlarged version of the earliest type of head found on a standing woman. The type lasted throughout the fifth century.

B] *Hand-made*

In contrast with most Greek communities in the fifth century, Corinthian coroplasts continued to produce hand-made figurines side by side with moulded ones. As a rule, the decoration was in glaze in the early part of the century, in matt paint thereafter.

Crude female figures with cylindrical bodies and rudimentary heads and arms continued to be made but only, it seems, for local use, as none of this date have been found outside the Corinthia. Groups of four such women performing a round dance, with a pipe-player in the centre, have recently been found in considerable numbers at a sanctuary in Corinth which may be as late as the fourth century.[1]

[1] *BCH* lxxxvii (1963), 725, fig. 9.

Animals are commoner than humans among the hand-made figurines, and, though far from realistic, they have a certain style. Commonest are horses, frequently ridden. Dogs and rams are also found.

Satyr-like creatures, evidently inspired by the satyric drama, have been found in considerable numbers in Corinth and also in Boeotia, whither they were exported and where they were perhaps imitated. The earliest, of the early fifth century, are crude, but towards the middle of the century they exhibit a more refined technique. The creatures sit propped up behind by their long tails. The heads, which are sometimes moulded, sometimes hand-made, indicate satyrs, monkeys, negroes, or (apparently) wearers of tragic masks. Two examples are shown on pls. 36C and E.

In the late fifth century these squatting creatures are succeeded by figures of monkeys with pestles and mortars in much the same style (pl. 36H), and in the first two-thirds of the fourth century by figures of mules carrying various loads, usually of a comic nature (pl. 36F).

ARGOS AND TEGEA

Argive terracottas of the fifth and fourth centuries have been found chiefly at the Argive Heraeum and Tiryns. They are not of great importance, being for the most part coarser and more solid versions of Corinthian types.

Tegeate terracottas follow much the same course as Argive.

LACONIA

Recorded Laconian terracottas of the fifth and fourth centuries are few and mostly without interest. An exception is a class of votive relief found at Amyclae comprising figures like Laconian stone reliefs and comprising seated men associated with snakes and kantharoi.

OLYNTHUS

The terracottas of Olynthus are noteworthy not for any originality or excellence of workmanship, but because the site has been excavated with unusual completeness, and has yielded the remains of a flourishing factory; and because the destruction of the city in 348 B.C. provides unusually good evidence for dating.

The types are for the most part derived from Rhodes, Attica, or Boeotia. The clay is distinctive: rather coarse, with much mica; generally orange in colour and lightly fired. Locally made terracottas start early in the fifth century and continue till the destruction of 348 B.C. Standing women, protomes, and (in the fourth century) imitations of Attic plastic lekythoi were especially popular.

THASOS

The production of terracottas continued in Thasos from the previous period. The latest pieces from the prolific North-West Deposit belong to the first half of the fifth century. In addition, a new deposit, the Valma Deposit, was discovered in 1960. It contained about 1,000 terracottas, varying in date from about 500 to the second century B.C.

East Greek types were still imitated; an example from this period is a copy of a Post-Aphrodite standing woman.

Protomes are common. They are made after the mid fifth century Rhodian model (cf. pl. 26c) but the best of them are finer than the models. A seated woman in a chiton and a symmetrical himation (fig. 25) holding a phiale in her right hand, and a bird to her breast with her left, is influenced by Rhodian *svelte* figures of the later fifth century.

FIG. 25. Seated woman. From Thasos. Late fifth century B.C.

CORCYRA

Corcyrean terracottas are distinguished by their clumsy workmanship, their restricted types and the clay of which they are made.

The commonest type, of the early fifth century and probably of Rhodian origin, is a solid piece with a flat back. A woman stands wearing a polos, chiton and symmetrical himation going over her head. In some examples both hands are held stiffly in front of the body; in others, the right hand holds a flower to her breast.

Large hollow-moulded figures of Artemis, some 50–60 cm. tall, also of the early fifth century and modelled on Corinthian types, were also made in Corcyra.

The clay is always lightly fired, fairly fine in quality, but containing coarse white particles; it varies in colour between green and cream.

Production does not seem to have started before 500 B.C. After the middle of the fifth century there is a gap in our knowledge until Hellenistic times. This gap is probably due to nothing more than lack of excavation, for existing Corcyrean pieces derive only from casual finds and from the limited Greek excavations of 1879.

SICILY

In spite of the considerable production of figurines in Sicily in the sixth century B.C. it was not till the fifth that a truly local idiom developed, to last till about 330 B.C.

The principal sites where Sicilian terracottas of the fifth and fourth centuries have been found are Gela, Camarina, Granmichele (the ancient name is not known), Acragas,

Syracuse, Megara Hyblaea and Selinus, where the Sanctuary of Demeter Malophoros continued to be a fruitful source of figurines. In addition, some excellent fourth century figurines have recently been discovered on the island of Lipari.

Some who have studied this material in detail claim to be able to distinguish local fabrics, and they may well be right. There is however such a strong family likeness in all Sicilian terracottas that they can profitably be studied together.

The principal subjects in the fifth century are standing women holding a pig; seated women with elaborate pectoral ornaments; and seated women with elaborate drapery (an imitation of a Locrian variety). In the fourth century, women holding a pig and a torch, and figures of Artemis were the most popular. Protomes were made throughout this period.

Sicilian terracottas were affected slightly by the arts of Rhodes, Attica and Locri, but in general exhibit little outside influence. They exercised considerable influence on the terracottas of the Greek colonies in Spain, the Balearics and Cyrenaica, and the Phoenician settlements in Western Sicily and Sardinia.

The terracottas of this period are hollow-moulded, with open undersides and with a hand-made back, generally without a vent. In some examples, as in Crete (p. 59), the back is omitted.

The clay is usually rather coarse, with a finer slip; slightly micaceous, lightly fired, and varying in colour between orange and green. The slip frequently has a greenish or cream tinge.

THE PRINCIPAL TYPES

1. *Standing women.* First, two imitations of foreign types. A common Locrian Late Archaic type (see p. 88), and the almost universal Second Attic type (cf. pl. 30F) were occasionally imitated. Later in the fifth century the Sicilian coroplasts produced elaborated versions of Severe Style types.

A woman holding a pig across her body with both hands, or holding it head downwards in her right hand, with her left hand raised to her breast, are two common types of the fifth century. There can be little doubt that these figures represent a votary with an offering to Demeter or Persephone, to whom the pig was sacred. Both types started about 500 B.C. and continued throughout the fifth century, basically unchanged, but echoing in the treatment of details the developments initiated by sculptors. The faces move from Late Archaic, through the Severe Style of the mid fifth century to the plump appearance which was typical of the late fifth century. Similarly, the drapery develops from the elaborate Late Archaic chiton and himation to the Early Classical peplos and thence to the richness of the late fifth century. Pl. 37D shows an example of the second quarter of the century; pl. 37F the third quarter; and pl. 37E of the last quarter.

Standing women holding a young pig head downwards in the left hand and a torch in the crook of her right arm served the same purpose in the fourth century. Pl. 37B shows a version of the early fourth century.

Standing figures of Artemis, datable by the style of the heads to the later fifth and the early fourth century, seem to have been made at Syracuse principally for dedication at the local temple of Artemis, where numbers have been found. The goddess is portrayed wearing high boots, and a chiton with a girdle and cross-bands, holding a bow and an arrow, and there are variations on this theme.

2. *Seated women.* The most characteristic Sicilian figurine of the first half of the fifth century is a seated woman identified by Blinkenberg with the Athena Lindia, tutelary deity of Lindus in Rhodes (pl. 37A). In most examples she sits stiffly on a wide stool, her hands on or beside her knees. She wears a polos and a peplos; across the top of the peplos run a number of chains supported at the sides by pins; from the chains hang pendants of various shapes, not unlike certain Rhodian gold pendants of the seventh century. Blinkenberg's identification with the Athena Lindia is not universally accepted, but is given added substance by the recent discovery of such a figure wearing also the aegis of Athena.

On pl. 37C is a more naturalistic version of the type, which is however probably contemporary with the others, to judge from the treatment of the face.

The bodies of these figures are always extremely flat, possibly in imitation of a primitive cult-image.

Another type of seated female figure which was especially popular at Selinus in the first half of the fifth century consists of close, but less skilled, copies of the Locrian types described overleaf.

Seated women after the middle of the fifth century are rare in Sicily.

3. *Actors.* Recent excavations on the island of Lipari have yielded great quantities of figurines of actors from Middle Comedy and Satyric Drama, and masks of Middle Comedy, Satyric Drama, and Tragedy. They were made around the middle and in the third quarter of the fourth century B.C. Numbers of the comic actors are copied from Attic models, but others are local creations.

4. *Other types.* Other types are a Hermes Kriophoros (carrying a ram); a reclining man; a squatting boy after the Rhodian model; a squatting Pan, perhaps a Cretan type.

5. *Protomes.* Protomes in imitation of the simpler Rhodian varieties were common in the first half of the fifth century.

6. *Busts.* Large female busts, up to 60 cm. or more in height, were a Sicilian speciality. The early fifth century is represented by a fine bust from Acragas. Examples of about 450 B.C. are recorded from Granmichele. Later versions of the late fifth century and the first two-thirds of the fourth, are recorded from Acragas and elsewhere. The finest of these busts may justifiably be ranked as works of sculpture.

LOCRI

Locrian terracottas of the fifth and fourth centuries have been found at Locri itself, at the Locrian colonies of Medma and Hipponium, at Naples and Pompeii, and in Sicily. One class of Locrian seated woman was imitated at Selinus in Sicily. The distinctive style is usually said to be basically East Greek.

The types in the fifth century are hollow-moulded figures of standing men and women with drapery rendered in great detail with almost metallic precision–a fact which is not surprising since Locri was a producer of first-class bronzes at this period. In the fourth century the output is mediocre in quality.

Other Locrian figurines bear a striking likeness to contemporary Boeotian figures, and one may assume that the ancient connection with mainland Locria was maintained down to the fifth and fourth centuries B.C.

But the most characteristic Locrian terracottas, and the best, are the votive reliefs, which are discussed below.

Locrian clay is of two kinds. The first is coarse, with a finer surface, containing much coarse mica (gold and silver) and frequently small white stones. It varies in colour between orange, pale orange and brown, and is usually fired at a high temperature. The second variety is pale in colour, finer in texture, rather powdery and is fired at a lower temperature. The decoration is in matt paint on a white slip.

THE PRINCIPAL TYPES

1. *Standing women.* Standing women of an orthodox Late Archaic type derived from Type 3 (p. 54) are fairly common in the first half of the fifth century. They wear a chiton and a transverse or a symmetrical himation.

Figures of Athena were made throughout the fifth century, varying in style in accordance with the changing fashions, and various female standing types, some of considerable merit, were current in the fourth.

2. *Seated women.* The characteristic Locrian seated women start about 500 B.C. and continue into the middle years of the fifth century (pl. 38A). They sit on a throne with an ornamental winged back, their feet on a footstool, usually wearing a peplos with a very long overfall and a symmetrical himation. In their hands they hold various objects, such as a phiale, a cock, or a dove. A predominant connection with Demeter and Persephone is evident, as in the reliefs which are discussed below.

The style, which is seen in sculpture in the Berlin Seated Goddess, and the Ludovisi and Boston Thrones,[1] is characterized by a meticulous rendering of detail, especially in the drapery. The heads vary in style from the Late Archaic to a local version of Early Classical. These figures were copied at Selinus in Sicily.

[1] Lawrence, *Classical Sculpture*, pls. 24, 30–33.

A few seated female figures were also made in the later fifth and the fourth centuries. Commonest are naked figures of about 350 B.C. in a seated position but lacking the seat, which was presumably supplied in another material.

3. *Standing men.* A youth with a cock resembles the popular Boeotian type, but differs in being draped. Figures of Hermes Kriophoros (carrying a ram) range from 500 to the middle years of the fifth century.

4. *Reclining men.* This type were also popular, and was probably of Rhodian origin.

5. *Reliefs.* The so-called Locrian reliefs are rectangular plaques, about 20–25 cm. square, with pictorial scenes in relief. They are equipped with holes for nailing or hanging. They are decorated in red, pink, blue, greenish grey and yellow and black over a white slip.

The majority have been found on the site of a sanctuary of Persephone at Locri which is mentioned by the historian Livy. A few however have been found at Medma and Hipponium, and one as far afield as Selinus. The bulk of the material is housed at Reggio, but there are examples at Naples, Taranto and elsewhere.

The style shows strong East Greek influence, such as we find in the Post-Aphrodite Group of figurines. It is characterized by an archaic love of stylized patterns formed by the texture of different kinds of drapery, and the folds and creases in which it falls. The plaques were made between 480 and 450 B.C. Although the later pieces exhibit certain characteristics which are recognizably Early Classical, their spirit is much more one of delayed archaism.

The subjects are all apparently concerned with the worship of Persephone as consort of Hades the King of the Underworld. Her abduction is depicted in two episodes: she is shown surprised by Hades while picking fruit, and carried off in a chariot drawn by two winged horses. Another group illustrates her wedding to Hades. She takes her wedding-garment out of a chest; it is carried in procession by an attendant. The nuptial bath is prepared; and we see her adorning herself for the ceremony.

The next group shows Hades and Persephone enthroned. Sometimes they are alone (pl. 38C); more frequently they receive offerings brought by divine visitors: Dionysus (pl. 38D), Hermes, or (less commonly) Apollo, Ares, or Artemis, or by apparently mortal women, or possibly nymphs.

Another group shows personages coming to worship Persephone, who is not indicated; two women put incense on an altar; the Dioscuri arrive on horseback; Aphrodite, attended by Hermes, sets out in a chariot drawn by Eros and his female counterpart.

Finally, Persephone or a priestess arrange sacred vessels on a chest; and Persephone discovers the infant Adonis in a wicker basket.

The object illustrated on pl. 38B is related to these reliefs, although, strictly speaking, it is not a true relief, since it is partly in the round; nor is it pierced for suspension. It represents an ornamental wooden chest, on which stand ritual objects for the worship of Persephone; a casket, a wicker basket, an alabastron (a scent-bottle of alabaster), a dove and a cheese. It bears a strong resemblance to the chest on which, in the relief mentioned above, Persephone arranges the sacred vessels.

TARENTUM

As elsewhere in the west, production on any considerable scale did not start here till about 500. From 500 to 330 the output was considerable, but the types were unusually restricted.

Sources from Tarentum include five votive deposits, of which one alone (the so-called Fondo Giovinazzo), contained some 30,000 figurines; and a number of tombs. A quantity of moulds have also come to light in the city, but their precise find-spot is not known. Exported figurines have also been discovered at Heraclea and Metapontum.

FIG. 26. Standing woman. From Tarentum. Early fifth century B.C.

The terracottas of this period are for the most part moulded as for a hollow piece, but without the back. Other peculiarities are noted below.

Tarentine clay is fine in texture, and usually contains much fine mica. It is always pale in colour, either cream, pale yellow, pale green or pale orange. It is usually lightly fired, with a powdery surface.

1. *Standing women*. The characteristic Tarentine standing female figure of the early fifth century (fig. 26) wears a chiton and a transverse himation and resembles the Attic type of pl. 30D, from which it was presumably derived. Around the middle of the fifth century the type is brought up to date and the women wear either the peplos or the chiton with the Early Classical form of the himation. Sometimes they hold a fawn, and should be identified with Artemis. Towards the end of the fifth century this variety gives place to figures of Artemis Bendis wearing a chiton and a lion's skin, the animal's muzzle forming a sort of cap (fig. 27). The type, with suitable modifications, continued well into the fourth century.

2. *Seated women*. In a variety of the early fifth century, a woman sits stiffly on a high-backed throne, hands on knees, wearing a polos and a chiton with overfall (pl. 34D). She has a long face with a long nose, protruding eyes and she smiles. Around the middle of the century the type is brought up to date (pl. 40B) and she now wears a polos, a peplos and a symmetrical himation going over her head. Her head, in the Early Classical style, has elaborately waved hair, massed over the ears.

In the fourth century a completely different kind of seated woman became popular at Tarentum and in the surrounding districts. These figures are not complete in themselves, but need a support, and were probably made to sit on wooden seats or thrones. The modelling is freer, and points the way to the Tanagra style (pl. 39B).

A more elaborate seated figure, and one of considerable merit, is shown on pl. 40A. Made in the early fourth century, it represents Aphrodite and Eros riding on a goose. Although of uncertain provenance, there are good reasons for regarding this piece as Tarentine. The style is that of Tarentum, and a replica of this piece (if not this very piece) was found at Rudiae nearby.

3. *Reclining men.* By far the commonest type of Tarentine terracotta is a reclining man, identifiable as Dionysus. Sometimes bearded, sometimes clean-shaven, he lies on a couch, holding in front of him a phiale or a kantharos. He wears an ornate stephane, frequently with a lotus-flower in relief on a raised central portion, and a himation which leaves the upper part of his body exposed. In some examples a woman, who must be Persephone, sits at his feet; in the fourth century she usually holds a child. Occasionally a naked youth in the role of a cup-bearer stands at his feet in place of the woman. The heads and the rendering of the figures were constantly brought up to date, and the type had an unusually long life, from about 500 to about 330 B.C.

FIG. 27. Artemis Bendis. Tarentine type. Late fifth century B.C.

These pieces are usually made without backs, and are supported behind by vertical struts. Much added detail is usually found. In the best pieces it was attached after moulding. Inferior varieties were sometimes moulded from the better pieces. In these, the details are naturally somewhat blurred. The average height for figurines of this class is about 20–25 cm., but they were occasionally made much larger, up to 60 cm. tall.

On pl. 39C is an unusually well-preserved example of the early fifth century. Pl. 39A shows another complete specimen, of the mid fourth century, where a woman sits at the god's feet.

4. *Reliefs.* A class of relief made at Tarentum throughout the fourth century is concerned with the exploits of the Dioscuri, the patrons of the city. The reliefs are made in the form of shrines, with a gabled roof, and are pierced for suspension. The subjects include these deities riding, driving a chariot, sacrificing, reclining at tables; the Kalydonian hunt; and the rape of the Leukippides.

Aesthetically these reliefs are disappointing when one compares the Locrian reliefs of the fifth century (p. 89), but they are interesting as illustrating a peculiarly Tarentine style.

SYBARIS

A few figurines have recently been discovered at Sybaris. Of the fourth century B.C., they bear a strong family likeness to those of Tarentum.

PAESTUM

The bulk of the surviving material for this period comes from the temples at Paestum itself, from Eboli, and from the sanctuary of the Argive Hera at the mouth of the river Silaris nearby. Paestan terracottas were also exported to Fratte, near Salerno, where they were imitated in the local clay. In spite of occupation by Lucanian invaders about 400 B.C., so far as the figurines and pottery are concerned, Paestum remained essentially Greek.

The types of the fifth and fourth centuries are very limited, being almost confined to seated figures of Hera, standing figures of Demeter or Persephone, and standing men.

THE PRINCIPAL TYPES

1. *Standing women.* A draped woman holds a young pig by its hind-legs in her right hand; with her left she holds a casket on her shoulder or against her breast. The type seems to have originated under Sicilian inspiration towards the end of the fifth century and to have continued well into the fourth. The pig and the casket are generally associated with Demeter and Persephone, and she should probably be regarded as one of these goddesses. Pl. 40D shows one of the earliest examples of the type, which was remarkably persistent.

In a related and equally popular version, she holds the pig against her breast.

2. *Seated women.* The most popular Paestan type is an enthroned goddess wearing a polos, chiton and symmetrical himation. Her hands rest on her lap, in the right a phiale and in the left a bowl of fruit. Figures of this type were found in large numbers on the site of temples dedicated to Hera, and it seems certain that that goddess is here represented, although the objects held in her hands are not her usual attributes.

The type evolved early in the fifth century, probably from the common Attic seated Athena of pl. 29, but was not produced in numbers till towards the end of the century, when a version evolved which was extremely popular and which probably lasted, without significant change, well into the fourth century (pl. 40E). The earlier versions differ slightly in the pose and in the objects held in the hands. One variety, of about 470 B.C., has an Eros on each shoulder, and perhaps represents Hera Eilithyia.

3. *Standing men.* A standing man is a less common alternative to the standing Demeter or Persephone of the late fifth and early fourth century; an example is shown on pl. 40C. He wears a himation over his left shoulder and draped round his hips. In his left hand he holds a bowl of fruit against his body; his right arm is by his side, the hand holding a young pig by the hind-legs.

4. *Hera Eilithyia.* A much finer type is represented by one example from the sanctuary at the mouth of the Sele (pl. 40F). A woman kneels in a graceful attitude, holding a dove in her right hand. With her left hand she draws aside her cloak, revealing her naked body. A child perches on either shoulder. She has been identified as Hera Eilithyia, goddess of childbirth. The workmanship is of a higher standard and the clay of a better quality than is usual for this fabric but there is no reason to doubt its local origin.
5. *Protomes.* Female protomes inspired by Rhodian models came into use about 450 B.C. and continued throughout the Classical period.
6. *Female busts.* Female busts with a flower springing from the top of the head make their first appearance at the sanctuary at the mouth of the Sele about 350 B.C., and continue into the Hellenistic period.

NAUCRATIS

Terracottas were still produced at Naucratis in the fifth and fourth centuries, but the surviving examples are too few for any systematic survey to be practicable. The clay is still the unattractive Nile mud.

CYRENAICA

The cities of Cyrenaica in North Africa formed an outpost of Greek culture between the Egyptians to the east and the Phoenicians to the west. Although there were Greek settlers in this region from as early as the seventh century, there is little evidence for the local manufacture of terracottas before about 470 B.C. From that date, production was plentiful until well into the Hellenistic period.

The principal sites which have yielded terracottas are Cyrene, Benghazi (the ancient Berenice) and Tocra (the ancient Teucheira). Unfortunately very little material from official excavations has been published. The earliest products are faithful but clumsy copies of Rhodian, Attic and Boeotian types. In the later fifth century the influence of the Western Greeks, especially those of Sicily and Tarentum, became predominant, and continued into the fourth century.

Cyrenaic clay varies considerably in appearance. It can be almost any colour (except green), but the commonest variety is a bright brick-red. It is generally coarse, sometimes finely slipped, and can be fired either hard or lightly. Fragments of shells (evidently in the sand with which the clay was tempered), are often present, and are a useful diagnostic feature. Mica is generally present in small quantities, and there are occasional white particles.

CYPRUS

The island of Cyprus has been beyond the scope of this survey since the Mycenaean period, for its art had moved outside the Greek orbit. In the fourth century B.C. however Cypriot art, and with it Cypriot figurines, resumed its place in the Greek world. Two areas in particular were producing figurines of distinctly Greek style: Achna and Kition (the modern Larnaka). The clay is pale in colour and rather coarse, and the workmanship is crude but confident.

CHAPTER 8

The Hellenistic Period, 330 B.C.-A.D. 100

INTRODUCTION

The widespread conquests of Alexander the Great between 333 and 322 B.C. gave rise to the Hellenistic civilization, which lasted for some three centuries or more, until it was finally swallowed up by the Roman Empire.

The Hellenistic world differed in two principal respects from the Classical. In the first place, the Greek horizons were greatly extended by the inclusion of vast tracts of the former Persian empire in Egypt and Western Asia. Henceforward the really great centres of Hellenism were not the cities of Old Greece, but the new foundations in the eastern territories: Alexandria, Antioch and Damascus.

In the second place, the regional peculiarities typical of Archaic and Classical Greek art were succeeded by a cultural uniformity unparalleled in Greek lands since the Mycenaean period. This uniformity was particularly noticeable, so far as terracottas are concerned, in the first part of the period, when the so-called Tanagra style reigned supreme throughout the Greek world, from 330 to 200 B.C.

After 200 B.C. the picture changes somewhat, but the underlying uniformity is still there. For the sake of convenience, we may end the Hellenistic period, so far as terracottas are concerned, in some areas about the time of Christ, in others about A.D. 100.

Although the general quality of Hellenistic terracottas is immeasurably higher than in any previous period, and although the quantity of surviving material is, if anything, greater, there is considerably less variety, and in consequence there is in fact rather less to say about this period.

The chronological fixed points on which to base a history of Hellenistic terracottas are much fewer than might be expected. Properly excavated grave-groups are rare and, where they exist, are less informative than in previous periods, since any associated pottery is seldom as closely datable as in earlier periods. Even the evidence of coins, although by no means useless, is somewhat invalidated by their long period of currency.

Moreover, the comparative evidence of sculpture, seldom a safe guide, is more than usually unreliable in this period.

We start however on firm ground. The beginning of the Early Hellenistic, or Tanagra, period is securely dated, since the Tanagra style is not represented at Olynthus, which was destroyed in 348 B.C., but is richly represented in the earliest cemeteries of Alexandria, which was founded in 331 B.C.

This gives us a date of *c.* 340–330 B.C. for the inception of the style. Fixed points in the third century to signpost the development of the Tanagra style are few but valuable. A grave in the Egyptian Delta has been dated just after 300 B.C. by the associated pottery. The destruction of Gela in 282 B.C. is a useful event for dating the latest figurines from that city. Further down the century, a tomb at Kerch in South Russia with provincial 'Tanagras' is dated by a coin to 250–225 B.C. In addition, various deposits in the Athenian Agora and at Corinth have been made to yield useful information.

The end of the Early Hellenistic period is by common consent placed about 200 B.C. There is no direct evidence for this date, but on balance it can scarcely be far out.

The beginning of the Late Hellenistic period is accordingly placed about 200 B.C. The first secure landmark after this date is the destruction of Corinth in 146 B.C. The second is the twofold destruction of Delos in 88 and 69 B.C. The rich haul of figurines from the houses and shops will in consequence date from the years immediately preceding the destructions.

Two groups of figurines from Priene can be dated with a fair degree of accuracy to the mid second and the first century B.C. respectively, and several groups from Tarsus are dated by coins and pottery to the Augustan period. The destruction of Pompeii in A.D. 79 gives a good *terminus ante quem* for objects found in its ruins; unfortunately terracottas were not numerous. A tomb at Salonica containing 48 terracottas can be dated by jewellery to the first or (less probably) the second century A.D. And deposits from the Athenian Agora have yielded important chronological information.

Hairdressing can also be a useful aid to chronology. At Myrina and Smyrna in particular certain female figurines or heads can be dated at various points in the first century A.D. by this means. Particularly informative are the Julio-Claudian club-knot on the back of the neck, and the unmistakable Neronian and Flavian-Trajanic hair-styles.

It is not easy to fix a point at which, so far as terracottas are concerned, the Late Hellenistic period ended. It probably ended earlier in the west than in the east. At Myrina the end was brought about by the earthquake of A.D. 106. The same general date seems to mark the end of the Smyrna series. In many areas there was no more terracotta production. In others, such as Athens, a new and very different style evolved (see p. 134)

THE TANAGRA STYLE

This style takes its name from the cemeteries of the Boeotian town of Tanagra, where great numbers of figurines were illicitly excavated in the seventies of last century. Many of them are familiar types of the Archaic and Classical periods, but others, made (as we now know) between 330 and 200 B.C., at once excited admiration by their unusual charm. For long it was believed that the style of these latter pieces, the so-called Tanagra style, was a local creation, which spread from Tanagra to the ends of the Hellenistic world; but evidence has been accumulating that in reality Athens was the cradle of the style.

The Tanagra repertoire consists of standing draped women and girls (the 'Tanagras' *par excellence*); women dancing, seated or playing knucklebones; half naked female figures probably representing Aphrodite, standing and seated; young men and boys standing and seated; figures of Eros flying; and a few grotesque female figures. The hallmark of the style are a complete naturalism; a real attempt to overcome the frontality to which sculpture and the minor arts were so long prone; and a particular method of rendering the drapery which was represented as tightly stretched over the figure, now completely revealing it, now concealing it with zig-zagging folds.

The typical Tanagra lady stands in a relaxed pose. She usually wears a chiton and over it a himation of fine linen, tightly draped so that it falls into contrasting stretches and folds. On her head she frequently wears a hat like the Chinese coolie hats of today. Her hairdressing is nearly always in the so-called *melon* style. The almost endless variety of these figures is attained by varying the stance, the position of the arms, and the fall of the drapery, and also by varying the way in which the head and limbs were fitted. It has been well said that all Tanagras are sisters but none of them are twins.

The other female figures and the male figures are treated in a similar way. The relaxed poses and the sweet, sentimental faces owe much to the art of Praxiteles.

In terracottas, the Tanagra style is the result of a development which started in the early fourth century, almost certainly in Athens. Although the evidence from Athens itself is as yet slight, we can trace the evolution of the style in areas apparently under Attic influence, such as Boeotia and Rhodes.

It is however inherently unlikely that this sequence was developed basically by the coroplasts themselves. At every stage it is probable that the coroplast's art was dependent on the sculptures of his day, which he either copied, or adapted to suit his needs.

Surviving sculptural prototypes for the Tanagra style itself are not as numerous as might be expected, but they do exist, both in the form of Greek originals and of Roman copies of Greek originals. Among the former we may note an Attic grave-relief, believed to be one of the last to be made before the sumptuary laws enacted between 317 and 307 B.C.; a statue of a boy from Eretria, and figures of Muses on a statue-base from Mantinea, which has been ascribed to Praxiteles.[1] Among the latter are the 'Maiden' and the 'Matron' from Herculaneum, and numbers of statues of Roman ladies who appended a Tanagra-style body to a portrait-head.[2]

The development of the Tanagra style between 330 and 200 B.C. is not easily traced, but Kleiner has made a credible attempt. His conclusions, in brief, are somewhat as follows.

The earliest examples (of the later fourth century) exhibit a balanced composition, in which the drapery serves to intensify the structure of the body. In the third century the poses become more relaxed and the drapery takes on an existence of its own, with angular folds and stretches, in conflict with the body. By the end of the century the conflict has exhausted itself and the style is finished.

Whom do these figures represent? The draped women in general look quite human, and we may accept them at their face-value. Yet an occasional attribute such as a fawn-skin, a mask, or a musical instrument, must indicate a Maenad or a Muse. Similarly, the boys are evidently studies of everyday life, but when equipped with wings can only represent Eros. Other deities are rare, but we would probably be right in recognizing Aphrodite in the half-naked women who sit, or lean against a pillar.

The solution of this problem is not easy, and is made no easier by the fact that we do not really know the purpose which these figures were meant to serve when placed in the tomb. We can only suggest that just as the vase painters represented deities, semi-deities and humans in precisely the same way, so these figures could at will be made to represent any of these categories.

Technically, Early Hellenistic terracottas show considerable advances over previous periods. The regular run-of-the-mill figurines may now reasonably claim to be regarded as real, if minor, works of art.

Instead of making a figure in one mould, the custom now was to make the principal parts of a figure such as head, trunk, limbs, etc. in different moulds and to assemble them after moulding; other portions were made by hand and added in the same way. The backs were sometimes moulded, as in the best figurines of previous periods, but frequently not. Sometimes, as a sort of compromise, the back was made in a mould but the modelling was reduced to a minimum.

Tanagras were gaily coloured in matt paint. The palette is rather less crude than before; a favourite shade for drapery is now a purplish pink made from rose madder.

[1] R. Horn, *Stehende weibliche Gewandstatuen* (Munich, 1931), pl. 5:1. Lawrence, *Classical Sculpture*, pl. 113. G. M. A. Richter, *Sculpture and Sculptors of the Greeks*, 2nd ed. (New Haven, 1950), figs. 679–81.

[2] J. D. Beazley and Bernard Ashmole, *Greek Sculpture and Painting* (Cambridge, 1932), figs. 157–8. Lawrence, *Classical Sculpture*, pl. 127.

THE LATE HELLENISTIC STYLE

About 200 B.C. a new style evolved, and lasted in some areas until about the time of Christ, in others till about A.D. 100. It is no longer a single universal style, as was the Tanagra style; nor however can we speak of a resumption of the local idioms such as we saw in the Archaic and Classical periods.

There are really two sides to the development of Late Hellenistic terracottas. In the first place, the Tanagra types continued for the three centuries with certain modifications, which effectively destroyed their original character, so that we can distinguish them at a glance from the true 'Tanagras'. In the second place we find more ambitious studies based on sculptures and small bronzes, such as the Aphrodite of Cnidus, Aphrodite taking off her sandal, the Crouching Aphrodite, the Farnese Heracles.

This double repertoire was seldom adopted in its entirety by any one district. Each community seems to have drawn on a common pool, located perhaps in some Asiatic centre. At Smyrna we find copies of statues of Heracles and Dionysus, and grotesques; at Myrina, draped women, Victories and Erotes; at Tarsus, Heracles and other deities; at Alexandria, grotesques and locally made combinations of Greek and Egyptian deities.

On the technical side, even greater use was made of assembling the figurines from separately made parts, many moulded, some hand-made. An Eros or a Victory from Myrina has been estimated to comprise the products of fourteen different moulds. Gilding, in imitation of gilt bronzes, was employed to a greater extent, especially at Smyrna. The use of a true lead-glaze has been observed in a few figurines from Smyrna and other centres in Asia Minor.

NOTE: In this chapter it has seemed advisable to alter the geographical order in the survey of the different fabrics, since for the Hellenistic period Attica and Boeotia should logically precede other areas.

ATTICA

Our sources for Attic terracottas of the Hellenistic period are few and far from satisfactory. In Athens the Acropolis has yielded a few figurines, and there is an interesting set (in Heidelberg), from the North Slope. The Sanctuary of the Nymph on the South Slope has also produced a certain amount of material. Another source is the Pnyx. A number of figurines, as yet unpublished, have been found in tombs of the Cerameicus. The chief source, however, is the Agora, where quantities of tantalizingly small fragments have been found in deposits of varying chronological reliability, covering the entire Hellenistic period. Outside Athens, a few figurines of this date have been found in the Cave of Pan at Eleusis. And a search among any collection of figurines from Tanagra will usually disclose a few whose clay proclaims them as Attic imports.

Although Athens was undoubtedly the cradle of the Tanagra style, surviving material is very rare in anything like complete condition. A few complete or near-complete examples were however found on the Acropolis, and the Sanctuary of the Nymph has yielded a number of standing 'Tanagras' in good condition, not free-standing figurines, but made for attachment to vases.

On pl. 41E and F are shown two of the better preserved standing 'Tanagras' from the Acropolis; one is quite complete, the other lacks only her head. The fragments of such figurines from the Agora, although more informative from a chronological point of view, are too fragmentary to admit of reproduction in a general survey.

The seated girl on pl. 41A was an Attic import to Tanagra, where it was found; the clay leaves no doubt of its Attic origin. The sweet face, recalling the art of Praxiteles, and the drapery, now bunched in rich folds, now stretched across her body, is typical of the style at its best. A related piece, lacking its head, was found in the Agora.[1]

A third century figure of a seated boy from Athens is shown on pl. 41C. He sits on a rock beside a primitive-looking statue of a bearded god. The boy is naked except for a himation over his right thigh and a wreath on his head.

Standing men and boys are common ingredients of the Tanagra style, and that on pl. 41D, recognized by its clay as Attic, is a good example. He wears a himation, high boots, and the Macedonian felt cap, the *kausia*. Both arms are hidden inside the himation; the right arm hangs by his side, and with the left hand he pulls the himation up to his chin. This is a very common Hellenistic type, which was sometimes (but probably not always) used to represent the young votary of a deity. Its complicated history has been traced by Dorothy Thompson.[2] The type originated in the third century B.C. either in Attica or in North Greece, and quickly spread throughout the Hellenistic world. This is an example of the early third century; an Alexandrian version of the late third century is shown on pl. 62B. Debased versions of the second century are found on many sites as widely separated as Demetrias, Samothrace and Troy.

The Eros on pl. 41B is seated on a rock, feeding a young swan which he holds in the crook of his left arm. His face recalls those of children on plastic lekythoi of the third quarter of the fourth century, but the representation of a childish rather than a youthful Eros is Early Hellenistic. A date in the later fourth century is therefore probable.

The Late Hellenistic period is even more deficient in complete figurines than the Early Hellenistic, but there are quantities of small fragments from the Agora to indicate that the craft continued unabated in Attica. The repertoire was drawn from the common Late Hellenistic stock. Production ceased with the wholesale destructions wrought by Sulla in 86 B.C., and was not resumed on any scale until the third century A.D.

Attic Hellenistic figurines are in general carefully made, but perhaps not as carefully as

[1] *Hesperia*, xxxi (1962), pl. 88, no. T139. [2] Thompson, *Troy Tcs*, 84.

in the Classical period. The 'Tanagras' differ principally from their Boeotian sisters in lacking a vent in the back. The clay varies from period to period. In the late fourth century it is generally friable in texture and pale orange (sometimes reddish) in colour. In the third century the fabric becomes hard and brittle and the colour is generally pale brown. In the second century two distinct clays are noted, a brownish clay, fired soft; and a light-coloured clay which seems, most surprisingly, on analysis to be imported from Corinth.

BOEOTIA

The term Boeotia is used here, as in previous chapters, to include the neighbouring districts and the island of Euboea.

The principal source for the Hellenistic period is comprised of the cemeteries of Tanagra, where terracottas had been buried with the dead since the sixth century B.C. (see p. 45). It was however the Hellenistic figurines which principally took the fancy of collectors and connoisseurs when the tombs were discovered and illicitly dug in the seventies of last century. These 'Tanagras' were principally figures of draped women and girls, but the term was also used to include other subjects in the same style and of the same date from this cemetery; seated women, young men and boys, deities, semi-deities and grotesques. The style, which originated not at Tanagra nor anywhere in Boeotia, but in Attica, is discussed above, on p. 97.

A very few similar figures have been found in official excavations at Halae and at Rhitsona.

The cemeteries of Chalcis and Eretria in Euboea have also yielded a number ot figurines, both officially and illicitly excavated. One chamber-tomb illicitly excavated at Eretria contained, *inter alia*, a female figurine in the Tanagra style (pl. 46A) and a large number of Erotes (see pl. 46B–C). This tomb is unfortunately not as good a chronological guide as might at first appear, since it was re-used on a number of occasions, and details of the separate interments were not kept. Kleiner, who went very carefully into the stylistic and other evidence, attributed the female figure to an interment of the second quarter of the third century B.C. and the Erotes to another of the third quarter of that century.

The dating of the Early Hellenistic or Tanagra period (the terms are synonymous) is discussed above, on p. 96. In brief, it ran from about 330 to about 200 B.C. In the Late Hellenistic period, from 200 B.C. to the first century A.D., it seems no longer to have been the custom in Boeotia to bury terracottas with the dead.

The characteristic Tanagra figurine is made up of a number of elements made separately and assembled before firing. In general, one mould was used for the front of the body, two for the head. The back of the figure was sometimes hand-made, at other times moulded – the moulded backs are sometimes as detailed as the front, sometimes taken from a summary mould, in which only the bare essentials are indicated (see pl. 42B). Vents are occasionally large and rectangular, as in the previous period (see p. 77), but are more commonly small (about 2–3 cm. across) and either rectangular or oval in shape. Occasionally the best-moulded backs have a small pin-hole vent unobtrusively placed. The smallest figures (those about 10 cm. tall and under) are sometimes solid, and so need no vent.

Many details were made separately (by hand or in moulds) and attached. Examples are hats, earrings, objects held in the hands, and bases. The latter, when found, are composed of a thin, rectangular plaque which was occasionally cut away underneath. Seated figures are sometimes completely open underneath.

The typical clay of Tanagra figures is fairly fine – finer than in the Classical period, with a shiny surface. It is very lightly fired, and is brown or pale brown in colour. A rare variety is finer in texture, with a greasy surface, and is a sealing-wax red colour.

Eretrian clay usually has a powdery surface and is brighter and cleaner in colour.

THE PRINCIPAL TYPES

1. *Standing women.* These are the 'Tanagras' *par excellence*. The outlines of this charming style, which originated in Attica, are given on p. 97. Draped figures of standing women, girls and children were found in their hundreds at Tanagra. A small selection of the almost endless repertoire is given on pls. 42–6.

The large-scale photographs on pl. 42 may serve to illustrate the whole class. A woman stands with her weight on her left leg, her right foot placed slightly to the side. She wears a chiton and a tightly draped himation which is drawn over her head. A coolie-type sun-hat is pinned to the himation on top of her head. Her arms are hidden in the himation and in her left hand, through the himation, she holds a woollen fillet. The head is small in relation to the body, in accordance with the canons of the fourth-century sculptor Lysippus.

The back view is not as carefully rendered as the front, a treatment reserved at Tanagra only for the best pieces. The small vent is now regularly found in place of the very large rectangular vent of Boeotian figurines of the Classical period.

On pls. 43C–E and 44C and E are variations on this theme, differing in the pose, the arrangement of the drapery, and the age of the subject.

Pl. 44E should be dated towards the end of the series, in the later third century, for here we find an ambitious attempt to render the folds of the chiton showing through the himation, a sculptors' trick which was first tentatively practised about 250 B.C.

A less common type, from a tomb at Eretria, is shown on pl. 46A. In this fine piece she leans gracefully to her left against a pillar. She was holding a kithara, which is now missing, so that she must be a Muse. Her date is about 275–250 B.C.

Figures of a woman naked to the waist, in a similar pose, are rather common. They must surely represent Aphrodite.

2. *Seated women.* The seated Tanagra woman was fairly common, but never as popular as her standing sister. One of the more attractive versions is shown on pl. 43A. When she is fully clothed she may generally be considered to be mortal, but the lady on pl. 43B, by virtue of her semi-nude condition, should more properly be regarded as Aphrodite.
3. *Astragal players.* The type of a woman crouching on one knee to play the popular game of knucklebones, or *astragala*, was created just before the Hellenistic period, about 360–350 B.C., for an example occurs at Olynthus. It was not however until the Hellenistic period that it became really popular as a vehicle for exhibiting the female figure in an interesting and unusual pose. An example of an Early Hellenistic design is shown on pl. 44A.

For a more elaborate version, which includes two players, compare the South Italian version of pl. 61A.
4. *Standing youths and boys.* This subject was popular, although never as popular as the female figures. All ages are represented, from childhood to young manhood. They may be depicted loosely draped in a short himation and carrying a lekythos or a strigil, on their way to the gymnasium (pl. 45F) or carrying a bag of knucklebones (pl. 45C). They are sometimes completely swathed in a long himation (pl. 45A and E). Occasionally a youth in armour is represented; a mould for such a figurine was found in the Athenian Agora.[1]
5. *Seated youths and boys.* This subject, too, had a certain popularity at Tanagra. In one of the better varieties (pl. 45B) he sits on a rock, wearing a long himation and a petasos.
6. *Erotes.* The Eros of Tanagra is no longer the youthful figure of the Classical period, but a chubby infant, made to be suspended in an attitude of flight. These Erotes, which may be naked or draped, usually carry some object in their hands, such as a musical instrument, a mirror, a dramatic mask or a fillet. Examples of almost every variety were found in the tomb at Eretria discussed above; they date from 250 to 225 B.C. Four are shown on pl. 46B–C.
7. *Ephedrismos.* A woman carries another on her shoulders. These groups apparently represent the game known as Ephedrismos, in which a player carried another as a forfeit.
8. *Grotesques.* These may be divided into two classes. The first class comprises characters taken from New Comedy, such as the Old Nurse, who is sometimes depicted standing, sometimes seated (pl. 44B). She is not a direct representation of an actor, like Attic figures of the mid fourth century (pl. 31A–B), but is rather a new creation influenced by such characters.

The second class comprises grossly fat women, either standing (pl. 44D) or seated. The standing variety can be dated about 350–325 from an Attic example from the Agora.[2] The seated versions are probably contemporary.

[1] *Hesperia*, xxvi (1957), pl. 34, no. 5.

[2] *Hesperia*, xxiii (1954), pl. 21.

CORINTH

The workshops situated in the Potters' Quarter were destroyed by an earthquake towards the end of the fourth century B.C. and were never rebuilt. Production of terracottas continued, however, at some other site as yet unidentified, throughout the Hellenistic period and beyond.

The sources of surviving material for this period are various deposits in Corinth itself; the Sanctuary of Demeter and Kore on Acrocorinth (which continued into the second century B.C.); and the Heraeum at Perachora.

The third century B.C. is represented by standing women of the Tanagra style (pl. 47C), a class which is not plentiful outside the Acrocorinth Deposit; by reclining men, often with women at their feet, as in earlier examples from Tarentum (pl. 47A); by boys riding horses (pl. 47D–E); and by figures of girls carrying an offering such as a fruit or a flower (pl. 47F), an archaistic throwback to the popular fifth century type of pl. 35E.

Pl. 47B shows a charming study of Thetis riding on a sea-monster and carrying his arms to Achilles, her son. To judge from the face of Thetis, this piece was made in the late fourth century B.C. Its find-spot is not recorded, but the attribution to Corinth is based not only on the clay but also on the occurrence of an identical fragment at Perachora.

The Late Hellenistic period is, in the present state of our knowledge, somewhat poorly represented.

The technical skill of the Corinthian coroplast was as high in the Hellenistic period as at any other time. Retouching is plentiful and is assisted by the fine texture of the clay. Colouring is gay, an unusually bright blue being especially popular.

The clay in common use is the usual fine-textured pale green or cream of earlier periods. A rather coarser reddish variety was also occasionally used in this period.

AEGINA

Little is known as yet of the Aeginetan terracotta industry at this (or any) period, but a class of Early Hellenistic figurines from that island is worthy of mention. These figurines all come from unauthorized sources, and nothing specific is known of their find-spots. The principal subjects are girls and boys, often carrying elaborate fans and other objects. On pl. 48A is a charming study of a boy in this fabric, holding an ornamental libation-vessel. On pl. 48D is a girl with a fan. The influence of the Tanagra style, and the independence of the Aeginetan coroplast, are both self-evident.

The clay is unmistakable. It is pale in colour, usually pale orange, fine in texture, with a waxy surface. It is very lightly fired, but the polychrome decoration survives better than usual.

NORTH GREECE

This large area may for convenience be subdivided into three main regions: Thessaly, Macedonia and Thrace.

A] *Thessaly*

The site of Demetrias-Pagasae (near the modern Volo) has produced a rich series of figurines from the Sanctuary of Pasikrata. The predominant types are Early Hellenistic draped women in the Tanagra style, and boys wearing the *kausia*, probably of the same period (cf. pl. 41D); but there are a few female figurines of later periods, some as late as the first century A.D. The clay is pale orange in colour, and fairly fine in texture.

B] *Macedonia*

A few figurines have been found at Pella, but not enough to give any idea of the quality or extent of the local industry.

A cemetery at Thessalonica (the modern Salonika) has yielded a number of terracottas in the Late Hellenistic style. One tomb contained 48 figurines including a Cnidian Aphrodite like those from Myrina (see p. 115). It is dated by jewellery to the first or (less probably) the early second century A.D.

Amphipolis is a rich source of terracottas from the fourth to the first century B.C. In the late fourth and third centuries the canonical Tanagra types were reproduced. In the second and first centuries B.C., we find uninspired versions of Late Hellenistic figures of Aphrodite and Eros such as abound at Myrina.

In addition, there are many figures of the gods Attis and Telesphoros. An example of the Attis figures is given on pl. 48F. He sits on a rock playing a syrinx or Pan-pipe; at his side is a shepherd's crook. He wears a short chiton, trousers, and a Phrygian cap. The type is not easy to date, but the costume and the face are paralleled in some otherwise dissimilar figures of Attis from Delos. We may therefore suggest a date in the second or first century B.C.

Telesphoros was a godling of recovery of illness, an associate of Asclepius. His figures could well be of the same date. Although rare in Hellenistic times, Telesphoros was a popular deity with the Romans.

The clay is orange in colour, and rather coarse in texture.

In 1964 a Hellenistic cemetery was discovered and partially excavated at Beroea. Two tomb-groups containing some excellent figurines have so far been published. One group consists of two draped women in the style popular at Myrina about 150 B.C. The other comprises a set of naked figures of the 'Oriental Aphrodite' (cf. pl. 50B), a seated woman, an Eros, and a group of Eros and Psyche. The date of the second tomb is about the first century B.C.

c] *Thrace*

A rich series of figurines and moulds has recently been excavated at Abdera. The types, which run from the fourth to the first century B.C., include Tanagra figures and later derivations, dancers, Erotes, satyrs, and the 'Oriental Aphrodite'.

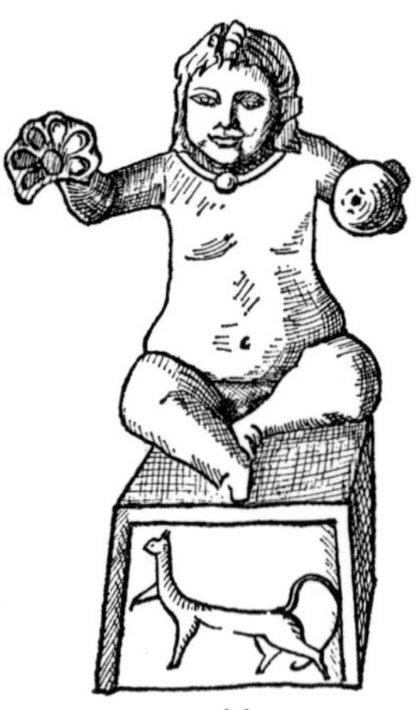

FIG. 28. Seated boy. From Bizye. First century A.D.

The clay is hard and homogeneous, of different shades of red, sometimes with a grey core. It is very micaceous, and is frequently tempered with sand, less frequently with ground-up stone.

A tomb at Bizye (the modern Vize) dated in the first century A.D., contained two figurines of children on elaborate moulded bases (fig. 28).

CORCYRA

Production of terracottas continued at Corcyra throughout the Hellenistic period. At first we find the ubiquitous Tanagras, then rather poor examples of the Late Hellenistic style. On pl. 48C is one of the better pieces. Asclepius, evidently copied from a statue, stands on an ornamental base in which his sacred snake is modelled in relief. This piece can be dated in the first century A.D. from the resemblance of the base to that of the Thracian figurine in fig. 28.

ITHACA

In the Archaic and Classical periods, the figurines from Ithaca were predominantly Corinthian imports. Towards the end of the fourth century B.C., however, there started a local production of female protomes, all probably representing Artemis. The clay is generally pink, sometimes misfired to grey.

THASOS

The production of terracottas in Thasos continued from the previous period. The Valma Deposit contained figurines of the third and second centuries B.C. Tanagra types are common and well produced, and are succeeded by a few later versions of those types. A recently discovered deposit at Evraiocastro carries the series down to the first century A.D. with a particularly nasty Aphrodite whose proportions are of that date.

SAMOTHRACE

Samothracian tombs of the Hellenistic period have yielded a number of attractive figurines. The common type of a boy wearing the *kausia*, as on pl. 62B, is represented by several fine examples. Tomb 25 was particularly rich in figurines in the style of the second century B.C. Among them are a flying Eros (pl. 48B) and a group comprising the Cypriot Eros playing a lyre accompanied by a boy, probably the young Adonis (pl. 48E). The identification of the Cypriot Eros is based on an inscription on the back of a replica of this piece from the same tomb.

The clay is a brightish orange in colour, with a powdery surface.

CYCLADES

A] *Delos*

The Early Hellenistic period is almost unrepresented at Delos, but this apparent gap in the series is almost certainly due to chance, and does not reflect the true position.

In the Late Hellenistic period the picture is very different. There is now for the first time evidence that terracottas were produced locally. The raw material for their manufacture was all imported, since Delos is entirely without suitable clay. Three, or perhaps four, factories are known to have been in existence when the town was destroyed (in 88 and again in 69 B.C.). We may assume that they were set up at least as early as the second century B.C., perhaps even in the third, about which too little at present is known.

Apart from the factories, terracottas have been found on Delos on the sites of the sanctuaries, public buildings and houses, and in tombs on the neighbouring island of Rheneia, where the Delians were buried.

The terracottas of this, materially the last stage of Delos (for the Roman occupation was negligible), are abundant, and chronologically of the highest importance, as they should all fall in the late second or the early first century B.C. They have been catalogued by Laumonier in a manner entirely worthy of their importance.

The types are drawn from the current Late Hellenistic repertoire, the closest resemblance being with the fabrics of Western Asia Minor, such as Smyrna, Myrina and Priene. Indeed a mould signed by Sosibios, a coroplast of Myrina, was actually found on Delos. In addition, a considerable number of figurines were either imported from Alexandria, or were copied from Alexandrian imports.

A few of the types most worthy of notice are illustrated on pl. 50. Later derivations of the Tanagra style (pl. 50D) show how minor alterations can have a major result. The larger head gives an entirely different bodily proportion, and the less plastic treatment of the drapery alters the superficial appearance of the figure. One could not call this treatment an improvement on the Tanagra style, but any attempt to inject new life into so familiar a subject is worthy of attention.

Another version of the standing woman breaks entirely new ground (pl. 50E). These large, coarsely made figures came into vogue in the second century in several areas.

The 'Oriental Aphrodite', so popular at Myrina, is also represented here both draped (pl. 50A) and naked (pl. 50B).

Another Aphrodite type equally popular in small bronzes and in terracottas, shows the goddess naked, leaning forward to untie her sandal (pl. 50F). Its occurrence at Delos is a useful means of dating this popular type. A Sicilian version is shown on pl. 59E.

The Eros in Oriental attire on pl. 50C is derived from the Erotes of the third century type represented in the chamber-tomb at Eretria (pl. 46B–C).

The clay varies from piece to piece. Indeed, the raw clay need not all have been imported from the same source. But the majority of Delian terracottas of this period are yellow-brown, light brown or red in colour.

B] *Melos*

The terracottas of Melos have no surprises. They follow in an undistinguished manner the general Hellenistic fashions. Figurines in the Tanagra style are succeeded by Late Hellenistic types of an unrelieved dullness.

The clay is like that of Melian reliefs (see p. 70), but rather greener, and harder fired.

C] *Paros*

A few fragments of Hellenistic figurines were found in the Delion at Paros.

D] *Thera*

The terracotta industry continued here throughout the Hellenistic period.

CRETE

Hellenistic Crete was a cultural backwater, and nothing outstanding can be expected from that quarter. The principal sources for Hellenistic terracottas are Axos, Knossos (where the Gypsades Deposit continues into the second century B.C.), and Gortyn; but a few strays from other sites makes it quite clear that figurines, as might be expected, were produced throughout the island.

In central Crete the Early Hellenistic period is represented by the Tanagra style at Knossos and Axos. The Gypsades Deposit at Knossos has yielded examples of almost every known Tanagra type, but in poor condition: shattered, rubbed and burnt. One of the few pieces in tolerable condition is shown on pl. 49C. In the Late Hellenistic period large coarsely made pieces were made at Knossos, Axos, and elsewhere. They are dated to the second century B.C. After that our knowledge is a blank.

On the basis of clay and style it has been possible to recognize as Knossian a few figurines of unknown provenance, as in the Classical period (see p. 59). The dancing woman on pl. 49B is one example. The one-piece construction and the absolute frontality make one think of the Classical period, but the freedom of movement and the opposed stretches of the drapery, in the Tanagra style, indicate that she comes just in the Hellenistic period. A date in the later fourth century is therefore probable.

In the south, the terracottas from Gortyn are as yet unpublished, but are exhibited in Heraclion. There seems in the late fourth century to have existed here a local style remarkably independent of the Tanagra tradition. As it was a singularly unattractive style, it is as well that it did not survive long. An example, of unknown provenance, but utterly typical, is shown on pl. 49F. A girl stands facing her front, wearing a short chiton and holding a young hare to her breast. Her face is full, and her long curly hair falls on her shoulders. The style of the face would suggest a date at the very beginning of the Early Hellenistic period, about 320 B.C.

For the clays of Crete, see above (p. 59).

RHODES

The production of terracottas continued in Rhodes into the Hellenistic period, but now only (it would seem) for the home market. Surviving examples from this period are few, but their high quality shows that Rhodian coroplasts had not lost their skill, and suggests that their output may have been considerable. The sources of what little Hellenistic material survives are Lindus and Camirus. There must also surely have been factories at Ialysus and in the town of Rhodes itself, but the evidence is so far lacking.

Although the 'Petit Depôt' at Lindus has been shown to be entirely pre-Hellenistic in date, a few figurines from other parts of that site do fall within the period under discussion. On pl. 49E is a figurine of a standing woman in the Tanagra style, from Camirus.

The clay, so far as Camirus and Lindus is concerned, is the same as in the Classical period.

SOUTH-WEST ASIA MINOR

A] *Cnidus*

The ancient city of Cnidus was refounded on a new site about 340 B.C., and a number of terracottas from that site testify to the early activity of coroplasts there. The material, mostly in London, comes from the excavations of C. T. Newton in the fifties of last century.

The finest figurines, of the Early Hellenistic period, come from the Sanctuary of Demeter. They consist principally of Tanagra figures and pitcher-bearers. The latter appear to run from about 340 to 300 (pl. 49D). In addition, a figure of a naked Silenus, shown on pl. 49A, is of some interest, as it is outside the usual early Hellenistic repertoire, but occurs in two other examples, one from Cyrenaica, the other adorning a polychrome vase of unknown origin, but datable in the late fourth century B.C.[1]

Terracottas from the Gymnasium, fragmentary and nondescript, seem to extend into the first century A.D.

The clay is generally like that of Rhodes at this date.

B] *Halicarnassus, Calymna, Nisyros*

The terracotta industry in these regions also continued in an undistinguished way. The types offer no surprises.

C] *Xanthus*

A few figurines are recorded from Xanthus and from the neighbouring city of Patara.

WESTERN ASIA MINOR

A] *Smyrna*

Smyrna was refounded about 288 B.C. by Lysimachus, one of Alexander's generals, some five miles from the site of the original foundation which had been destroyed in 627 B.C. and never re-occupied. The new city soon became one of the most important in Asia Minor, and has existed on the same site up to the present time.

Terracottas allegedly from this site exist in most important museums, and in the majority of cases the alleged provenance is probably correct. Unfortunately however no official excavations have been undertaken here, and all the material comes from illicit operations conducted towards the end of last century. It consists almost entirely of fragments; heads broken from figurines, less commonly headless torsos or separate limbs. Only very occasionally have complete, or near-complete, figures been preserved. These fragments were formerly believed to have come from a cemetery, but later opinion had it that they came from the ruins of houses. This last view is possible, but it is on the whole more likely that we have here part of a large votive deposit. The few moulds which are also alleged to come from Smyrna must however have come from a factory.

The vast preponderance of heads over bodies is surprising. In all probability the figurines were found in fragments, and the robbers found that the most profitable course was to fill their sacks almost entirely with heads, destroying or abandoning the torsos.

Owing to the unsatisfactory nature of the excavations, the dates of these terracottas can only be established by internal evidence. For reasons which will be given below, this evidence suggests that they were made in the first century B.C. and the first century A.D.

[1] See Winter, 2, 394:7. The vase is now in the British Museum (Reg. no. 1947. 7-14.20).

Smyrna terracottas fall into three principal categories, which will be considered below: copies of famous statues (nearly all male); female figures in later versions of the Tanagra tradition; and grotesques and actors.

These outstanding figurines were widely exported. Examples have been reported from Myrina, Priene, Pergamon, Troy, Tarsus, Delos, Athens, Cyprus and South Russia, and their influence on local fabrics was considerable.

Style and technique are unmistakable. The clay is generally orange or pale orange in colour, with a very fine shiny surface, and frequently a grey core. The figurines were made up of many separately moulded sections, the backs were modelled as carefully as the fronts, and retouching was plentiful and careful. The general effect was of a metal rather than a clay figure, an effect which was enhanced by the custom of completely or partially gilding the figurines (especially those copying works of sculpture) in imitation of gilt bronzes.

As an alternative method of decoration a true lead-glaze, green or yellow in colour, was occasionally used.

Makers' signatures are found, and would doubtless be more common had more bodies been preserved.

THE PRINCIPAL TYPES

1. *Copies of sculptures*. The Smyrna terracotta *par excellence* is a large figurine, sometimes as tall as 80 cm., partly or completely gilt, which was copied or adapted from a famous work of sculpture, usually of a male athletic variety. Owing to the fragmentary nature of the surviving material it is seldom possible to identify the sculptural models, but a few of the fortunate exceptions are reproduced on pls. 51 and 52.

On pl. 51E is an almost complete copy of the famous Diadumenos, or athlete crowning himself, by Polycleitus. And on pl. 51C is the head from a copy of the Doryphoros, or youth carrying a spear, by the same sculptor.

Pl. 51D shows a headless male figure, a copy of a statue of Zeus of the middle of the fifth century.[1] There are traces of gilding. The complete figurine would have been over 50 cm. tall. A head from a figurine of the same, or a related, type is shown on pl. 51A.

Heracles was another favourite subject. The bearded Farnese type has been recognized in a fragmentary figurine from the Loeb Collection in Munich:[2] a head of this type is shown on pl. 51B. A head of a beardless Heracles, perhaps Heracles in the Garden of the Hesperides, is shown on pl. 52A.

On pl. 52F is an almost complete figure of Hermes. The influence of the sculptor Lysippus is evident in the pose and in the proportions.

[1] A. Furtwängler, *Masterpieces of Greek Sculpture* (London, 1895), 212, fig. 90. I owe this reference to D. E. Strong.

[2] Sieveking, *Samml. Loeb*, ii, 47.

Other favourite subjects (known principally from the heads alone) are Dionysus, Apollo, Ares, satyrs, and the Ephesian Artemis (cf. pl. 58E). Portraits of Hellenistic kings, their heads set on heroic nude bodies, have been tentatively identified, but the evidence is not entirely convincing.

These copies of statues are generally dated in the first century B.C., a dating confirmed by the occurrence of a few fragments in this style at Delos; but dated deposits at Tarsus (see p. 123), where other comparable pieces have been found, would suggest that the manufacture of figurines in this style continued into the first century A.D.

2. *Female figures.* Many of the Smyrna heads are feminine, but the evidence as to the kind of bodies to which they belonged is in most cases entirely absent. The heads are some of them in the Late Hellenistic style, of which a good example is shown in pl. 52B. By analogy with comparable pieces from Myrina, it is probable that the bodies were either draped standing women in developments of the Tanagra style (cf. pl. 53C) or were figures of Aphrodite, draped, semi-nude or naked (cf. pl. 54D).

Another class of heads betray a date in the first century A.D. by their coiffures, which reflect the fashions made popular by successive Roman empresses of that century. The head on pl. 52C, an unusually fine example, can be dated to the closing years of the first century A.D., or perhaps even the beginning of the second, by the Flavian-Trajanic style of the hairdressing.

A third class of heads belong to the seated 'Oriental Aphrodite' type so popular at Myrina (pl. 56A) and Delos (pl. 50A) in the first century B.C.

3. *Grotesques.* Figures of men and women with gross faces and deformed bodies were made in quantity at Smyrna and other East Greek sites, and at Alexandria. It is not clear where this surprising fashion originated, but statistical evidence would suggest that it was either at Smyrna or at Alexandria.

The date for this class is well established by examples from Delos (first century B.C.) and Pompeii (first century A.D.). A female grotesque in Paris with Flavian-Trajanic hairdressing carries it to the end of the first century A.D.[1] The whole class probably falls within these two centuries.

Many of these figures are believed to represent actors in the Mimes, where deformed people were apparently employed. Others may well be pathological studies of disease. The running slave on pl. 52D and E could well be a character in a mime.

Under this general heading we may also include the few figures of actors from the New Comedy, represented mostly by heads, which occur at Smyrna.

B] *Myrina*

A small and unimportant town situated halfway between Smyrna and Pergamon,

[1] Mollard-Besques, *Tc grecques*, pl. XXII:4.

Myrina possesses today an importance out of all proportion to its original status. The reason for this importance is the vast quantity of terracottas excavated in its cemeteries.

Some 5,000 tombs were here excavated towards the end of last century. The excavations were at first clandestine, but in 1880 were undertaken by French archaeologists, who continued until prevented by the new Turkish law of 1884. Excavations were later continued by the Athenian Archaeological Society. The terracottas which formed so notable a feature of the tombs were distributed principally between the museums at Istanbul, Athens and Paris, but few principal museums are without a number of representative specimens, and the Museum of Fine Arts in Boston has a particularly good collection.

Although a few pieces of the Archaic and Classical periods have been found, the vast majority of Myrina terracottas date from the Hellenistic period.

It is most unfortunate that only in some six instances did the excavators record tomb-groups, and then only in part, so that the importance of this cemetery for chronological information is comparatively slight. It has however great importance in other respects, since it is the source of a vast quantity of authenticated Hellenistic terracottas of high quality and in good condition.

The figurines from Myrina have been the subject of two important studies; the catalogue of those in Boston by Dorothy Burr (Thompson) and that of those in the Louvre by Simone Mollard-Besques.

The task of dating these terracottas was made somewhat easier by the fact that many of them are inscribed on the back with the name of the maker. Sometimes the full name is given, in the genitive; sometimes an abbreviation or a monogram. Figurines bearing the same signature may generally be regarded as being more or less contemporary. But certain signatures, such as Diphilos, apparently denote a firm rather than one particular craftsman; and some firms could last as long as a century, as did that of Diphilos, or even longer.

The general development has been worked out by Dorothy Thompson and her conclusions still hold good today.

Down to 200 B.C., as might be expected, we find the Tanagra style in a particularly pure form; draped women, children, childish Erotes, masks, and a few animals. There are no signatures.

From 200 to 130 B.C. the style continues the Tanagra tradition, with greater freedom. The popular types are draped women, children, childish and now also youthful Erotes, and Victories. The earliest signatures occur in this period: Agestratos and Hyperbolos.

From 130 to 60 B.C. production increases, the style becomes more emphatic, and the repertoire is increased to include mythological subjects, and groups such as those on the Frontispiece and pl. 54A. Signatures include Aglaophon and Menestratos.

From 60 B.C. to A.D. 30 (when a severe earthquake occurred) figurines and signatures are most numerous. The repertoire includes draped women, Aphrodite, sirens, grotesques, actors, Erotes (childish and youthful), the seated 'Oriental Aphrodite', mythological subjects and copies of statues. The style is coarser than before. Among the signatures are: Hieron and Sodamos, who were active around the middle of the first century B.C.; Diphilos, Attalikos, Menophilos, Pythodoros, Artemon, Papias (a colleague of Diphilos), Amyntas, Aglaophon (again); and a few Roman names, Maecius, Gaius, Antistius.

From A.D. 30 to 106, when a second earthquake put an end to the coroplast's art at Myrina, there are fewer figurines. The repertoire is as before, and the modelling is sharp, with a metallic style and careless retouching. The pupils of the eyes are clearly indicated. The signatures include Diphilos (whose shop continued until about A.D. 50), Spinthax, and the Romans Bassus and Varius.

The clay is fairly fine in texture, usually with mica. It is generally orange in colour, but a pale orange and (in the latest examples) a dark red clay are also found.

The backs are generally unworked, and often hand-made. Vents are normally oval; occasionally rectangular (especially in 'Tanagras'); very occasionally triangular.

THE PRINCIPAL TYPES

1. *Draped women.* We start with a typical 'Tanagra' of the second half of the third century B.C. (pl. 53B). She stands in a relaxed pose, wearing a chiton and a himation which she has drawn over her head. This figurine is one of the finest examples of the Tanagra style to come from any site. The next draped woman illustrated is that shown on pl. 53A, one of the largest of the Myrina figurines – it is almost 50 cm. tall – which is dated in the first half of the first century B.C. She wears a chiton and himation, and leans gracefully to her left against a pillar, on which she rests her left elbow. The pose and the drapery are unchanged from the Tanagra period, but she breathes the spirit of an entirely new age.

The first century A.D. is represented by a figure of a Muse (pl. 53C). She was originally playing a lyre, but the instrument is now missing, and her hands are empty. Again, a complete change in feeling. The dull style, the mechanical folds and the metallic finish bear witness to Roman taste. An unpleasing piece, but typical of its era.

The first century A.D. is also represented by the exquisite figure on pl. 54D of Aphrodite putting on her necklace; the necklace, which existed in another material, has perished. The maker of this masterpiece, Menophilos, whose name (abbreviated to Meno) is inscribed on the back, is well known at Myrina for mediocre work. This figure, which comes as a surprise, shows the influence of the terracottas of Smyrna. Confirmation of a date in the early first century A.D. is given by the occurrence of a similar figurine among the few found at Pompeii.[1] The peculiar looped appearance of the drapery is seen also at Palmyra, from where it found its way into the repertoire of Indian sculptors.

Among the draped women we may also include the popular figures of the so-called Venus Genitrix type, based on the famous statue of about 400 B.C., possibly the 'Aphrodite in the Gardens' of Alcamenes.[2] Few of these figures are signed; an exception is one of the finest, on pl. 54B, which is by Diphilos.

2. *Victories.* Winged female figures in an attitude of flight became very popular at Myrina from the second century B.C. onwards. In Classical times figures of this kind represented the goddess of Victory, but by the Hellenistic period, although still no doubt technically regarded as Victories, they had lost their original function, and their purpose was now purely decorative.

The type of the Victory of Paeonios at Olympia was followed.[3] The figure stands out against the drapery, which appears to be blown backwards; one leg is advanced; and in one hand she frequently carries some object such as a wreath or fillet, a vase, a mask, or castanets.

The figure on pl. 54C is by the greatest craftsman at Myrina. His name is not known, but his career has been investigated by Dorothy Thompson and Simone Mollard-Besques. He specialized in winged figures – Victories and Erotes – in the early second century B.C. The figure illustrated is one of three in Boston made from the same moulds, but acquiring a different personality by the different set and treatment of the heads. Another masterpiece by the same hand is the famous Heyl Aphrodite in Berlin.[4]

3. *Aphrodite.* The half-naked Aphrodite leaning against a pillar originated in the Tanagra period; more elaborate versions were made thereafter. The figure on pl. 53D, signed by Aglaophon, was made about 150 B.C. Here she is shown leaning against an archaic statue, possibly of herself, possibly of a priestess or a votary.

Completely naked figures of Aphrodite were made from the second century B.C. onwards. In a particularly attractive version on pl. 53E she is depicted crowning a herm of Dionysus. The rich modelling is in the best second century tradition, while the treatment of the herm, paralleled at Delos, suggests a date towards the end of that century.

Adaptations of the famous Cnidian Aphrodite of Praxiteles were extremely popular in the early first century A.D. They were made principally in the workshop of Diphilos, and are of a nastiness almost unparalleled in Greek terracottas (fig. 29).

4. *Oriental Aphrodite.* This term, coined by Pottier and perpetuated by Simone Mollard-Besques, is used to denote three separate varieties of female figures seated, but without a seat (it was presumably supplied in some perishable material). It is, in truth, still

[1] H. von Rohden, *Die Terracotten von Pompeii* (Stuttgart, 1880), pl. XXVIII:3.
[2] Lawrence, *Classical Sculpture*, pl. 72.
[3] ibid., pl. 68.
[4] Burr, *Boston Myrinas*, 59, fig. 13.

undecided whether a goddess or her servant, as Dorothy Thompson holds, is indicated. These figures are common on East Greek sites: Smyrna, Myrina, Priene, Troy, Delos, Samothrace, Thasos. It is not certain where this class originated, but it is convenient to discuss it at this point, as all these varieties are particularly well represented at Myrina. All are dated in the first century B.C.

A] Naked, with melon-hairdressing, like the Delian example on pl. 50B. The treatment of the arms varies. In some examples one arm is at the side, the other raised to the breast;

FIG. 29. Copy of Cnidian Aphrodite. From Myrina. Late first century B.C.

FIG. 30. Female half-figure. From Priene. Mid second century B.C.

in others both arms are at the sides; in yet others, the arms were made separately and attached with wires, so that they could be moved up and down, like the dolls of the fifth and fourth centuries.

B] Naked, but wearing a tall and elaborate headdress, high-soled sandals, and much jewellery. The arms are movable.

C] As B, but wearing a high-girdled sleeveless chiton (pl. 56A).

5. *Female busts*. Figures of women unusually well modelled, but terminating just below the breasts, are about 25 cm. tall and wear an unusual amount of jewellery, carefully indicated. Similar busts were found at Priene (fig. 30). They were made in one of the best periods, the early second century B.C.

6. *Youths*. Figures of youths wearing a himation were popular in the late first century B.C. and the early first century A.D. These pieces are frequently signed, most often with

the names of Amyntas, Attalikos, Diphilos, Menophilos and Bassus. One arm is usually at his side, the other bent across his chest. Often, as in pl. 56E, he has a quiver on his back. Occasionally he holds a manuscript scroll in both hands.

A slightly younger boy was popular about the same time, wearing a chlamys and accompanied by a pet goose or a dog. The example on pl. 56B, with a dog, is signed by Diphilos.

On pl. 56D a more unusual type, of the first century A.D., depicts a composite deity, Dionysus-Sabazius. The effeminacy of the body and of the pose are typical of this period.

7. *Erotes.* Erotes were extremely popular at Myrina throughout the Hellenistic period. In the Tanagra period (down to 200 B.C.) only the childish version is found. Thereafter he is portrayed impartially at any age between infancy and young manhood. A selection from the many varieties is shown on pl. 55.

On pl. 55A a childish Eros, lightly draped, is flying down to earth. In his left hand he holds a pyxis, and in his right he lifts up his drapery. This charming study is dated in the first half of the second century B.C. An equally attractive portrayal of a naked Eros is shown on pl. 55B; its date is the middle of the second century B.C.

A well-defined group of childish Erotes is dated about the middle of the first century B.C. These Erotes are characterized by a very metallic treatment, probably borrowed from the art of Smyrna, and a multiplicity of applied ornamentation. The figure on pl. 55D is a conflation of the Greek Eros with the Egyptian Harpocrates. He is basically an Eros, but the headdress and the cornucopia indicate his *alter ego*, the Egyptian god of plenty. A bronze from the Mahdia shipwreck dating from the early first century B.C. is related to this group, which apparently emanated from the workshop of Diphilos.[1]

In pl. 55C a youthful Eros stands beside a winged female figure, evidently Psyche, whom he loosely embraces. This group was made in the early first century B.C. The almost mechanical combination of a young Eros and a draped woman of Tanagra affinities is surprisingly successful.

8. *Seated groups.* Genre pieces of this nature were made in the later second century B.C., and are among the most charming of the Myrina creations. On pl. 54A is a group of a man and a woman on a couch; evidently a nuptial scene, but whether human or divine it is not possible to say. A related piece on the Frontispiece shows two women on a couch. This is usually interpreted as an older woman instructing a bride in the secrets of the marriage-bed. The bride holds in her left hand a model of a hare, doubtless a love-gift from her husband.

9. *Actors and grotesques.* Actors from the New Comedy are common in the second and first centuries B.C. On pl. 56C is a slave of the second half of the first century B.C.

Grotesques, many of whom probably represent actors in the mimes, are found in the

[1] W. Fuchs, *Der Schiffsfund von Mahdia* (Tübingen, 1963), pl. 14.

first century B.C. These are more fully discussed in connection with Smyrna, where they were especially popular (see p. 112).

c] *Kyme*

A number of figurines came to light at Kyme in Aeolis from the French excavations of 1881 and the Czechoslovak of 1925. They are now in Istanbul and in the Louvre.

Kyme and Myrina were very near neighbours, and it is no surprise that the figurines of these two cities are remarkably alike in choice of subjects, in style, and in clay. The principal differences lie in the coarser workmanship of most of the figurines of Kyme and in their occasional use, in the first century B.C., of a true lead-glaze as an alternative to the almost universal matt paint. This glaze, which was also used at Smyrna (see p. 111), is greenish brown in colour.

A few makers' signatures are recorded, among them that of Phanites, whose wares were exported to Myrina.

D] *Larisa*

The workshops of Larisa continued just into the Hellenistic period. They probably ceased with the destruction of the city by the Gauls 279 B.C. The most popular types are standing and seated women in the Tanagra tradition. The clay is as before (see p. 69).

E] *Priene*

An Ionian city in the Maeander valley opposite Miletus, Priene remained unimportant until it was rebuilt on a new site about 350 B.C. A few figurines were recovered by the Society of Dilettanti at the Temple of Athena Polias in 1869, and are now in the British Museum. The vast majority of the material, however, comes from the German excavations of the eighteen-nineties, and are divided between Berlin and Istanbul.

The figurines of Priene, which run from the later fourth century B.C. to about the time of Christ, are of excellent quality. They all come from temples and houses, for the cemeteries have not yet been dug. They would doubtless prove an even more fruitful source of figurines if they should ever be excavated.

Those from the houses cover the second and first centuries B.C. In a period when chronological evidence is all too rare, Priene provides two important dated groups: a group of houses whose destruction about 150 B.C. (at the hands of Orophernes) is attested by associated coins; and another group whose destruction is dated by associated pottery to the first century B.C.

So far as temples are concerned, that of Demeter and Kore has yielded a rich series of figurines of the later fourth and the third century B.C. The Temple of Athena Polias was less productive. The material from that site is restricted to a fine female statuette of the first century B.C. (pl. 57D), and a few fragments.

The figurines of Priene are very like the better-known products of Myrina, but are distinguished by the different clay and by a few types which are not found at Myrina. Signatures are common. The following are recorded: Gerasimos, Menekrates, Moschos, Pytheas (?), Theodotos; and the abbreviations NO and OS.

The clay is fine in texture, with a waxy surface, and is usually very micaceous. The colour, always bright and clear, varies between pale orange and brown. The figurines are lightly fired, and the surface in consequence tends to crumble away. Gilding was occasionally employed instead of the usual polychrome decoration.

THE PRINCIPAL TYPES

1. *Standing women.* A votive deposit at the Temple of Demeter and Kore produced a number of figurines in the Tanagra style. Two such figurines, of a woman and a girl respectively, as shown on pl. 57A and B.

A typical figurine of the second century, from one of the houses destroyed about 150 B.C., is shown on pl. 57C. It has lost its head since the original publication, but it is still an important piece. The pose, the flamboyant style, and the transparent drapery all reveal the influence of contemporary Pergamene sculpture.

The figurine on pl. 57E comes from one of the houses destroyed in the first century B.C. In some respects it is close to the Tanagra tradition of some two centuries earlier, and serves to illustrate the remarkable tenacity of the main lines of that style. Pl. 57D shows a contemporary piece, from the Temple of Athena Polias. The date is given by the resemblance of the head to one from a house destroyed in the first century B.C.

The end of the first century B.C. or the beginning of the first century A.D. is represented by a series of female figurines in the style of fig. 29 (from Myrina). The standing woman of pl. 57F (signed by Gerasimos) is linked by maker and find-spot (a house) to one such type, and must have been made also about the time of Christ; a dull, but not entirely worthless piece.

2. *Dancing women.* On pl. 58C is a figure of a girl dancing, on a rectangular flanged base; it is signed by Theodotos. Although in many ways recalling dancing figures of the mid fourth century (cf. pl. 34C), this figurine comes from a house whose contents can on general grounds be dated in the late first century B.C.

3. *Aphrodite taking off her sandal.* This popular Late Hellenistic type is well represented at Priene. Its occurrence at Delos (cf. pl. 50F) serves to date it in the late second or early first century B.C.

4. '*Oriental Aphrodite*'. The clothed version of this common East Greek type (cf. pls. 50A, 56A) is also found at Priene. It also dates in the late second or early first century B.C.

5. *Female busts.* Female busts cut off just below the level of the breasts occur in several

examples (fig. 30, p. 116). They are unusually large and made with care. Similar busts were made at Myrina.

6. *Flying Erotes.* Figures of a flying Eros very like pl. 55B (from Myrina) are well represented in the group of houses destroyed about 150 B.C. They are just as charming as their contemporaries from Myrina.

7. *Groups and genre-scenes.* Groups and genre-scenes very like those from Myrina are also found at Priene. A local creation of unusual charm is however shown on pl. 58A. It comes from a house destroyed in the first century B.C. A negro boy is depicted pulling a thorn out of his foot. Although clearly inspired by a famous sculpture[1] it has been transformed by the coroplast into a human document, a sympathetic study of a racial type.

8. *Mythological creatures.* An extremely spirited rendering of a centaur comes from one of the houses destroyed about 150 B.C. (pl. 58B), and a satyr, equally spirited, with a goat leaping over his shoulder, from one of those destroyed in the first century B.C. Another mythological piece shows a nymph in the embrace of Pan.

9. *Grotesques.* Grotesques like those found principally at Smyrna and Alexandria, but common throughout Eastern Greece, occur also at Priene, where they were made in the first century B.C. More unusual are indecent female figures, believed to represent Baubo, which were offered in the Temple of Demeter and Kore in the third century B.C. They were apparently a local creation.

10. *Animals.* Figures of pigs, sacred to Demeter, were found in the third century votive deposit of the Temple of Demeter and Kore.

11. *Masks.* A fine series of dramatic masks, all apparently from the New Comedy, decorated the walls of a house destroyed about 150 B.C.

F] *Ephesus*

Production of terracottas continued at Ephesus into the Hellenistic period. The evidence, which comes mostly from J. T. Wood's excavations of the sixties and seventies of last century, is not plentiful, but it is clear that this was no creative centre of the coroplast's art.

The style was the usual one for this part of the world, and needs no further comment. One type however deserves particular mention, and that is the multiple-breasted goddess on pl. 58E. The identification of this type as the 'Diana of the Ephesians' rests soundly on sculptural and numismatic evidence, but this is the only surviving terracotta recorded as coming from Ephesus itself. The only similar ones with recorded provenance come from Smyrna, and serve to date the type in the first century B.C. or the first A.D. But this one is apparently not of Smyrna clay or workmanship, and the alleged find-spot, although not soundly based, may provisionally be accepted. The clay could certainly be Ephesian.

[1] Lawrence, *Classical Sculpture*, pl. 119a.

G] *Sardis*

A tomb at Sardis, dated by a coin to around 200 B.C. or rather later, contained a few figurines of types familiar at Myrina.

H] *Pergamon*

Pergamon, a hill-top city in North-West Asia Minor, does not enter history until the third century B.C., when, under the Attalid dynasty, it became the capital of a rich and important kingdom. The kings of Pergamon were enlightened patrons of the arts, and Pergamene sculptures of the third and second centuries B.C. are among the finest of the Hellenistic world.

The figurines from this important site (now divided between Berlin and the local museum at Bergama) derive mostly from the German excavations from 1878 onwards. A few had been acquired earlier, in 1839, by Thomas Burgon, and are now in the British Museum.

Pergamene figurines are all too little known, but a comprehensive study of them is now being prepared. There is evidently a wide range of subjects and a varied style. The local coroplasts were evidently influenced by the sculptures of their city.

Some idea of the quality of Pergamene figurines is provided by the contents of a rich tomb at the site of the town of Gambrion, nearby. It is dated by a coin to the mid second century B.C. and contained the following figurines: Silenus with the infant Dionysus; Erotes; boys; Aphrodite.

Pergamene clay varies between pale brown and yellow in colour, is fine in texture with a glossy surface, and has no mica. It resembles that of Smyrna.

I] *Troy*

The Hellenistic terracottas from the Classical Ilion (Troy IX of the excavators) originate from three sources: the excavations of Frank Calvert in the eighteen-fifties, of Schliemann in 1870–94, and above all of the American archaeologists of the University of Cincinnati in 1932–8. The figurines are for the most part dull, provincial, and badly preserved; but those from the American excavations have been studied so thoroughly (by Dorothy Thompson) as to acquire an importance out of all proportion to their aesthetic worth. The material is for the most part in Istanbul and at Çannakale.

The figurines from Ilion are for the most part of local workmanship, and date between the third and the first centuries B.C. Draped women in the Tanagra style and a Late Hellenistic development of it, were made throughout this period. Dancing women cover the second and first centuries B.C. Seated figures of the goddess Cybele were made from the third to the first centuries B.C., and seated naked women (the 'Oriental Aphrodite') as on pl. 50B, throughout the second and first centuries.

Figures of boys wearing a *kausia* (as on pl. 62B) range from the late third to the first century B.C. Finally, relief-plaques of riders, evidently a local creation, were made in the third and second centuries B.C.

Trojan clay is sandy and fairly micaceous, fired medium to hard. The colour is described as ranging from dusky buff to tan, with a grey core.

BLACK SEA COASTS

A] *Amisos*

Amisos (the modern Samsoun), a Milesian colony on the north coast of Asia Minor, became in the Hellenistic period an important centre for the manufacture of terracottas. There is a fine collection in Istanbul, and there are other examples in the Louvre; all unfortunately from illicit excavations.

The repertoire covers the usual Hellenistic types, but they are treated with unusual freshness. Favourite subjects are: draped women, Muses (pl. 58D), Cybele, Isis, Aphrodite, Heracles (bearded and beardless), Hermes, genre-scenes, children, grotesques, animals and (a local speciality) comic masks of Dionysus; young men and women, satyrs and actors. As might be expected, there are resemblances to the figurines of Myrina and Priene.

The workmanship is perhaps somewhat crude, but there is rich polychrome decoration, and the occasional use of gilding. The moulds were some of clay, some of plaster. The clay is usually soft, pale yellow or dark brown in colour, with a grey core.

B] *South Russia*

In the Classical period the Greek and semi-Greek communities on the northern shores of the Black Sea had been keen importers of Greek figurines, and had to a limited extent supplemented the imports from their own resources.

In the Hellenistic period they continued to import, but local workshops were set up to an increasing extent. Remains of such workshops have been discovered at Kerch and Chersonesus. The latter site produced a fine collection of moulds in second century style.

The principal site where figurines have been found are Olbia, Theodosia, Panticapaeum (the modern Kerch, the source of most surviving South Russian terracottas), Myrmekion and Phanagoria.

A generous range of Early and Late Hellenistic types survives, especially from Kerch, but the workmanship is in general second-rate. The factories continued into the Roman period.

In certain instances local clays have been noted. That of Panticapaeum has several varieties: pale green and lightly fired, pink or orange and fired harder. That of Theodosia is fine and yellowish; of Olbia, reddish and friable, with a smooth surface.

TARSUS

Tarsus was an important city in Cilicia in Hellenistic and Roman times. Terracottas had been found by treasure-hunters in the mid nineteenth century, but our principal source of the material, and of our knowledge of it, comes from the American excavations of 1934 and subsequent years.

The figurines of Tarsus range in date from the late third century B.C. to the third century A.D. They are without merit; derivative in repertoire and provincial in style. But considerable chronological importance attaches to certain dated groups of the late first century B.C. and the early first century A.D., a period for which in most fabrics precise chronological evidence is singularly lacking.

The repertoire is varied: a few Tanagra types; deities, comprising Aphrodite, Athena, Apollo Citharoedus (playing the lyre), Dionysus, and above all Heracles, bearded and beardless; a number of Egyptian deities, Harpocrates, Isis, Serapis; grotesques; and a series of comic and tragic theatrical masks of the second century A.D. Almost every representation tends to wear an ivy-wreath, which may almost be regarded as the hall-mark of Tarsus. There are no makers' signatures.

All surviving moulds are of plaster, and many of the figurines show the bead-like spotting characteristic of the products of such moulds (see p. 2). The early pieces are mostly made in two moulds, for front and back. More elaborate pieces are occasionally found later, but the extreme intricacy of Myrina is not found. Occasionally in the first century B.C. the terracottas of Tarsus were decorated with a lead-glaze, like that on pottery from this centre. For the clay of Tarsus one cannot do better than quote the excavators: 'The two most characteristic clays of Tarsus are a buff tending to red or orange and a buff tending to cream or greenish white. Both are exceedingly fine and close-grained although the reddish buff is somewhat finer. Both show occasional lime inclusions.'

CYPRUS

As was stated above (p. 94), throughout the fourth century B.C. Cypriot art, and with it Cypriot terracottas, was moving back into the Greek orbit, which it had left after the Mycenaean age. By the end of the century the process was complete and Cypriot terracottas of the Hellenistic period are purely Greek. An Early Hellenistic phase in the Tanagra style is succeeded by a Late Hellenistic which has much in common with that of Asia Minor, Myrina in particular.

The principal sites where Hellenistic figurines have been found are Kition (the modern Larnaka), Amathus, Curium and Salamis. The standard of workmanship is on the whole high. Backs are hand-made, with circular, less commonly rectangular, and occasionally arch-shaped vents. The clay is generally pale in colour, varying from cream to pale orange or light brown, and rather coarse. That of Curium however is dark brown or brownish red in colour, and definitely coarse in texture.

SYRIA

The Hellenistic terracottas of Syria are represented particularly well by the contents of a sanctuary at Kharayeb, near Sidon, which are now to be found in Beirut. The repertoire includes the usual Hellenistic subjects, on which a few Egyptian and Western Asiatic themes were occasionally grafted. The deposit ranges in date from the late fourth to the first century B.C.

The style is somewhat clumsy and provincial. The clay is usually reddish and fairly well levigated, but contains particles of chalk. There is however another variety which is very pale in colour. The degree of firing is usually light in both varieties.

SICILY

The Sicilian terracotta industry continued into the Hellenistic period till at least the first century B.C. The quantity of surviving material is, apart from Centorbi, considerably diminished in the Early Hellenistic period and even more diminished in the Late Hellenistic; but it may well be that this scarcity is due to the chances of discovery and does not represent the true position.

The principal sources are as follows: Centuripae (the modern Centorbi, which covers the entire Hellenistic period); Syracuse (which probably also covers the entire period); and Acragas, Gela, Morgantina, Soloeis (the modern Solunto, near Palermo), and Selinus, where little but the Early Hellenistic period is so far represented. Gela is particularly important chronologically by virtue of its destruction in 282 B.C.; Morgantina by virtue of a dated deposit of 278–250. With Sicily we may include the island of Lipari, where a number of excellent Early Hellenistic figurines have been discovered.

The workmanship is of a high standard. The decoration is carefully done; particularly effective is a lustrous pink which looks at first sight like a glaze, but is in fact a highly refined clay. Backs are hand-made, with round vents. The repertoire recalls in many respects that of Tarentum.

THE PRINCIPAL TYPES

After the Early Hellenistic period, the surviving material is virtually restricted to Centorbi, but was probably in fact typical of all Sicily.

1. *Standing draped women.* Figurines in the orthodox Tanagra style are succeeded by derivatives of the style of second century B.C. date.

2. *Aphrodite* (?) *standing*. Half-naked women standing in various relaxed poses, probably (but not certainly) to be identified with Aphrodite, are very common. They are all, it would seem, of the second century B.C. One example is shown on pl. 59C; the object which she held in her hand is unfortunately missing.
3. *Women dancing*. There are a few dancing women in the Early Hellenistic style; many more in the style of the second century B.C., where their drapery swirls round their bodies in the rapid movement of the dance (pl. 59B).
4. *Seated women*. The second century B.C. saw many figurines of women seated on a rock. Some are fully draped, others are half-naked; all were probably intended as Muses.
5. '*Oriental Aphrodite*.' The simple, naked, version of the 'Oriental Aphrodite' (cf. pl. 50B) occurs rarely in the late fourth or the third century.
6. *Ephedrismos*. A popular type of the second century B.C. consists of a draped woman, presumably Aphrodite, carrying Eros on her shoulders (pl. 59D). These groups apparently represent the game known as Ephedrismos, in which a player carried another over her shoulders as a forfeit (see p. 103).
7. *Aphrodite undoing her sandal*. Two varieties of this popular Hellenistic subject are known from Sicily: a draped and a naked version, both of the second century B.C. The latter is illustrated on pl. 59E.
8. *Dionysus and Ariadne* (?). A naked man and a draped woman standing side by side should possibly be interpreted as Dionysus and Ariadne.
9. *Erotes*. Chubby winged infants of the Early Hellenistic period are succeeded by more sophisticated young men of the second century B.C., most of them partially draped.
10. *Mythological figures*. Figures from mythology include Thetis on a sea-monster (second century B.C.), a satyr recalling one from Priene of the first century B.C.; Pan assailing a nymph (first century B.C.); and Scylla (second or first century B.C.).
11. *Herms*. A herm of Priapus recalls a figurine from Delos of the late second or early first century B.C.
12. *Masks*. Numbers of tragic and comic masks should probably be dated in the second century B.C.
13. *Ornamental plates*. Ornamental plates pierced for suspension are a Sicilian speciality. They include a flower out of which emerges a bust of Eros holding a mirror (pl. 59A); a flower in the centre of which is the head of a Gorgon, seen full-face; and a circular composition of Eros and Psyche kissing. Their date is about the second century B.C.
14. *Busts*. Large female busts like those from Myrina and Priene were also made in Sicily (see pp. 116, 119).

LOCRI

The Locrian terracotta industry continued into the Hellenistic period. The Tanagra style of the Early Hellenistic period is adequately represented; the Late Hellenistic, on present evidence, has little to show in the way of figurines.

APULIA

A] *Tarentum*

The principal coroplastic centre in Apulia in the Hellenistic age was Tarentum. In spite of their city's disasters at the hands of Rome, the Tarentine coroplasts maintained, down to the first century A.D. and perhaps beyond, their earlier reputation for productivity, competence and originality.

The universal Tanagra style was here reproduced in a manner nearer to that of mainland Greece than was usual in the west, and was succeeded by a Late Hellenistic phase of unusual brilliance which can be traced into the first century A.D.

The clay is of the same pale shades and friable texture as before. The decoration has survived to a greater degree than at most sites, rose-madder being particularly common. Spool-shaped bases, thrown on the wheel, are a Tarentine speciality in this period.

THE PRINCIPAL TYPES

1. *Standing women*. Draped standing women in the Tanagra style abound, and are succeeded by Late Hellenistic derivatives of the style. Half-naked women follow the same sequence.
2. *Dancing women*. Women dancing, their drapery swirling round them, are common in the second century B.C. (cf. pl. 59B). Less common is a naked woman performing a rather more stately dance.
3. *Seated women*. Seated draped women, like their more common standing sisters, follow a singular sequence from the Tanagra style to the Late Hellenistic. Half-naked female figures seated on a rectangular block are a popular Tarentine type, and are unknown elsewhere; an example is shown on pl. 60D. Since another example (in Tarentum) holds a satyric mask, we may deduce that all of this type (most of whom have lost the object once in their hands) are intended as Muses.
4. *Reclining woman*. A half-naked reclining woman rendered in semi-relief and seen from above, would also seem to be a Tarentine speciality. The date is the second century B.C.
5. *Ephedrismos*. A second century ephedrismos group (cf. p. 106 and pl. 59D) was common at Tarentum. Here Aphrodite may be either naked or draped.
6. *Aphrodite removing her sandal*. Two versions of the popular Hellenistic type were known at Tarentum, as in Sicily: naked, as on pls. 50F and 59E, and draped.

7. *Victory*. Standing draped figures of Victory were common in the second and first centuries B.C.
8. *Dionysus and Ariadne* (?). A group similar to the Sicilian type (p. 125) was also popular at Tarentum in the second century B.C.
9. *Acrobats*. Acrobats of both sexes, but more commonly female, occur in the second and first centuries B.C.
10. *Boys*. Naked boys are found in the Tanagra style of the Early Hellenistic period.
11. *Erotes*. Figures of Eros run the full gamut from the late fourth to the first century B.C.
12. *Actors*. There are numbers of comic actors of the second and first centuries B.C. in very much the same style as the Myrina actors (cf. pl. 56C).
13. *Gladiators*. Figures of gladiators may be dated to the first century A.D. from their resemblance to a piece from Pompeii.
14. *Masks*. Tragic masks should probably be dated in the second or first century B.C. Crooked-faced masks from farce, however, must be as late as the first century A.D., since a similar mask was found at Pompeii.

B] *Other Apulian Sites*

The principal sites in Apulia, apart from Tarentum, to produce figurines in the Hellenistic period include Egnatia (also written Gnathia), Canusium (the modern Canosa), and Rubi (the modern Ruvo). All have their own characteristics, but the overriding influence of Tarentum is plain.

Egnatia follows Tarentum closely in the choice of types and in the appearance of the clay. Orthodox standing women in the Tanagra style and contemporary pitcher-bearers like those from Cnidus (cf. pl. 49D) are succeeded by Late Hellenistic Victories, Erotes, and children riding on animals.

At Canosa the Early Hellenistic period is marked not only by orthodox Tanagra figures (pl. 60B), but also by large and ostentatious polychrome vases decorated lavishly with figurines in this style. In the second century B.C., in addition to the usual Late Hellenistic repertoire, we find larger figurines of women with outstretched arms. These so-called *orantes* (praying women) can be as tall as one metre. Among more orthodox Late Hellenistic pieces, a series of dancing girls of the second century in the British Museum is worthy of note. One is illustrated on pl. 60C. The heads and bodies of all are made in the same moulds, but the set of the heads and the arrangement of the (handmade) arms gives to each girl an individuality of her own. The clay of Canosa is like that of Tarentum, but somewhat coarser.

Ruvo produced some fine Tanagras; the woman seated on a rock (a Muse?) of pl. 61C is a good example. A speciality of the second century is a kneeling figure of Aphrodite emerging in birth from a scallop-shell, the open valves of which are spread out beside her like a pair of wings. The theme is known in many fabrics, but this precise arrangement, perhaps the most effective, was evidently invented at Ruvo, where many examples have been found. An example is shown on pl. 60A. The clay of Ruvo is like that of Tarentum, but the surface is less friable.

PAESTUM

The production of figurines continued at Paestum at least into the second century B.C. They have been discovered not only at Paestum itself, but also in considerable quantities at the Heraeum on the mouth of the Silaris nearby.

The workmanship is fairly good. Backs are hand-made, with round or oval vents. Bases are often moulded in one piece with the front of the figurine.

The Tanagra period is richly represented; the Late Hellenistic somewhat scantily. The post-Tanagra material, such as it is, seems to peter out about 150 B.C.

THE PRINCIPAL TYPES

1. *Standing, draped women.* Standing women in the Tanagra style of 330–200 B.C. are extremely common. So far as style is concerned, they offer no surprises, but the tremendous range of sizes is most unusual. In addition to the orthodox pieces of about 20 cm. tall we find on the one hand midgets of some 5 cm.; on the other, giants up to 1 metre tall. Occasionally, in figurines of the normal size, the woman stands with a palm-tree at her right side.

There are also a few draped standing women in a second century version of the Tanagra style.

2. *Seated women.* A seated version of the Tanagra style occurs, but is rare.
3. *Dancing women.* There are a few second century dancing women, with their skirts twirling round.
4. *Erotes.* A few third century Erotes in the Tanagra style are found.
5. *Protomes.* Protomes, now in the Tanagra style, continue from the previous period, and should probably be dated in the late fourth century.
6. *Female busts.* Busts of a woman with a flower emerging from the top of her head continue from the previous period into the late fourth century.

CAMPANIA

The principal Campanian cities to produce figurines in the Hellenistic period are Cumae, Capua, Nola and Pompeii. Of these cities only the first was technically Greek, but in this period all were producing figurines of a uniformly Greek type.

The first three sites are conveniently considered first. The Early Hellenistic period is represented by plentiful figurines in the Tanagra style. The Late Hellenistic period is less well represented, but the evidence, such as it is, points to the survival of the craft in this area into the first century A.D.

The clay is brown in colour, micaceous, and somewhat coarse in texture. Backs are normally hand-made, with circular vents. The workmanship in general is crude.

The Early Hellenistic period is fully represented by orthodox standing draped women in the Tanagra style. Another type comprises a woman leaning against a pillar (pl. 61B); a provincial version of the Eretrian example on pl. 46A.

The group of two knucklebone players on pl. 61A is said to have been found at Capua, and there is no reason to doubt this assertion, but the high quality of the work and the appearance of the clay suggest that it was made in a rather more accomplished centre. Tarentum is a strong possibility, but the group could still be the work of an unusually talented Capuan coroplast using an unusually refined clay; there can be no certainty in the present state of our knowledge. The group is a combination of two women knucklebone players of a type which evolved slightly before the Tanagra period, but which gained its greatest popularity in the course of that period. The figures are tongued into the large rectangular base. The style of the faces suggests that this minor masterpiece was made about 330 B.C.

A second century type from Nola is worthy of mention. It comprises a large flying Eros which exists in a number of surviving examples. He looks somewhat like a type of Eros from Myrina, but wears cross-straps across his chest, a female ornament borrowed from his mother Aphrodite. The back, exceptionally, is moulded, and the vent is a stick-hole.

The Late Hellenistic period is represented by other types, but surviving examples are few in number and, in general, unoriginal and inferior.

The case of Pompeii is rather different. A few figurines in the Tanagra style were recovered from Samnite tombs of the third century B.C., but the Pompeian material comes for the most part from houses, and so dates from the last period of occupation, before the eruption of A.D. 79. Unfortunately such an excellent piece of chronological evidence is not particularly useful for the present survey, since terracottas are rare at Pompeii, being replaced in popular esteem by small bronzes. Nevertheless, the few terracottas from the ruins have their importance in this respect. For example, a figurine very like that on pl. 54D was found there, and serves to date that piece.

EGYPT

The best of the Hellenistic terracottas of Egypt were made in Alexandria, and all were probably inspired by her products. Founded by Alexander the Great in 331 B.C., the city was settled with Greeks and Macedonians, and rapidly, under the successive Ptolemies, became one of the leading artistic and intellectual centres of the Hellenistic world.

The cemeteries of the Greeks and Macedonians, to the east of the city, have yielded a rich harvest of terracottas, whose surface decoration, thanks to the aridity of the Egyptian climate, has survived unusually complete. Their bright colours, which are their most noticeable feature, were in fact common to all Hellenistic terracottas, but in no other region have they survived to anything like the same extent. The principal cemeteries are named after the modern suburbs of Chatby, Hadra, Ibrahimiya and Moustafa Pasha. These cemeteries came into use early in the life of the city. There is some dispute as to when they went out of use, but so far as terracottas are concerned, Chatby seems to end about 200 B.C., Hadra some fifty years later.

Unfortunately, the individual tomb-groups from these cemeteries were not recorded by the excavators, and much valuable chronological information was thereby lost. A tomb-group from an unidentified site in the Delta has however been preserved and is now in Leiden. It can be dated by the pottery to the early third century B.C.

The Greek settlement at Naucratis, where terracottas had been produced from the seventh century B.C., may well have continued to produce terracottas in the Hellenistic period, and the numbers of figurines in the Tanagra and Late Hellenistic styles from that site may well be local products. It was not however till after 200 B.C. that terracottas were produced throughout Ptolemaic Egypt. This popularity resulted in a contamination of Greek with the local Egyptian taste, and produced a hybrid Graeco-Egyptian style which lasted into the Roman era.

Certain Alexandrian sites have produced material for this latter period; in particular a votive deposit at Ras-el-Soda, east of the city, which dates from about the first century B.C. But it is the Fayoum which has produced the greatest number, and which has given its name to the whole class.

The Hellenistic terracottas of Egypt are best considered under two heads, which we may term *Alexandrian* and *Graeco-Egyptian*.

A] *Alexandrian*

This style may be dated roughly between the foundation of Alexandria in 331 B.C. and about 200 B.C. All the terracottas from Chatby cemetery, and most of those from Hadra, belong to this style. The style is for the most part the Tanagra style carried out in Egyptian clay; usually, the coarse brownish clay (the so-called Nile mud) of which the figures from Naucratis had been made in previous centuries (see p. 56). The draped women of pl. 62D–F and Colour Plate D could well be mistaken for the products of Tanagra but for their different clay, and for a slighter coarser, heavier feel. On pl. 62B is a boy wearing the Macedonian hat, the *kausia*. This type originated in the third century B.C.

D. Woman holding an ointment-jar. From Alexandria. 330–200 B.C. British Museum

on the Greek mainland and persisted well into the second and perhaps beyond. The original Attic version is shown on pl. 41D. It used to be believed that the Alexandrian Tanagras were made by immigrant Boeotian craftsmen, but now that the origins of this style have been shown to lie not in Boeotia but in Attica, it seems more probable that it was in fact introduced by Athenians.

There is however one variety of this period which seems to be entirely an Alexandrian creation. The clay in this case is fine and rather dense in texture and pale in colour, ranging from pale brown to pale yellow. The raw material is found in certain desert wadis, and is vastly superior in appearance to the Nile mud. The figurines, in the form of standing boys and girls, are rather more solid than the Tanagra types, and the base is moulded in one piece with the figurine. Pl. 62A and C belong to this group.

B] *Graeco-Egyptian*

By about 200 B.C. the Greek settlers in Alexandria and in the countryside were intermarrying with the Egyptians and were ceasing to be a completely alien aristocracy. One result of this fusion was the creation of a mixed Graeco-Egyptian art, of which terracottas formed a humble part. These Graeco-Egyptian figurines continued to be made under the Roman Empire. The best were made in Alexandria, but provincial versions were made in many localities, especially in the Fayoum, the district after which the whole class is sometimes called. A votive deposit at Ras-el-Soda, east of Alexandria, shows the new style in the first century B.C.

These terracottas fall into several groups. First, grotesques like those of Smyrna and other Asiatic sites were made in vast quantities. Some were apparently actors in the mimes, others not. It seems probable that the origin of these grotesques is to be sought at Alexandria or Smyrna (see p. 112).

Secondly, rather clumsy copies of famous statues attained considerable popularity. The Heracles on pl. 63D falls into this category. It is dated in the late second or early first century B.C. since a similar head came from a deposit of that date in the Athenian Agora.[1]

Thirdly, we find a combination of Greek and Egyptian religious types such as Isis (pl. 63F), Bes (pl. 63A), Baubo (pl. 63B) and Harpocrates (pl. 63C). The naked woman on pl. 63E, a common type, appears to be a combination of Aphrodite and Isis. An exact dating for these types is not easy, but the Baubo could be as early as the first century B.C., since the subject is represented at Delos. The Bes was probably made in the first century A.D., since a similar figurine was found at Pompeii.[2]

Technically, Graeco-Egyptian terracottas are clumsy work, made with few moulds and a minimum of effort. The walls are thick, and the clay is generally the coarse Nile mud of earlier periods. Two other varieties of clay are however occasionally met: a

[1] *Hesperia*, xxxiv (1965), pl. 18, no. 4a. [2] von Rohden, op. cit., pl. L.2.

coarse red clay with a red 'Roman' glaze, and a grey clay with a black glaze. These two fabrics are probably the same in origin, but fired respectively in an oxidizing and in a reducing atmosphere.

CYRENAICA

The cities of Cyrenaica continued the production of terracottas in the Hellenistic period. In the late fourth and third centuries B.C. the style is the ubiquitous Tanagra style. Whether it reached Cyrenaica from mainland Greece or from Ptolemaic Egypt is uncertain, but the strong resemblance between the Alexandrian and the Cyrenaic Tanagras suggests the latter direction. Local characteristics are a somewhat larger size than usual, a coarser treatment, and the frequent appearance of a thick fillet on the women's heads. Pl. 64A and B show typical Cyrenaic figurines of this period. Pl. 64C, a girl seated, with a writing tablet on her knees, is another Tanagra type which must belong to the third century B.C.

In the second and first centuries B.C. the style was very much that of the East Greek world. Connections with Egypt were apparently broken, for Cyrenaica has little to show of the Graeco-Egyptian style of these centuries, but for the small kalathos so popular on figures of Serapis and of Ptolemaic kings and queens, which is worn by many Cyrenaic female figures.

Pl. 64D shows a woman dancing, a common type throughout the Hellenistic world. This style belongs to the second century B.C.

The standing woman on pl. 64E is a direct continuation of the Tanagra tradition, but the treatment of the drapery is different and the larger head gives different proportions to the body. She wears the Ptolemaic kalathos. This stage of development may be dated to the late second or early first century B.C. from its occurrence in a house of that date at Delos.

Finally, the Aphrodite on pl. 64F, leaning to her right against a pillar, should be roughly contemporary with the foregoing, to judge from the style of the head and the bodily proportions.

The principal sources of terracottas are, as before, the cities of Cyrene, Benghazi and Tocra.

Cyrenaic figurines tend, as in the Classical period, to be coarsely made, with thick walls. The backs are hand-made, and the vents are almost invariably circular.

The clay is as before (p. 93), with the brick-red variety predominating.

CHAPTER 9

Epilogue

The Greek coroplastic tradition seems to have come to an end at different times in different areas. In some places it expired about the time of Christ; in others it lingered on till the end of the first century A.D.; in a few exceptional centres, of which the most important are Athens and Corinth, feeble copies of Greek sculptures and bronzes continued to be made in terracotta even as late as the early third century A.D.

This early collapse of a Hellenistic craft was by no means typical of the Roman Empire; in many fields the Hellenistic spirit flourished for some three centuries or more of Roman rule. The principal cause of the growing unpopularity of terracotta was the increasing cheapness of bronze, which was now placed within the reach of quite modest purses as a material for statuettes.

During the second century of our era a new inspiration gave a temporary extension of life to this dying craft in Athens and Corinth and perhaps elsewhere in the eastern part of the Empire. New types arose under Oriental and Egyptian influence, and there evolved a crude but vigorous peasant art of religious subjects and children's toys, very different from the basically sculptural nature of the Hellenistic tradition. This new fashion lasted till the end of the fourth century A.D., when the craft finally died out. It was too deeply rooted in paganism to survive the triumph of Christianity.

The history of terracottas in the western provinces of the Roman Empire, which had never been Greek, is different again, and is outside the scope of this survey.

Bibliography

References to publications before 1903 are not as a rule quoted in this bibliography, as excellent site-lists up to that date are given in Winter, i, pp. I–CXXX. See also Mollard-Besques, *Tc grecques*, 119.

Where a reference covers more than one page, in many cases only the first page is quoted; e.g. *AA* xvi (1901), 134, rather than 134–65, or 134 ff.

For the abbreviations used, see p. xliv.

GENERAL WORKS

S. Mollard-Besques, *Les terres cuites grecques* (Paris, 1963).

T. B. L. Webster, *Greek Terracottas* (Harmondsworth, 1950).

R. A. Higgins, *Greek Terracotta Figures* (London, 1963).

Winter, *Typen*, i, ii.

CATALOGUES OF IMPORTANT COLLECTIONS

A] *Museums*

ALEXANDRIA, Graeco-Roman Museum. E. Breccia, *Terrecotte figurate greche e greco-egizie del Museo di Alexandria* i, ii (Bergamo, 1930, 1934).

ATHENS, National Museum. J. Martha, *Catalogue des figurines en terre cuite du Musée de la Société Archéologique d' Athènes* (Paris, 1880).

BERLIN, Königliche (*now* Staatliche) Museen. W. Weber, *Die Ägyptisch-griechisch Terrakotten* (Berlin, 1914).

COPENHAGEN, National Museum. N. Breitenstein, *Catalogue of the Terracottas in the Danish National Museum* (Copenhagen, 1941).

COPENHAGEN, Ny Carlsberg Glyptotek. V. H. Poulsen, *Catalogue des terres cuites grecques et romaines* (Copenhagen, 1949).

DELOS, Museum. A. Laumonier, *Délos*, xxiii.

ISTANBUL, Archaeological Museum. G. Mendel, *Catalogue des figurines greques de terre cuite, Musées impériaux ottomans* (Constantinople, 1908).

LEIPZIG, Archaeological Institute. E. Paul, *Antike Welt in Ton* (Leipzig, 1959).

LONDON, British Museum. H. B. Walters, *Catalogue of the Terracottas in the British Museum* (1903). R. A. Higgins, *Catalogue of the Terracottas in the . . . British Museum*, i, *Greek, 730–330 B.C.*

(1954); ii, *Plastic Vases of the Seventh and Sixth Centuries B.C. Plastic Lekythoi of the Fourth Century B.C.* (1959).

MADRID, Archaeological Museum. A. Laumonier, *Catalogue de terres cuites du Musée Archéologique de Madrid* (Bordeaux, Paris, 1921).

MYKONOS, Museum. A. Laumonier, *Délos*, xxiii.

NAPLES, Museo Nazionale. A. Levi, *Le terrecotte figurate del Mus. Naz. di Napoli* (Florence, 1926).

PARIS, Louvre Museum. S. Mollard-Besques, *Catalogue raisonné des figurines et reliefs en terre cuite*, i (1954), ii (1963). L. Heuzey, *Les figurines antiques de terre cuite du Musée du Louvre* (Paris, 1883).

B] *Private Collections*

Fouquet (Cairo). P. Perdrizet, *Les terres cuites grecques d'Égypte de la Collection Fouquet* (Nancy, Paris, Strasbourg, 1921).

Loeb (Munich). J. Sieveking, *Die Terrakotten der Sammlung Loeb*, i, ii (Munich, 1916). id., *Bronzen, Terrakotten, Vasen der Sammlung Loeb* (Munich, 1930).

INTRODUCTION

THE COROPLAST'S CRAFT

Corolla Ludwig Curtius (Stuttgart, 1937), 95.

PURPOSE

Grave-goods. *Olynthus*, xiv, 43 ff. And excavation reports generally.
Votive offerings. W. H. D. Rouse, *Greek Votive Offerings* (Cambridge, 1902). *RM* xii (1897), 253 f. (Acragas); *BMC* i, 102 ff. (Halicarnassus). *Lindos*, i.
In houses. *Olynthus*, iv, vii, xiv. *Délos*, xxiii.
Dolls. *AJA* xxxiv (1930), 455 ff. *Antike Kunst*, i (1958), 41 ff. *BMC* i, passim.
Plastic vases. Maximova, *Vases plastiques*. *BMC* ii.

EVIDENCE FROM OTHER ARTS

P. Paris, *Elatée* (Paris, 1892), 158.
C. Blümel, *Berlin Sculpture Cat.*, iii (1928), pl. 36.
Mollard-Besques, *Tc grecques*, 9, and fig. 3.
Antike Kunst, i (1958), 41 ff.

EVIDENCE FROM ANCIENT TEXTS

Mollard-Besques, op. cit., 5 ff.
BMC (1903), xxvi ff.

DRESS

BMC i, 12 ff.

FORGERIES

O. Kurz, *Fakes, a Handbook for Collectors and Students* (London, 1948), 144 ff.

1. TECHNICAL PROCESSES

GENERAL

BMC i, 3, and refs.
Mollard-Besques, *Tc grecques*, 14.

CLAYS

AJA lxvii (1963), 389; lxviii (1964), 221.
Hesperia, xxxiv (1965), 34, 53.

ANCIENT WORKSHOPS

Athens, Agora. *Hesperia*, xxi (1952), 120.
Athens, Pnyx. *Hesperia*, Suppl. vii (1943), 140.
Athens, Cerameicus. *Corinth*, xv, pt 1, 86, n. 11.
Corinth. *Corinth*, xv, pt 1.
Delos. *Délos*, xxiii, 18.
Olynthus. *Olynthus*, ii, 109; iv, 92; vii, 4.
Abdera. *PAE* 1952, 272.
Pergamon. A. Conze, *Pergamon*, i, 2 (Berlin, 1913), 255.
Acragas. *RM* xii (1897), 253.
Tarentum. *Corinth*, xv, pt 1, 86, n. 11.
Naucratis. *JHS* xxv (1905), 132 f., fig. 12.
Kerch. Minns, *Scythians and Greeks*, 363.
Chersonnese. ibid., 364.

ARCHETYPES

BMC i, 4, n. 1, and refs.
Hesperia, xxxii (1963), 88.

MOULDS AND MOULDING

General. *BMC* i, 3, n. 4. *BSA* xlvii (1952), 217. *RM* lxviii (1961), 150.
Plaster moulds. Thompson, *Troy Tcs*, 16. *Hesperia*, xxxiv (1965), 35.
Direct cutting of moulds. Boardman, *Cretan Collection*, 109, n. 6.

PIGMENTS AND DECORATION

General. *BMC* i, 5, 7, and refs.
'Glaze'. *AJA* lxiv (1960), 307. J. V. Noble, *The Techniques of Painted Attic Pottery* (London and New York, 1966).
True vitreous glaze. *Tarsus*, i, 302. Mollard-Besques, *Tc grecques*, 29.

2. THE EARLIEST TERRACOTTAS

ANATOLIA

Haçilar. *ILN* 11:ii:1961.

CRETE

Knossos. Evans, *Palace*, i, 44 ff. Pendlebury, *AC*, 38 ff. Zervos, *Crète*, figs. 56–61. *Bulletin of Institute of Archaeology*, iv (1964), 55 ff. *BSA* lix (1964), 237.
Palaikastro. *Palaikastro*, 131, fig. 113.

CYCLADES

C. Zervos, *L'art des Cyclades* (Paris, 1957), figs. 204 ff. (frying pans); 238–9 (bear).

GREECE

Neolithic

Nea Nikomedia. *ILN* 18:iv:1964, 604 f.
Sesklo. A. J. B. Wace and M. S. Thompson, *Prehistoric Thessaly* (Cambridge, 1912), 68, fig. 35. Tsountas, *Dimini and Sesklo*, 290 ff.
Chaeronea. op. cit., 200, fig. 141.
Thespiae. *Hesperia*, xxviii (1959), pl. 74.
Eutresis. *Archaeology*, xii (1959), 64.
Lerna. *Hesperia*, xxv (1956), 175 ff.
Tiryns. G. Karo, *Führer durch Tiryns* (Athens, 1934), 37, fig. 12.

Early Helladic

RE xxii, pt 2, 1439.
Zygouries. Blegen, *Zygouries*, 185, pl. 21.
Lerna. *ILN* 12:i:1957, fig. 12.
Kalamata. *BSA* lii (1957) pl. 50, 6.
(Anchors). *Hesperia*, xxv (1956), pl. 47; xxvi (1957), pl. 42c; xxix (1960), 297.

3. THE MIDDLE BRONZE AGE

MIDDLE MINOAN

Kr. Chr. v (1951), 96 ff.
Marinatos and Hirmer, pls. 14–17.
Zervos, *Crète*, figs. 224–406 passim.
Petsofa. *BSA* ix (1902–3), 356 ff.
Trapeza. *BSA* xxxvi (1935–6), 121, no. 14.
Phaestos. Marinatos and Hirmer, pl. 19.
Mesara. S. A. Xanthoudides, *Vaulted Tombs of Mesara* (London, 1924).

MIDDLE HELLADIC

RE xxii, pt 2, 1463.
Eleusis. *PAE* 1955, 70, pl. 19b.

4. THE LATE BRONZE AGE

LATE MINOAN

Household Goddess

Kr. Chr. xii (1958), 179 ff.
Nilssen, *MMR*², 289 ff.
Gazi. *AE* 1937, 286 ff. Marinatos and Hirmer, pls. 128–31.
Karphi. *BSA* xxxviii (1937–8), pl. XXXI; lv (1960), pl. XIV. Marinatos and Hirmer, pls. 135–7.
Knossos. Evans, *Palace*, ii, 340, fig. 193.

Hand-made figures

Knossos. Evans, *Palace*, ii, 339, fig. 192.
Palaikastro. *Palaikastro*, 88, fig. 71.

Kamilari. *Arch. Rep. for 1959–60*, 19. *Ann.* xxiii–xxiv (1961–2), 7 ff.
Hagia Triada. Evans, *Palace*, iv, 25, fig. 13a (incorrectly attributed to Phaestos).

Plastic rhyta

Karphi. *BSA* lv (1960), pl. 13.
Pseira. R. B. Seager, *Excavations on the Island of Pseira* (Philadelphia, 1910), 23, fig. 7; 31, pl. 9. Marinatos and Hirmer, pl. 90.

MYCENAEAN

Hand-made figures

General. A. Furumark, *The Chronology of Mycenaean Pottery* (Stockholm, 1941), 86. Blegen, *Prosymna*, 355. Wace, *Chamber Tombs*, 215. G. E. Mylonas, *Ancient Mycenae* (Princeton, 1957), 78. Nilssen, *MMR*², 303. *Opuscula Atheniensia*, v (1965), 47. *ADelt* xviii (1963), pt B.1, pls. 86–8. *Ann.* xli–xlii (1963–4), 7. For the twelfth century, Nilssen, *MMR*, 113, fig. 32 (Asine).
Standing women. Furumark, op. cit., 87. Lord W. Taylour, *The Mycenaeans* (London, 1964), 81, pl. 26 (the earliest example).
Two women and child. *Aegean and Near East*, pl. XV, 9. L. R. Palmer, *Mycenaeans and Minoans* (London, 1965), 135.
Bread-maker. *Ann.* viii–ix (1946–8), 15 ff.
Mourner. *PAE* 1953, 99. *Ergon for 1961*, 15, fig. 11; *for 1960*, 190. *AJA* lxx (1966), 43.
Seated woman. *Aegean and Near East*, 113 ff. *Kr. Chr.* v (1951), 398 ff. *PAE* 1955, pl. 26. *Ann.* xiii–xiv (1930–1), 306–7.
Throne. *Aegean and Near East*, 110 ff. Richter, *Furniture*, figs. 8–19.
Couches and sacred marriage. J. G. Szilagyi and L. Castiglione, *Museum d. bildenden Künste, Griechisch-Römische Sammlung, Führer* (Budapest, 1957), pl. II, 2. Blegen, *Prosymna*, ii, fig. 156, no. 421. Richter, *Furniture*, figs. 22–5.
Chariot-group. Wace, *Chamber Tombs*, pl. 24a. Blegen, *Prosymna*, i, 365; ii, figs. 617–18. C. F. A. Schaeffer, *Ugaritica*, ii (Paris, 1949), 231, fig. 97, 13.
Ploughing. Blegen, *Prosymna*, i, 363 f.; ii, figs. 614, 616.
Rider. *BSA* xlviii (1953), 84 ff. Blegen, *Prosymna*, ii, fig. 615.
Goddess riding. *Aegean and Near East*, pl. XIV, no. 4.
Bull-jumper. ibid., 124 f. and refs. *Opuscula Atheniensia*, v (1965), pl. VI.
Bulls. Blegen, *Prosymna*, i, 361 ff.; ii, figs. 614, 616. *BMC* A23, B3–4.
Deer. *PAE* 1956, pl. 16.
Tripods. Blegen, *Prosymna*, i, 367; ii, fig. 632. Richter, *Furniture*, figs. 21, 26, 27.

Wheel-made figures

Human. Winter, i, 3:4. *Ergon for 1962*, 96 f., figs. 115–16 (Mycenae). ibid., 118, fig. 139 (Pylos).
Animal. *JdI* lviii (1943), 183 ff. (Athens, and general study). Marinatos and Hirmer, pl. 134 (Phaestos). *AE* 1892, 14, pl. 3; *AM* lii (1927), 38 ff. (Amyclae). Perrot and Chipiez, vi, 822, fig. 397 (Mycenae). *Fouilles de Delphes*, v, 15, fig. 61. *Ann.* xiii–xiv (1930–1), pl. 22 (Ialysus).

5. THE DARK AGES

CRETE

Anavlochos. *BCH* lv (1931), 365.
Archanes. Marinatos and Hirmer, pls. 138–9.

Arkades. *Ann.* x–xii (1927–9), 303.
Gortyn. *Ann.* xvii–xviii (1955–6), 241.
Knossos, Spring Chamber. Evans, *Palace*, ii, 123.
Knossos, Khaniale Tekke. *BSA* xlix (1954), 221, fig. 5, pl. 20, no. 1.
Phaestos. *ILN* 3:viii:1963, 162, fig. 1. *Ann.* xxiii–xxiv (1961–2), 410, fig. 52; see also ibid., 500, fig. 193.
Hagia Triada. *Ann.* iii–iv (1941–3), 52.
Dictaean Cave. Boardman, *Cretan Collection.*
Vrokastro. E. H. Hall, *Excavations in Eastern Crete, Vrokastro* (Philadelphia, 1914), 102, fig. 56.

SAMOS

AM lxv (1940), 57; lxvi (1941), 1; lxxiv (1959), 10; lxxvi (1961), 25. *AA* 1964, 493.

MILETUS

Ist. Mitt. ix–x (1959–60), 58, pls. 61, 73.

RHODES

Bell-doll. *Cl. Rh.* iii, 149, fig. 142.
Wheel-made figures. *Lindos*, i, pls. 82–3.
Hand-made figures. ibid., pl. 80, no. 1860. *Cl. Rh.* iii, 100; vi–vii, 292.

COS

AA 1936, 178.
Boll. d'Arte xxxv, (1950), 320.

ATTICA

Bell-dolls

Kerameikos, iv, pl. 31.
Hesperia, xxx (1961), pl. XXX, no. 54.
AA 1948–9, 29 ff. (suggested Balkan origin).

Wheel-made figures

Deer. *Kerameikos*, iv, 20, pl. 26.
Cock. op. cit., v, pt 1, pl. 144.
Pomegranate. ibid., pl. 118.
Horse with amphorae. ibid., pl. 144, no. 1311. *BCH* lxxxvii (1963), 429, fig. 17. G. M. A. Richter, *Handbook of Greek Art* (London, 1959), 219, fig. 323a.

Hand-made figures

Horse. *Kerameikos*, v, pt 1, 127 f., pls. 142–3.
Enthroned goddess. *Hesperia*. Suppl. ii (1939), 65, fig. 41. *BCH* lxxxvii (1963), 415, figs. 8–9, pl. XII. *B. Metr. Mus.*, iii (1944–5), 240 (with mourning woman).
Mourning woman. *Hesperia*, Suppl. ii, 54, fig. 36.
Chariot-group. ibid., 65 f., fig. 42.
Dog. ibid., 62, fig. 40.
Bird. ibid., 62, fig. 40.
Centaur. *ADelt* xix (1964), pt B.1, pl. 55.

BOEOTIA

Bell-dolls

Grace, *Arch. Sc. Boeo.*
Mon. Piot, i (1894), 21.
Winter, i, 6 passim.
AJA xxxiv (1930), 458.
V. Müller, *Frühe Plastik in Griechenland u. Vorderasien* (Augsburg, 1929), fig. 264.
Breitenstein, no. 110.
Louvre Cat., i, B 52–4.

LACONIA

Sparta. Dawkins, *Artemis Orthia*, 145 ff.
Amyclae. *AE* 1892, pl. 4, 4 and 5. *AM* lv (1930), Beil. 42–3. Grace, *Arch. Sc. Boeo.*, 77 ff. *BSA* xxxiii (1932–3), 68, n. 1.

OLYMPIA

Olympia, Ergebnisse, iv, pl. XVII.
AM lxxvii (1963), 3 ff.

AEGINA

Furtwängler, *Aegina*, 375.

6. THE SEVENTH AND SIXTH CENTURIES B.C.

GENERAL

T. J. Dunbabin, *The Greeks and their Eastern Neighbours* (London, 1957).
Jenkins, *Dedalica.*

CRETE

General

Boardman, *Cretan Collection.*
P. Demargne, *La Crète Dédalique* (Paris, 1947).
MMS iii, pt 2 (1931).
Knoblauch, 114 ff.

Sites

Anavlochos. *BCH* lv (1931), 365 ff.
Arkades. *Ann.* x–xii (1927–9).
Axos. Mostly unpublished (at Canea). But see *AM* lxxvii (1962), Beil. 22:4.
Gortyn. *Ann.* xvi–xviii (1956–8), 242.
Kavousi. *Kr. Chr.* x (1956), 15 ff.
Knossos. The figurines from Gypsades will shortly be published by the author in *BSA.*
Lato. *BCH* liii (1929), 383. *RA* xxi (1913), 278 ff.
Praisos. *BSA* viii (1901–2), 271; xi (1904–5), 243. *AJA* v (1901), 371. *BMC* i, 157 ff.
Siteia. *Louvre Cat.*, i, 28. *AA* 1937, 231.

Plaques

Dedalic. Most sites; see above.
Charioteer (?). *BMC* i, no. 582.

Warrior. *BMC* i, no. 575.
Sphinx and griffin. Boardman, *Cretan Collection*, 110 ff.
Demon. *Perachora*, i, 230, pl. 102, no. 180. Waldstein, *Argive Heraeum*, ii, 49, pl. 49, 1.
Narrative. *Antike Plastik*, 113, fig. 1. *Ann.* xvii-xviii (1955–6), 260, fig. 56; pl. I. *Perachora*, i, 230, pl. 102, no. 179.

Dedalic heads on crude bodies

Ann. xvii–xviii (1955–6), 257, and pl. IV.

RHODES

Sites (in Rhodes)

Camirus. *Cl. Rh.* iv, vi–vii. *BMC* i, 19 ff.
Ialysus. *Cl. Rh.* iii, viii.
Lindus. *Lindos*, i.

Subgeometric figurines

Cl. Rh. vi–vii, 71–2.
BMC i, nos. 5–6.

Dedalic plaques

BMC i, nos. 16–18.

Dedalic figurines

BMC i, nos. 6–32 passim.
Knoblauch, 139 ff.

GORGONEION GROUP

General

Maximova, *Vases plastiques*, 167 ff.
BMC ii, 9 ff.
Knoblauch, 132, 141 ff.

Sites

It is impossible to list the countless sites where figurines and plastic vases of the Gorgoneion and Aphrodite Groups have been recorded. For recent discoveries, see *Boll. d'Arte*, xlvii (1962), 153 (Tarentum), and ibid., xlv (1960), 247 (Catana).

Types

Female bust. *BMC* ii, nos 1608 ff.
Male bust. *BMC* ii, no. 1613.
Gorgoneion bust. *BMC* ii, no. 1619.
Female figure. H. S. Jones, *The Sculptures of the Palazzo Conservatori* (Oxford, 1926), pl. 76, Castellani III, 20. *AM* lxvi (1941), pl. 31, no. 28; lxxiv (1959), 30, Beil. 66:3.
Siren. *BMC* ii, no. 1629.
Other types. *BMC* ii, nos. 1620–54.

APHRODITE GROUP

General

Maximova, op. cit., passim.
BMC i, nos. 47 ff.

Lindos, i, 503 ff.
Knoblauch, 133, 145 ff.
Boll. d'Arte, xlvii (1962), 153 ff. An important publication of tomb-groups from Tarentum, giving firm dates for many Aphrodite types. As a result, my dates in *BMC* i have been substantially raised, in many cases by a quarter of a century.

Sites

See above (Gorgoneion Group). Add J. Boardman, J. Hayes, *Excavations at Tocra, 1963–1965* (London, 1966), 151.

Types

Standing woman, Type A. Buschor, *Altsam. Standbild*, figs. 121–3. *MA* xxxii (1927), pl. 38:9. *Perachora*, i, pl. 112, no. 278.
Type B. *BMC* i, no. 49.
Type C. *BMC* i, nos. 57–8. *Boll. d'Arte*, xlvii, 162, fig. 17. With wings, *Délos*, xxiii, no. 60.
Type D. *BMC* i, 48, n. 5. *MA* i (1890), 805. *Boll. d'Arte*, xlvii, 160, fig. 13.
Type E. *BMC* i, 48, n. 6. Winter, i, 41:3. *Boll. d'Arte*, xlvii, 164, fig. 20d.
Type F. *BMC* i, 48, n. 6.
Type G. *BMC* i, no. 59.
Type H. *Bull. Ant. Besch.*, 1939, 3, fig. 1. *MA* xxxii (1927), pl. 38:7.
Seated woman, normal. *BMC* i, no. 63. *Ann.* xxi–xxii (1959–60), 206, fig. 182a.
large. *BMC* i, no. 65.
with polos. *BMC* i, no. 68.
Siren. *BMC* i, no. 75. *Boll. d'Arte*, xlvii, 156, fig. 6. *Corinth*, xiii, pl. 90, no. 157, x.
Standing man. *BMC* i, 71, n. 6. Knoblauch, 150, nos. 165–7. *Louvre Cat.*, i, B 200–1. *Boll. d'Arte*, xlvii, 163, fig. 18.
Seated man. *BMC* i, no. 79.
Seated pair. *BMC* i, no. 80.
Reclining man. *BMC*, i, no. 81. *Louvre Cat.*, i, B 190.
Kneeling figures. *BMC* i, nos. 82–4. *Boll. d'Arte*, xlvii, 163, fig. 19b.
Crouching dwarfs. *BMC* i, no. 86. *Boll. d'Arte*, xlvii, 167, fig. 24.
Other types. *BMC* i, nos. 95–103.

IONIA

Samos. See Ch. 5. Add J. Boehlau, *Aus ionischen und italischen Nekropolen* (Leipzig, 1898). Buschor, *Alsam. Standbild. BMC* i, no. 523 (satyr-mask).
Ephesus. Hogarth, *Ephesus. BMC* i, nos. 529 ff. Mendel, 201.
Miletus. *Ist. Mitt.*, vii (1957), pl. 43.

COS

AA 1901, 134.
Mendel, 128 ff.
Knoblauch, 163.
Louvre Cat., i, B 187–90.

AEOLIS

K. Schefold and J. Boehlau, *Larisa am Hermos*, iii (Berlin, 1942).

CYCLADES

Thera. *Thera*, ii, 24, 77, 306; iii, 78. *AM* lxxiii (1958), 119.
Siphnos. *BSA* xliv (1949), 19.
Paros. O. Rubensohn, *Das Delion von Paros* (Wiesbaden, 1962).
Naxos. *AA* 1940, 284, fig. 86.
Delos. *Délos*, xxiii (1956).

THASOS

BCH lxxxii (1958), 808; lxxxiii (1959), 778.
Archaeology, xiii (1960), 97.

LEMNOS

AM xxxi (1906), 63; xxxiii (1908), 65.
AA 1930, 142.
Knoblauch, 166–7.

ATTICA

General

Knoblauch, 173 ff.

Sites

Athens, Agora. *Hesperia*, ii (1933), 619 ff. (700–650).
Hesperia, vii (1938), 420 ff. (650–625).
Hesperia, Suppl. ii (1939), 193 ff. (700–650).
Acropolis. *Acrop. Mus. Cat.*, ii, 345 ff.
(N. Slope.) *Hesperia*, iv (1935), 193 ff.
Hesperia, vii (1938), 200 ff. (550–500).
Sanctuary of Nymph. *PAE* 1957, 25 f.
Pnyx. *Hesperia*, Suppl. vii (1943), 112 ff.
Cerameicus. Karo, *An Attic Cemetery*.
Eleusis. Winter, i, 23–5.
Brauron. *PAE* 1949, 89. *Ergon for 1961*, 29.
Menidi. *JdI* xiv (1899), 122.

Hand-made figurines

Women. *Hesperia*, iv, 194; vii, 201, 421; Suppl. vii, 135. Winter, i, 24 passim.
Warriors. *Hesperia*, ii, 616.
Horses, riders. *Hesperia*, ii, 617 ff.; iv, 197; vii, 201, 421; Suppl. ii, 62. Winter, i, 7:3 and 25:3.
Chariot-groups. *Hesperia*, ii, 619; Suppl. ii, 66, 193. *JdI* xiv (1899), 122, fig. 26. Winter, i, 25:2.
Funeral group. *AJA* lxi (1957), pl. 84:9.

Figurines with moulded heads and crude bodies

Flat body (free-standing). *Hesperia*, iv, 204, 206; Suppl. vii, 135. Winter, i, 29 and 31 passim. Breitenstein, no. 173.
Flat body (attached to vases). Karo, *An Attic Cemetery*, pls. 15–16. *AA* 1932, 198, fig. 5. *BSA* xlv (1950), 197. *Arch. Rep. for 1963–4*, 4, fig. 1 (c. 575).
Cylindrical body. Karo, op. cit., pl. 16. *Ergon for 1961*, 29, fig. 29.

Plaques in semi-relief

Hesperia, ii, 619.

Protomes

Subdedalic. Winter, i, 240:4. *PAE* 1949, 89; 1957, pl. 3a:3.
With rayed headress. Winter, i, 238:6. *Louvre Cat.*, i, B 92.
With rectangular body. Winter, i, 238:2. *PAE* 1957, pl. 3a:2.

MEGARA

BMC i, nos. 646, 649, 650, 653.
Louvre Cat., i, 5 ff.

BOEOTIA, ETC.

General

Grace, *Arch. Sc. Boeo.*
BMC i, 203 ff.
Louvre Cat, i, 9 ff.
Knoblauch, 189 ff.

Sites

Rhitsona. P. N. Ure, *Black Glaze Pottery from Rhitsona in Boeotia* (Oxford, 1913). id., *Sixth and Fifth Century Pottery from Rhitsona* (Oxford, 1927). id., *Aryballoi.*
Tanagra. Winter, i, passim. Otherwise unpublished.

Female figurines

Cylindrical, primitive. Ure, *Aryballoi*, 54.
Mouse-face. *BMC* i, no. 761.
Bird-face. *BMC* i, no. 775.
With fully modelled heads. Grace, op. cit., 27.
With moulded heads and wheel-made bodies. *Louvre Cat.*, i, B 99, 100.

Animals

Horses, riders. Ure, *Aryballoi*, 61 ff. *BMC* i, nos. 770 ff., 782.
Bird. *BMC* i, no. 794.
Dog with hare. *BMC* i, nos. 773, 789.
Monkey. *BMC* i, no. 774.

Genre-figures

Ploughing scene. *Louvre Cat.*, i, B 103.
Chariot-group. ibid., B 105.
Woman with loaves. ibid., B 111.

CORINTH

General

Knoblauch, 125 ff.
BMC i, 240 ff.
AJA lxvii (1963), 389 ff. (clay).

Sites

Corinth. *Corinth*, xii, 9 ff.; xv, pts i and ii (the workshops in the Potters' Quarter).
Acrocorinth. *Hesperia*, xxxiv (1965), 7.
Perachora. *Perachora*, i, 191 ff.

Solygeia. *Archaeology*, xv (1962), 191. *Ergon for 1958*, 114 ff.
Ithaca, *BSA* xxxix (1938–9), 38 ff.

AEGINA

Plaques. *AE* 1895, pl. 12. Furtwängler, *Aegina*, 384, pl. 111:2 and 3. Jenkins, *Dedalica*, pls. 2:8 and 3:4.
Head. Jenkins, op. cit., pl. 1:2.

ARGOLID

General

Perachora, i, 241 ff.
Knoblauch, 131.

Sites

Argos. *AJA* xliii (1939), 410 ff.
Argive Heraeum. Waldstein, *Argive Heraeum*, ii, 1 ff.
Tiryns. *Tiryns*, i, 51 ff.

Figurines

Hand-made, flat bodies. Waldstein, *Argive Heraeum*, ii, 16 ff.
  rectangular bodies. B.M. 1956. 5–18.1. *Louvre Cat.*, i, B 153.
Moulded heads, hand-made flat bodies. *BSA* xxxii (1931–2), 23 ff.
Masks. G. Karo, *Führer durch Tiryns* (Athens, 1934), 47, fig. 17.

TEGEA

BMC i, 272.

LACONIA

BSA xxxiii (1932–3), 66 ff. and refs., p. 66.
BMC i, 277.

SICILY

General

AA 1954, 465 ff.
A. Q. van Ufford, *Les terres-cuites Siciliennes* (Assen. 1941).
R. Kekulé, *Die Terracotten von Sicilien* (Berlin, Stuttgart, 1884).
Langlotz and Hirmer, pls. 19 ff.

Sites

Catania. *Boll. d'Arte*, xlv (1960), 247 ff.
Gela. *NS* 1956, 203; 1960, 227; 1962, 340. *MA* xvii (1907); xliv (1958), 204 (Butera); xlvi (1963), 3. *BMC* i, 297.
Megara Hyblaea. *MA* i (1890), 690 ff. *Mélanges d'Archéologie et d'Histoire*, lxxvi (1964), 25 ff. *NS* 1954, 396 ff.
Palermo. V. Tusa, *Una statuetta di terracotta di tipo dedalico* (Palermo, 1964).
Selinus. *MA* xxxii (1927).

Types

Dedalic plaques. *MA* xxxii, pl. 37:1–8. *Arch. Rep. for 1960–1*, 46. Tusa, op. cit.
Sixth century derivations of above. Winter, i, 104, 6–8. Van Ufford, op. cit., fig. 47.

Kouroi. *MA* xxxii, pl. 41:7. *NS* 1954, 396, fig. 6.
Seated women, moulded. *MA* xxxii, pl. 37:9, 11.
Imitations of Aphrodite Group. *MA* xxxii, pls. 39–54. *MA* i, pl. 9.
Protomes. See Ch. 7.

LOCRI

Sites

Locri. Levi, *Tc Napoli*, 6 ff. *Critica d'Arte*, vi (1941), 49 ff. *Atti Magna Grecia*, iv (1961), 67. Winter, i, 103. Zanotti-Bianco, 127.
Medma. *NS* 1913, Suppl., 55. Zanotti-Bianco, 95.

Types

Standing women, Type 1. *Atti Magna Grecia*, iv, pls. 28–30 passim. *Critica d'Arte*, vi, pls. 28:9, 31:15. *NS* 1913, Suppl., 83, fig. 92. Winter, i, 103: 8, 9. Langlotz and Hirmer, pl. 6.
Type 2, *Critica d'Arte*, vi, pl. 27:5. *Atti Magna Grecia*, iv, pls. 28–9, nos. 55–9. Zanotti-Bianco, pls. 114, 116.
Type 3. *NS* 1913, Suppl., 85, fig. 95 (left) and 88, fig. 98.
Seated women, Type 4. *Atti Magna Grecia*, iv, pl. 31, no. 67. *Critica d'Arte*, vi, pl. 31:13, 14. *NS* 1913, Suppl., 90, fig. 102. Langlotz and Hirmer, pl. 18.
Type 5. Zanotti-Bianco, pl. 117.
Kouroi. Winter, 1, 177:5.
Kriophoros. *NS* 1913, Suppl., 119, fig. 159.
Imitations of Aphrodite Group. *Critica d'Arte*, vi, pl. 31, nos. 12, 16. *Atti Magna Grecia*, iv, pl. 32, no. 70. Winter, 1, 105:4. Zanotti-Bianco, pl. 115.
Protomes. *Atti Magna Grecia*, iv, pls. 34–6.

TARENTUM

Wuilleumier, 396.
Moulded figurines. *JHS* vii (1886), 23 ff. Winter, i, 103:4, 177:4, 6.
Wheel-made figurine. Winter, i, 103:1. *AM* lxxvii (1962), Beil. 22:5.

PAESTUM

Zanotti-Bianco, pls. 53–4.

SYBARIS

Critica d'Arte, vi (1941), pls. 25–6.

CROTON

NS 1911, Suppl., 116, fig. 99.

METAPONTUM

JHS lix (1939), 219.
NS 1940, 95.
Langlotz and Hirmer, pl. 5 (left).

NAUCRATIS

BMC i, 404 and refs.

7. THE FIFTH AND FOURTH CENTURIES B.C.

GENERAL

Poulsen, *Strenge Stil.*

CRETE

General

MA, vi (1896), 153.

Sites

Hyrtakina. *AE* 1942–4, Suppl., 36, fig. 2.
Arkouda Cave. *BCH* lxxxv (1961), 897, figs. 6–7.
Olous. Mostly unpublished, but see *BCH* lxxxv (1961), 871.
Praisos. See Ch. 6.
Kamilari. *BCH* lxxxii (1958), 794.
Knossos. Mostly unpublished; see Ch. 6. See also *Arch. Rep. for 1957*, 23; *for 1958*, 20; *for 1959–60*, 24; *for 1960–61*, 25. Hitherto unrecognized Knossian figurines: *Louvre Cat.*, i, C 115–22; ii, pl. 3c, 4g; *BMC* i, nos. 567, 939, 940, and *BMC* (1903), C 60. Laumonier, *Madrid Tcs*, pl. XLVI, 1; XLVII, 1–3.
Lato. *RA* xxi (1913), 278 ff.

RHODES

Sites

See Ch. 6. Add:
Rhodes (city). *Cl. Rh.* vi–vii, 445–67.
Note. For the fourth century virtually the only site, apart from the city of Rhodes, is the so-called *Petit Depôt* at Lindus (*Lindos*, i, 55, nos. 2866–3144 passim.) Blinkenberg dated the deposit after 300 B.C., but it should be dated 400–330 B.C. (see *Hesperia*, xxi (1952), 119, n. 13).

Standing women

Late Archaic. *BMC* i, no. 111.
First Attic style. *BMC* i, no. 204.
'Svelte'. *BMC* i, no. 284.
Fourth century version. *Lindos*, i, nos. 3049–53.
Second Attic style. ibid., nos. 2288–90.
Severe Style, with himation. *BMC* i, nos. 210–13.
Fourth century, with himation. *Lindos*, i, nos. 3054–8, 3064–73.
Athena. ibid., nos. 2868–70.
Pitcher-bearer. ibid., nos. 3003–12.
Canephoros. ibid., nos. 3014–16.
With pig. ibid., nos. 3030–6.
With torch. ibid., nos. 3018–22.
Dancing. ibid., nos. 2968–85.

Seated women

Late Archaic. *BMC* i, no. 121.
As above, with Severe Style head. *BMC* i, no. 225.
Second Attic style. *BMC* i, no. 224.
'Svelte'. *BMC* i, no. 288.

Fourth century. *Lindos*, i, nos. 2951–60.
With child. ibid., nos. 2944–50. *BMC* i, no. 229.

Women playing knucklebones

Lindos, i, no. 2967.

Standing men

Fifth century. *BMC* i, no. 248.
Fourth century. *Lindos*, i, nos. 2872–5 and 2901–2.

Other types

See *BMC* i, 109–297 passim.

Protomes

Straight-sided. *BMC* i, nos. 134–46, 241, 294. *Lindos*, i, nos. 3091–109.
Modelled. *BMC* i, nos. 147, 239, 295. *Lindos*, i, nos. 3110–131.

POST-APHRODITE GROUP

Lindos, i, 518.
BMC i, nos. 109, 119, 120.

IONIA

Samos. *BMC* i, nos. 524–6.
Ephesus. Hogarth, *Ephesus*. *BMC* i, nos. 545 ff. Mendel, 201.

HALICARNASSUS, ETC.

Halicarnassus. *BMC* i, 102.
Cos. See Ch. 6. Add *Ann.* viii–ix (1925–6), 253, 310. *Cl. Rh.* i, 100.
Calymna. *BMC* i, nos. 326–7, 352, 443, 460, 490–2.
Nisyros. *Louvre Cat.*, i, C 126–8. *Cl. Rh.* vi–vii, 513.

AEOLIS

Troy (In-Tepe). Mendel, 175, pl. IV, nos. 1867–9. Winter, ii, 198:1; ii, 145:6; ii, 200:3. Thompson, *Troy Tcs*, 62.
Troy. *BMC* i, no. 566.
Assos. Winter, i, 54, passim, etc. Mendel, 161.
Dardanus. *BMC* i, nos. 563–5.
Larisa. K. Schefold and J. Boehlau, *Larisa am Hermos*, iii (Berlin, 1942).
Lesbos. *BMC* i, nos. 562, 569, 571. Mendel, 159.

MELOS

General

P. Jacobsthal, *Die Melischen Reliefs* (Berlin, 1931).
JHS lix (1939), 65.
B. Metr. Mus., xxvii (1932), 45.
BCH lxxxii (1958), 27 ff.
AJA lxii (1958), 313 ff.
BMC i, 165 ff.
BMQ xxvi (1962–3), 101, pl. LIIc.

Subjects

The numbers in brackets are those of Jacobsthal's catalogue. Other references are given only in cases new to Jacobsthal.

Artemis and hind. [16–18]. *AJA* xlv (1941), 342–3, fig. 1.
Aphrodite and Eros in chariot. [46, 84.]
Aphrodite on bird. [49.]
Drunken Dionysus. [86.]
Helle on ram. [5, 31, 69, 70.]
Phrixus with ram. [3, 4, 101–2.]
Eos and Kephalos. [10–13, 75.]
Sphinx carrying off youth. [7–9, 85.]
Woman being carried off. [100.]
Centaur seizing woman. *BMQ* xxvi (1962–3), 101, p. LIIc.
Death of Actaeon. [24–6, 60, 97–8.]
Bellerophon. [19, 20, 82–3.] *BCH* lxxxii (1958), pl. IV.
Perseus and Medusa. [61–2.]
Death of Niobids. [81.] *JHS* lix (1939), pl. VIIIb.
Scylla. [71–4.]
Theseus and Triton. [3.]
Theseus and sow. [99.]
Kalydonian hunt. [27, 59, 103.]
Peleus and Atalanta. [80.]
Peleus and Thetis. [14, 15.]
Thetis with arms of Achilles. [21, 47.]
Ajax and Cassandra. [65–7.]
Ransom of Hector. *AJA* lxii (1958), 313 ff.
Electra and Orestes. [1, 2, 94, 104–5.]
Odysseus: foot-washing. [95–6.]
Odysseus and Penelope. [87–93.] *BCH* lxxxii (1958), pl. II:2.
Hippalectryon. [51.]
Siren. [52–4.]
Sphinx. [55–8.]
Pipe-player, dancing-girl, and man. [78–9.]
Girl lyre-player and man. [76–7.]
Dancer with castanets. [28–30, 35–45.]
Dancer with kalathos. [64.]
Boy riding. [63.]
Woman walking. [6.]
Woman sacrificing. [32–3.]
Sacrifice of a deer. [68.]
Greek and barbarian fighting. [22–3.]
Warrior and slave. [106.]
Two horses (fragt.). [50.]
Satyr (fragt.). [4.]

PAROS

See Ch. 6.

DELOS

See Ch. 6.

ATTICA

General

Poulsen, *Strenge Stil*, 48.
Neutsch, *Studien*, 2.
BMC i, 171.

Sites

Athens, Acropolis. See Ch. 6.
Pnyx. See Ch. 6.
Cerameicus. See Ch. 6. Add *ADelt* xviii (1963), pt B.I, pl. 27 (tomb-group of 400–375 B.C.).
Agora. *Hesperia*, xv (1946), 330 (early fifth century).
Syntagma Square. *AE* 1958, Suppl., 1.
Plato's Academy. *Ergon for 1958*, 10.
Brauron. *Ergon for 1961*, 31; *for 1962*, 26. *AJA* lxvii (1963), pl. 63, fig. 9. *Pictures from Greece*, May 1962, 14.

Types

See *BMC* i, 171.
For actors, add M. Bieber, *History of the Greek and Roman Theatre* (2nd ed., Princeton, 1961), 36, esp. figs. 185–98 (New York sets).

BOEOTIA, ETC.

General

BMC i, 203.
Louvre Cat., i, 9, 87.

Sites

Thebes. Kabeirion. Unpublished but for *AM* xv (1890) and Winter, i, passim.
Thespiae. Polyandrion. *AM* lxv (1940), 8.
Tanagra. Unpublished, but see Winter, i, passim.
Halae. *Hesperia*, xi (1942), 365.
Rhitsona. See Ch. 6.
Delphi. *Fouilles de Delphes*, v, pls. XXII–XXV.

Genre-groups

Winter, i, 33–5.
JHS lxxxii (1962), 121 (cooks, etc.).
Louvre Cat., i, 17.
Festschrift f. James Loeb (Munich, 1930), 51.

Other types

See *BMC* i, 213.

CORINTH

Sites

See Ch. 6. Add:
Corinth. *Hesperia*, xxxi (1962), pl. 41. *Corinth*, xiii, passim.
Argos. *ADelt* xv (1933–5), 21.
Arta. *Ergon for 1957*, 52.

Types

See *BMC* i, 245. Add:
Victory relief. *Hesperia*, xxxi (1962), pl. 41a. *Ergon for 1957*, 52, fig. 54.

ARGOS

See Ch. 6. Add:
ADelt xv (1933–5), 21; xviii (1963), pt B.I, pls. 75–7.

LACONIA

Sites

See Ch. 6. Add:
Amyclae. *PAE* 1956, pls. 104–5. *AJA* lxi (1957), pls. 84–5.

OLYNTHUS

Olynthus iv, vii, xiv.

THASOS

See Ch. 6. Add:
BCH lxxxv (1961), 920 (Valma Deposit).

CORCYRA

BMC i, 295.
BCH xv (1891), 1.
ADelt. xviii (1963), pt B.II, pls. 201 ff.

SICILY

General

See Ch. 6. Add Langlotz and Hirmer, pls. 34 ff.

Sites

Acragas. P. Marconi, *Agrigento* (Florence, 1929). id., *Agrigento Arcaica* (Rome, 1933). *MA* xlvi (1963), 114 ff.
Camarina. G. Libertini, *Il Museo Biscari* (Milan, Rome, 1930), i, 216 ff.
Catania. *Boll. d'Arte*, xlv (1960), 247 ff.
Gela. See Ch. 6. Add *Archaeologia Classica*, ix (1957), 44 ff. and 153 ff.
Granmichele. *MA* vii (1897), 216 ff.
Megara Hyblaea. *MA* i (1890), 690 ff. Langlotz and Hirmer, pl. 130.
Selinus. *MA* xxxii (1927).
Syracuse. *NS* 1900, 353 ff.; 1943, 33 ff.; 1954, 302 ff.
Lipari. L. Bernabo-Brea and E. M. Cavalier. *Meligunis-Lipara*, ii (Palermo, 1965).

Types

See *BMC* i, 297 ff.

LOCRI

Sites

See Ch. 6.

Reliefs

Ausonia, iii (1908), 136.
Boll. d'Arte, iii (1909), 406 ff., 463 ff.
Atti Magna Grecia, i (1954), 71.
BMC i, 324, 330.
RE xiii, 1355 ff.
T. J. Dunbabin, *The Western Greeks* (Oxford, 1948), 293.
Langlotz and Hirmer, pls. 71 ff.

Figurines

See *BMC* i, 330, and refs. Add:
Seated naked women. Zanotti-Bianco, pls. 124, 125.

TARENTUM

General

Wuilleumier, 393.
Levi, *Tc. Napoli*, 24.
BMC i, 336.
Louvre Cat., i, 59, 123.
Zanotti-Bianco, 67.

Sites

Tarentum, Fondo Giovinazzo. *BMC* i, 336, n. 1. Wuilleumier, 339.
Another deposit. ibid., 395. *NS* 1936–7, 151.
Tombs. ibid., 111.
Heraclea. *Boll. D'Arte*, xlvi (1961), 133.
Metapontum. *NS* 1936–7, 443; 1940, 64.

Figurines and reliefs

BMC i, 336.

SYBARIS

ILN 8:xii:1962.

PAESTUM

Sites

Paestum. Levi, *Tc Napoli*, 97. *Louvre Cat.*, i, 155. *Archaeology*, vii (1954), 206. *AA* 1956, 373. Zanotti-Bianco, 67. Langlotz and Hirmer, pls. 65–6.
Foce del Sele. *NS* 1937–8, 207. *JHS* lvii (1937), 243. Zanotti-Bianco, 43.
Fratte. *NS* 1952, 86.

NAUCRATIS

See Ch. 6.

CYRENAICA

BMC i, 378.
Louvre Cat., i, 113.

CYPRUS

L. P. Di Cesnola, *A Descriptive Atlas of the Cesnola Collection of Cypriote Antiquities in the Metropolitan Museum of Art, New York* (New York, 1894).
BMC (1903), 42.

SOUTH RUSSIA

E. H. Minns, *Scythians and Greeks* (Cambridge, 1913).
Compte rendu de la Commission Impériale Archéologique (St Petersburg, 1859–88).
Arch. Rep. for 1962–3, 39.
K. Michalowski, *Mirmeki* (Warsaw, 1958).
M. M. Kobylina, *Terracotta Statuettes from Panticapaeum and Phanagoria* (Moscow, 1961, in Russian).

8. THE HELLENISTIC PERIOD

GENERAL

Kleiner, *Tanagrafiguren.*
R. Horn, *Stehende weibliche Gewandstatuen* (Munich, 1931).
AJA lxx (1966), 51.

ATTICA

Athens, Agora. *Hesperia*, xxi (1952), 116; xxiii (1954), 72; xxvi (1957), 108; xxviii (1959), 127; xxxi (1962), 244; xxxii (1963), 276; xxxiv (1965), 34; xxxv (1966), 252.
Athens, Pnyx. See Ch. 6.
Athens, Acropolis. *Acrop. Mus. Cat.*, ii, 387. Neutsch, *Studien*, passim (N. Slope).
Athens, Sanctuary of the Nymph. *Ergon for 1957*, 10, fig. 8. *PAE* 1957, pl. 3.
Eleusis, Cave of Pan. *ADelt* xvi (1960), pl. 42.
Vouliagmeni. *AE* 1938, 30.

BOEOTIA

Tanagra. Kleiner, *Tanagrafiguren*. R. Kekulé, *Griechische Thonfiguren aus Tanagra* (Stuttgart, 1878).
Thebes. *ADelt* iii (1917), 242, fig. 174.
Halae. See Ch. 7.
Rhitsona. See Ch. 6.
Eretria. Kleiner, op. cit., 19 (Boston tomb-group). *BMC* (1903), C 191–204. *PAE* 1956, pl. 38.
Chalcis. G. A. Papabasileiou, *Περὶ τῶν 'εν Εὐβοίᾳ 'αρχαίων τάφων* (Athens, 1910).

CORINTH

See Chs. 6 & 7. Add: *Hesperia*, xvii (1948), 197.

NORTH GREECE

General

Olynthus, xiv, 1.

Sites

Demetrias. A. S. Arvanitopoulos, *Γραπταὶ στῆλαι Δημητριάδος Παγασῶν* (Athens, 1928), 46.
Amphipolis. *BCH* xxi (1897), 515. *PAE* 1934, 89. *Ergon for 1957*, 38; *for 1958*, 76; *for 1959*, 38.

Pella. *ADelt* xvi (1960), pt A, pls. 84–5.
Thessalonica (Salonika). *PAE* 1951, 171.
Abdera. D. Lazarides, *Πήλινα εἰδώλια Ἀβδήρων* (Athens, 1960). *PAE* 1952, 267; 1954, 170.
Beroea. *BCH* lxxxix (1965), 794.
Bizye (Vize) Tumulus B (first cent. A.D.). *AA* lvi (1941), 182.

CORCYRA

BMC (1903), C 42–66 and 92–7. *ADelt* xviii (1963), pt. B 2, 159.

ITHACA

BSA xxxix (1938–9), 38 ff.

THASOS

See Ch. 7. Add: *BCH* lxxxvii (1963), 860; lxxxix (1965), 924 (Evraiocastro); op. cit., 934.

SAMOTHRACE

Archaeology, xii (1959), 163; xvii (1964), 185.
Arch. Rep. for 1955, 26, fig. 25.

CYCLADES

Delos. See Ch. 6. Add: *BCH* lxxxiv (1960), 854.
Melos. *BMC* (1903), C 69–81.
Paros. See Ch. 6.
Thera. *Thera*, iii, 171.

CRETE

See Ch. 7.

RHODES

Lindus. *Lindos*, i, nos. 2923 (?), 2984, 3090b.
Camirus. *Cl. Rh.* vi–vii, 297. *BMC* (1903), C 482.

SOUTH-WEST ASIA MINOR

Cnidus. *BMC* (1903), C 421–88, passim.
Halicarnassus. ibid., C 489–518.
Calymna. ibid., C 469 ff.
Nisyros. Mendel, 156.
Xanthus. *Fouilles de Xanthus*, i, pl. LVI.
Patara. *ILN*, 21:iii:1953, 448, fig. 3.

WESTERN ASIA MINOR

Smyrna. *Mélanges Graux* (Paris, 1884), 143. *BCH* lxx (1946), 312, and refs. *Editions TEL, Encyclopédie Photographique de l'Art*, i–iii, *Le Musée du Louvre* (Paris, 1935–8), 236–46. Mendel, 210. Sieveking, *Samml. Loeb*, ii, passim. Unpublished heads in the British Museum: 1909. 5–23.3 to 9 ('from Smyrna'); 1914. 5–16.5 to 10 ('from the neighbourhood of Smyrna'); 1907. 5–19.8 to 50 (no provenance).

Myrina. E. Pottier and S. Reinach, *La Nécropole de Myrina* (Paris, 1887–8). Burr, *Boston Myrinas*. *BCH* lxxvii (1953), 1, and refs. *Louvre Cat.*, ii. *Revue du Louvre*, xiv (1964), 299 (the Coroplast of the Victories). Mendel, 278.

Priene. *Priene*, passim. Mendel, 227. For group of 150 B.C., figs. 382–3, 389, 390, 406, 416, 418, 428–30, 446–50, 564. For group of first century B.C., figs. 405, 417, 420, 424, 434–5. See *PW*, Suppl. ix, s.v. 'Priene'.

Ephesus. *BMC* (1903), C 449–65.

Sardis. *AJA* xxvi (1922), 401, fig. 9.

Pergamon. A. Conze, *Pergamon*, i, 2 (Berlin, 1913), 255. *Türk Tarih* iv (1940), 3; *AA* 1937, 267 (Gambrion). The terracottas of Pergamon are being published by Eva Hoffmann.

Kyme. *Annual of the Archaeological Museum of Constantinople*, ix (1960). *BMC* (1903), C 459. Mendel, 441. Pottier and Reinach, op. cit., 506.

Larisa. See Ch. 6.

Troy. Thompson, *Troy Tcs*. Mendel, 178.

BLACK SEA

Amisos. Mendel, 196, 588. Thompson, *Troy Tcs*, 15.

South Russia. See Ch. 7.

TARSUS

Tarsus, i.

CYPRUS

See Ch. 7.

SYRIA

M. Chehab, *Les terres cuites de Kharayeb* (*Bulletin du Musée de Beyrouth*, xi, Paris, 1953–4).

SICILY

General

See Ch. 7.

Sites

Acragas. See Ch. 7.

Centuripae. G. Libertini, *Centuripe* (Catania, 1926). *NS* 1947, 259. *BMC* (1903), D 1–49 passim. Langlotz and Hirmer, pls. 144, 148 (right), 150, 160.

Gela. See Ch. 7.

Morgantina. *AJA* lxiv (1960), 126, pl. 21:3 (deposit of 275–250).

Soloeis. R. Kekulé, *Die Terracotten von Sicilien* (Berlin, Stuttgart, 1884), 41, etc.

Syracuse. *NS* 1951, 289.

Lipari. See Ch. 7.

LOCRI

Atti Magna Grecia, iv (1961), pls. XLV ff.

NS 1942, 219 ff. (Rhegion); 1946, 141 ff.

APULIA

Tarentum. See Ch. 7. Add: *NS* 1940, 314. Langlotz and Hirmer, pls. XIV–XIX, 133 ff. Zanotti-Bianco, 185.

Egnatia. Levi, *Tc Napoli*, 82. *AA* 1956, 263.

Canusium. *RM* xxix (1914), 90, 260. P. Jacobsthal, *Early Celtic Art* (Oxford, 1944), 146. Levi, *Tc Napoli*, 55.
Rubi, Levi, *Tc Napoli*, 69.

PAESTUM

See Ch. 7. Add: *Atti Magna Grecia*, vi–vii (1965–6), 23 ff.

CAMPANIA

Capua, Levi, *Tc Napoli*, 116.
Cumae. *MA* xxii (1913). Levi, *Tc Napoli*, 106.
Nola, Levi, *Tc Napoli*, 133.
Pompeii. H. von Rohden, *Die Terracotten von Pompeii* (Stuttgart, 1880). Levi, *Tc Napoli*, 181.

EGYPT

General

P. Graindor, *Terres cuites de l'Égypte gréco-romaine* (Gent, 1939).
P. Perdrizet, *Terres cuites de la Collection Fouquet* (Nancy, Paris, Strasbourg, 1921).
W. Weber, *Königliche Museen zu Berlin, Die Agyptisch-griechischen Terracotten* (Berlin, 1914).
W. D. van Wijngaarden, *De Grieks-Egyptische Terracotta's in het Rijksmuseum van Oudheden* (Leiden, 1958).
Revue des Études Anciennes, xlviii (1941), 122.
Kleiner, *Tanagrafiguren*, 26.

Sites

Alexandria. E. Breccia, *Terrecotte figurate greche e greco-egizie del Museo di Alexandria* (Bergamo, 1930, 1934). J. Vogt, *Expedition Ernst von Sieglin, Ausgrabungen in Alexandria*, ii, *Terrakotten* (Leipzig, 1924).
Alexandria, Chatby. E. Breccia, *La necropoli di Sciatbi* (Cairo, 1912).
Alexandria, Hadra. *Annuaire du Musée Gréco-romain*, iii (1940–50), 1.
Alexandria, Mustafa Pasha. op. cit., i (1933–5), 11.
Alexandria, Ras el Soda. op. cit., iii (1940–50), 28.
Naucratis. See Ch. 6.
Delta. M. I. Rostovsteff, *Social and Economic History of the Hellenistic World* (Oxford, 1941), pl. XX. *AJA* liv (1950), 443. (Tomb-group of early third century B.C.)
Fayoum. C. M. Kaufmann, *Ägyptische Terrakotten der griechisch-römischen und koptischen Epoche* (Cairo, 1913).

CYRENAICA

BMC (1903), C 701–859.
L. Heuzey, *Figurines antiques de terre cuite* (Paris, 1883), pls. 40–56.
Laumonier, *Madrid Tc*, pls. XXVII–XLI.

ROMAN TERRACOTTAS

Clairève Grandjouan, *The Athenian Agora*, vi: *Terracottas and Plastic Lamps of the Roman Period* (Princeton, 1961).
Corinth, xii, passim.

Glossary

AEGIS: A breastplate, decorated with a gorgon's head in the centre, worn by Athena.
ARCHAIC: The style and period after Geometric. 700–480 B.C.
ARCHETYPE: See p. 2.
ATTIC: For all practical purposes, synonymous with Athenian.
CHITON: See p. lii.
CLASSICAL: The style and period after Archaic. 480–330 B.C.
COROPLAST. A maker of terracotta figurines.
EARLY CLASSICAL: The first phase of the Classical period. 480–440 B.C. See also SEVERE STYLE.
FIGURINE: A statuette. The term is restricted in this book to statuettes of terracotta.
GEOMETRIC: The style and period after Protogeometric. 900–700 B.C.
HELLENISTIC: The style and period after Classical. Generally 330–27 B.C., but in this book the end of the Hellenistic period is in some places extended to A.D. 100.
HERM: A pillar topped by a human or divine head.
HIMATION: See p. lii.
KALATHOS: A basket-shaped headdress worn by goddesses.
KANTHAROS (plural *Kantharoi*): A wine-cup with two high handles.
KAUSIA: See p. liii.
KOINE: A style common to a large area.
KORE: An alternative name for Persephone.
KOUROS (plural, *kouroi*): An archaic figure of a naked standing man.
LEKYTHOS (plural, *lekythoi*): A form of oil-flask.
MICA: A shiny mineral, silver or gold in appearance, found in small crystals in many clays.
MICACEOUS: Containing mica.
MIME: A kind of play which originated in the Hellenistic period and became very

popular under the Roman Empire. Masks were not worn, but persons of a naturally grotesque appearance were employed as actors.

MINOAN: Cretan, of the Bronze Age. Named after Minos, the legendary king of Knossos.

MYCENAEAN: A term applied to the Late Bronze Age culture of Greece.

PATRIX: Synonymous with Archetype.

PEPLOS: See p. lii.

PHIALE: A saucer-shaped vessel used for pouring libations.

PILOS: See p. liii.

PLASTIC VASE: A vase in human, animal or vegetable shape.

POLOS: A cylindrical headdress worn by deities.

PROTOGEOMETRIC: The style and period after Mycenaean and before Geometric. 1050–900 B.C.

PROTOME: The upper part of a human figure, made for suspension, and lacking a separate back.

RHYTON: A vessel (frequently in animal form), used for pouring libations.

SEVERE STYLE: The style of the Early Classical period.

STEPHANE: A hair-ornament in the shape of a crown.

TANAGRA: The term 'a Tanagra' is used for the sake of brevity to denote a figurine of a draped standing woman in the Tanagra style of 330–200 B.C., wherever made.

VENT: A hole cut in the back of a figurine to facilitate the escape of hot air during firing.

VOTARY: A worshipper.

Index of Sites

This index is restricted to sites where figurines or moulds have actually been found. It does not cover the Bibliography, except where new material is found therein. For the orthography see p. xlviii.

Index of Coroplasts

General Index

This index does not cover the Glossary, nor the Bibliography, except in a few cases where new material is mentioned therein. Geographical regions are included, but not individual sites, which will be found in the *Index of Sites*.

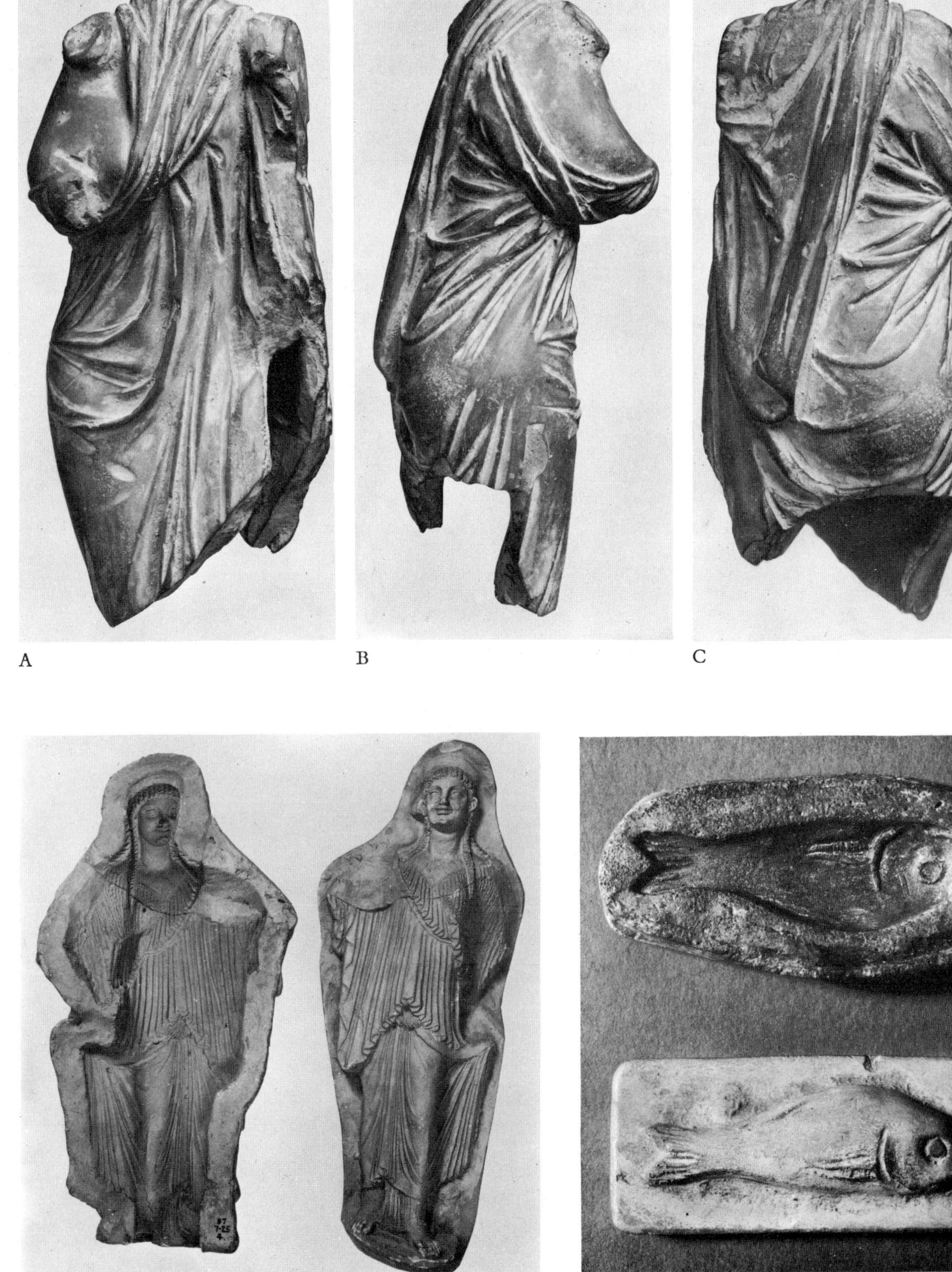

A B C

D E

2 Neolithic, about 4000–3000 B.C.

A

B

C

D

E

A

B

C D E

4 Mycenaean, 1400–1200 B.C.

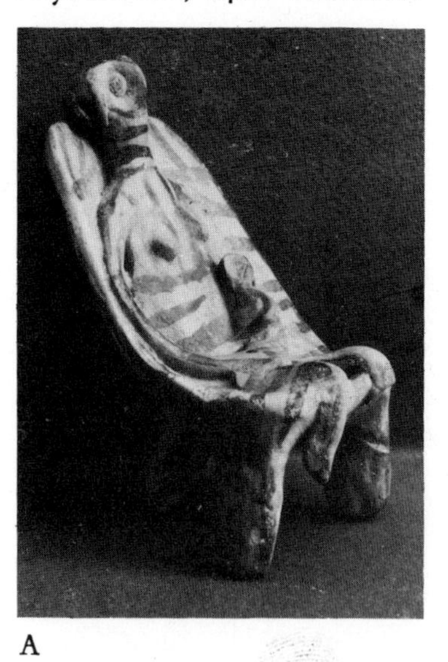

A

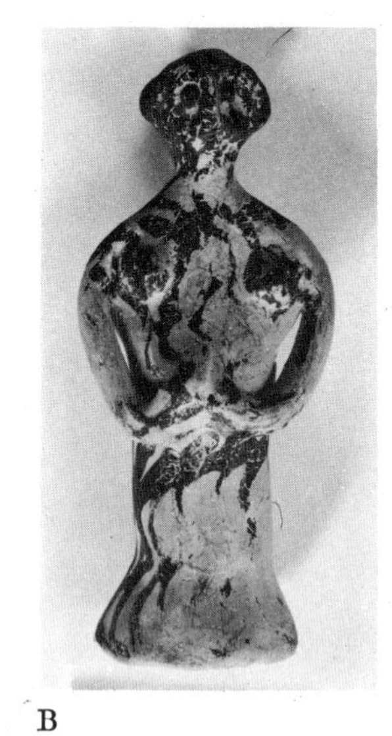

B

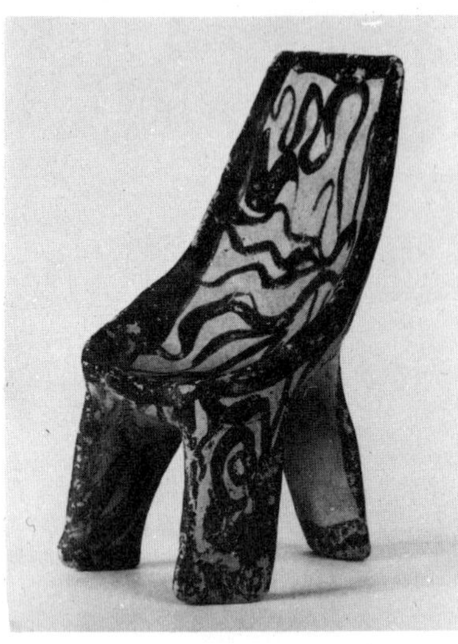

C

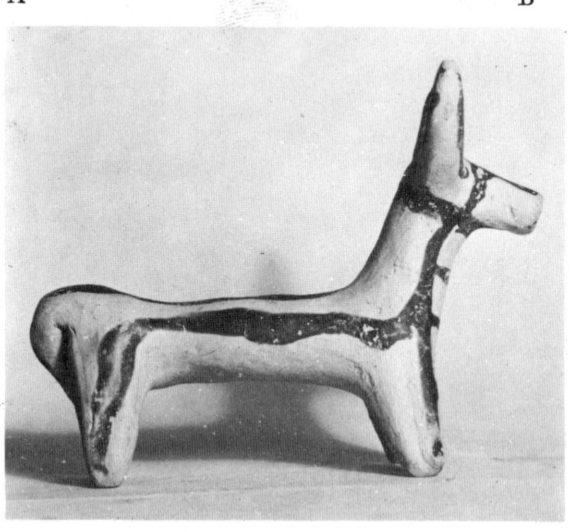

D

E

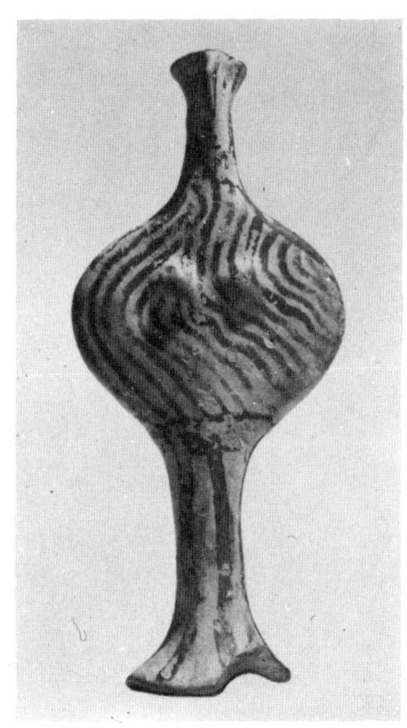

F

G

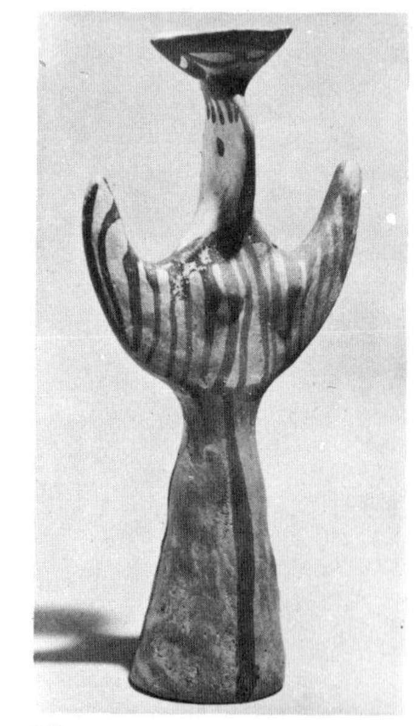

H

A

B

C

D

6 Greek Islands, tenth to eighth centuries B.C.

A

B

C

D

E

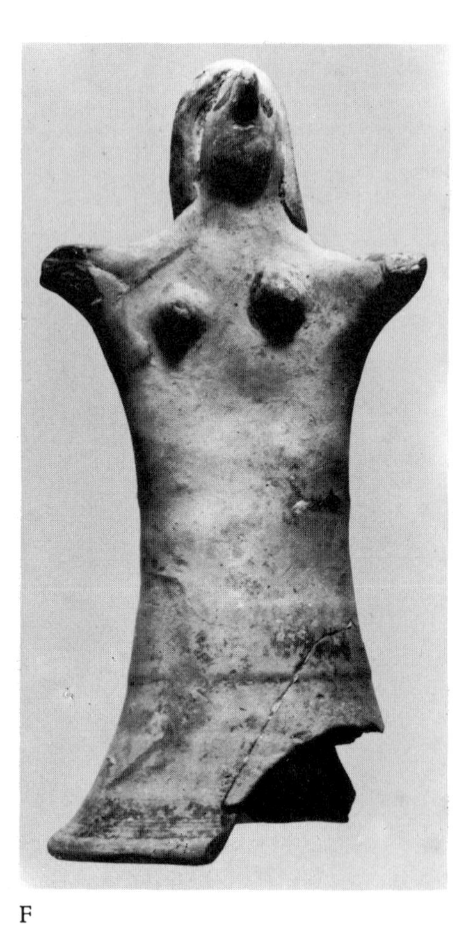

F

A

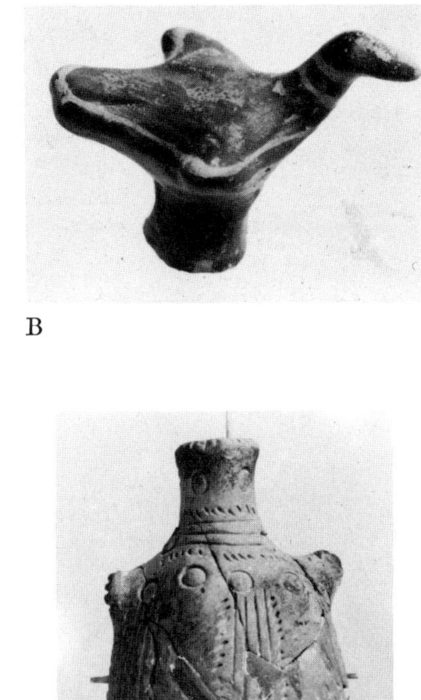

B

C

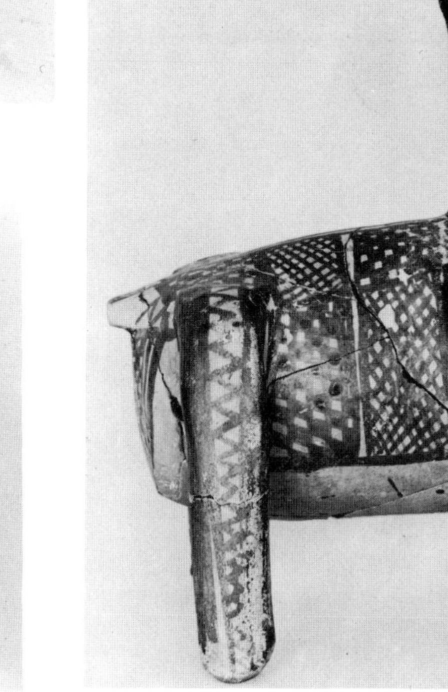

D

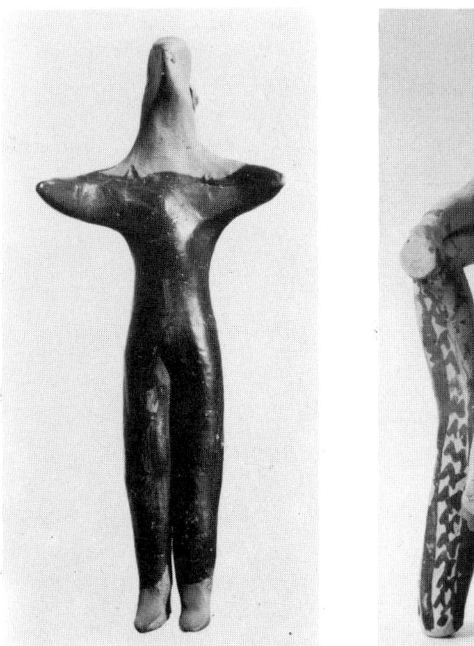

E

F

G

A

B

A

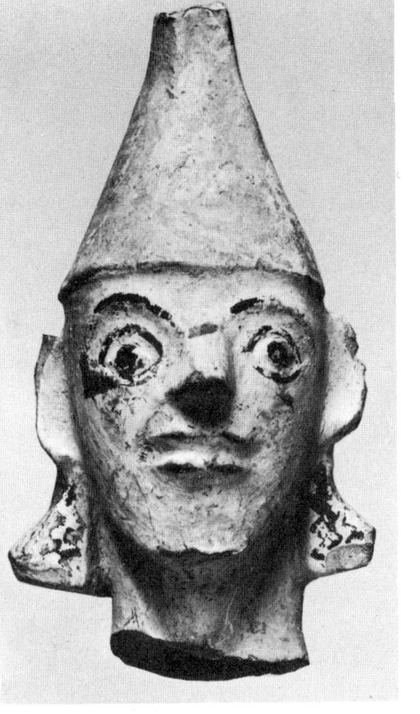

B

C

D

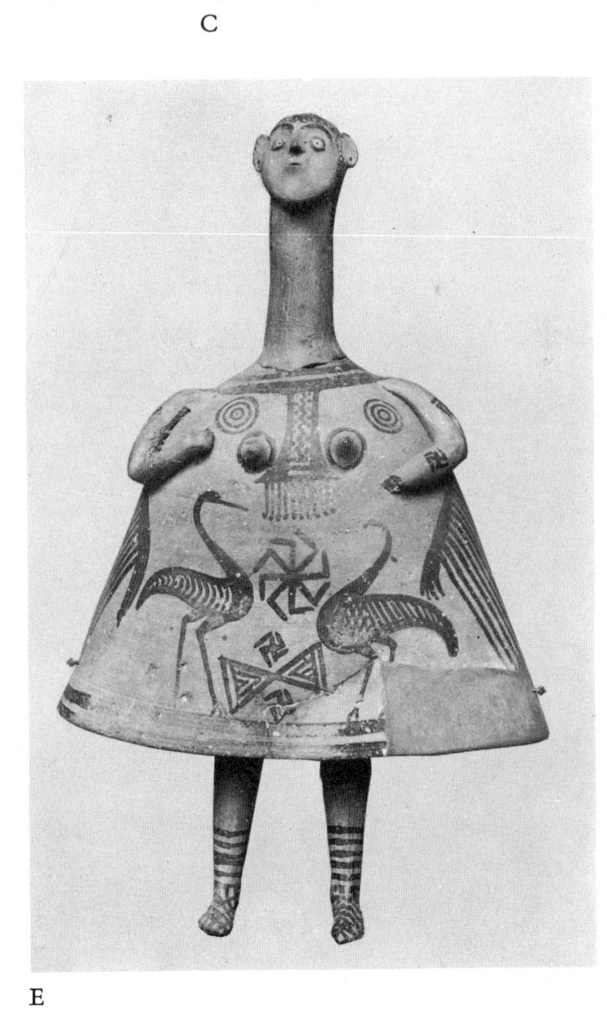

E

10 Crete, seventh century B.C.

A

B

C

D

E

F

A

B

C

D

E

A

B

C

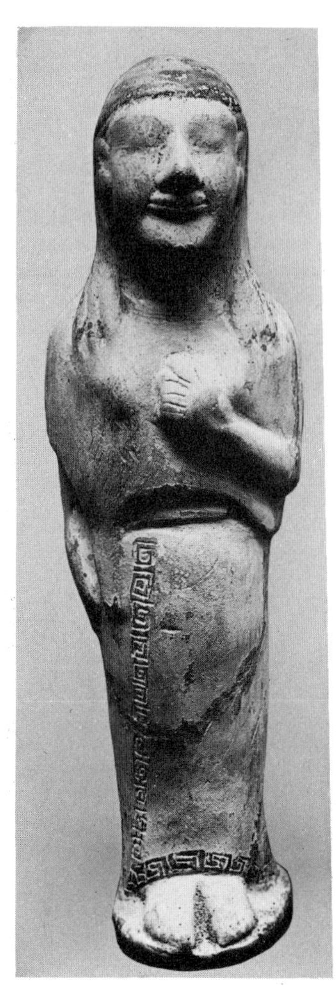
D

E

F

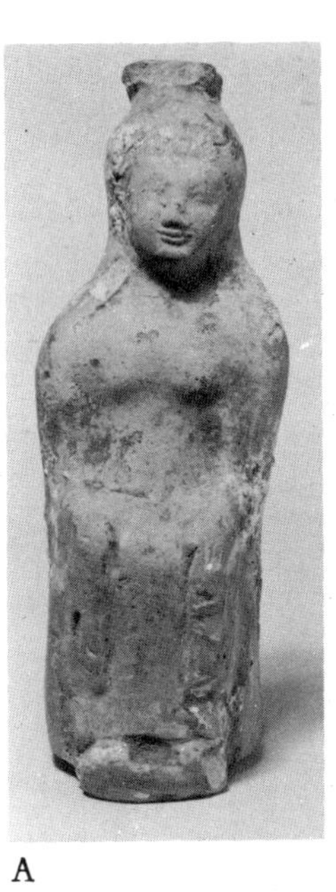

A

B

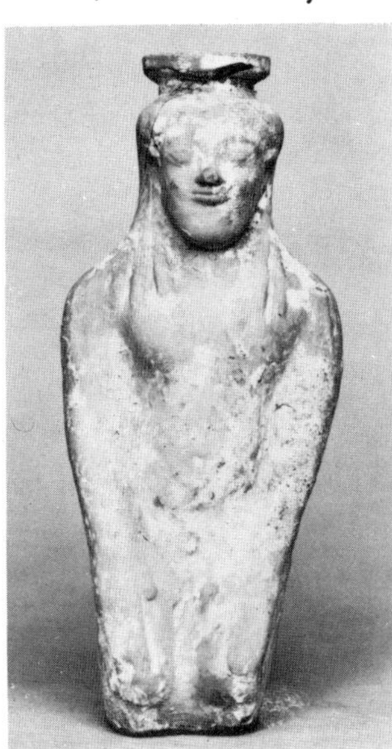

C

D

E

F

A

B

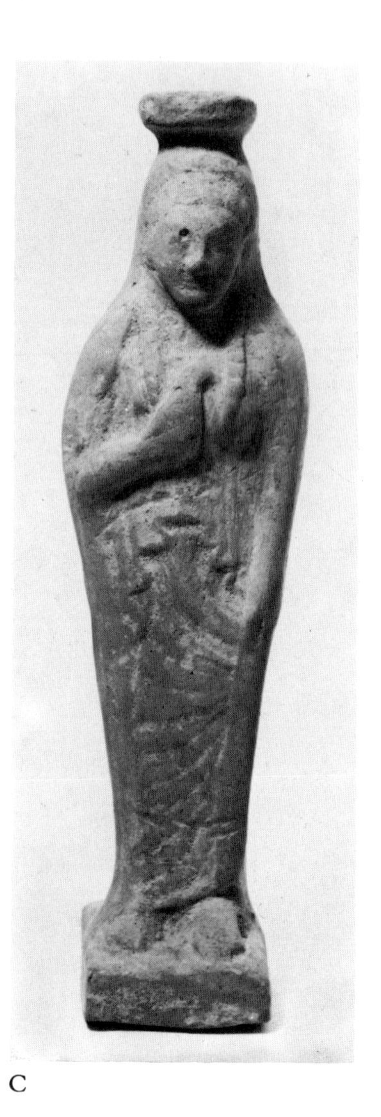

C

D

E

A

B

C

D

E F G H

Attica, sixth century B.C.

A

B

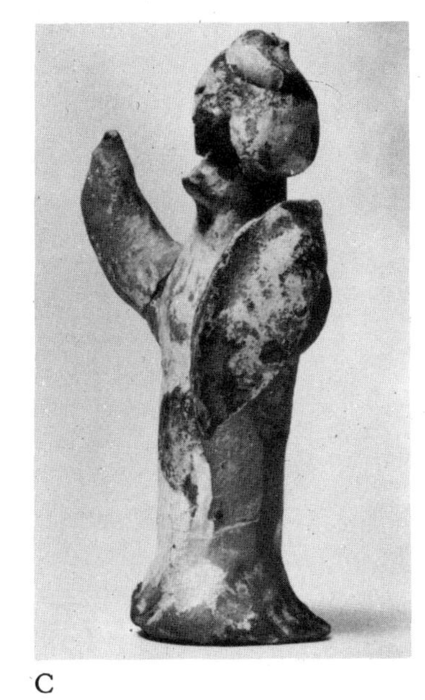
C

D

E

18 Boeotia, sixth century B.C.

A

B

C

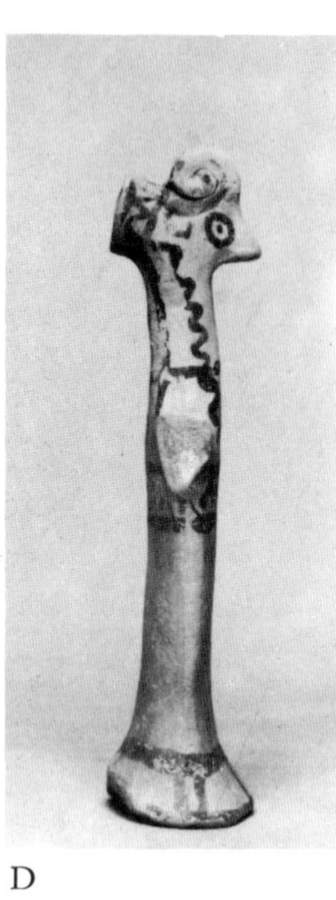

D

E

F

G

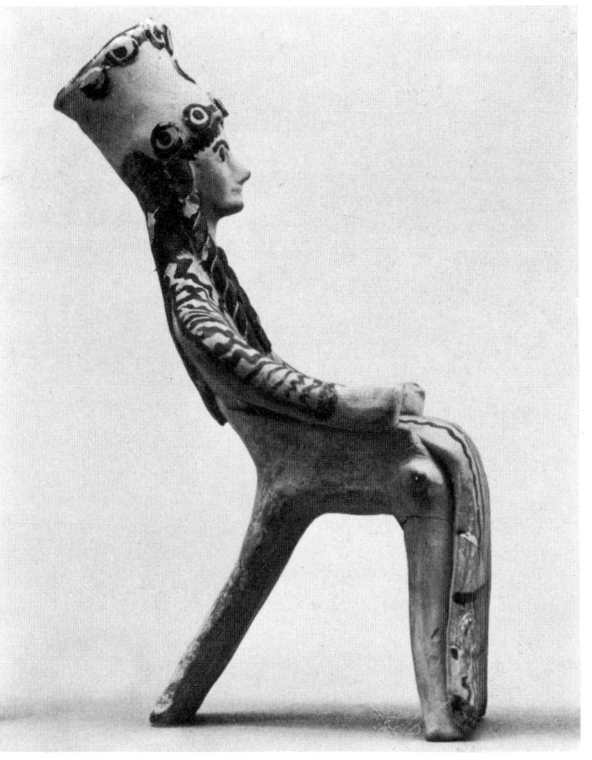

A

B

C

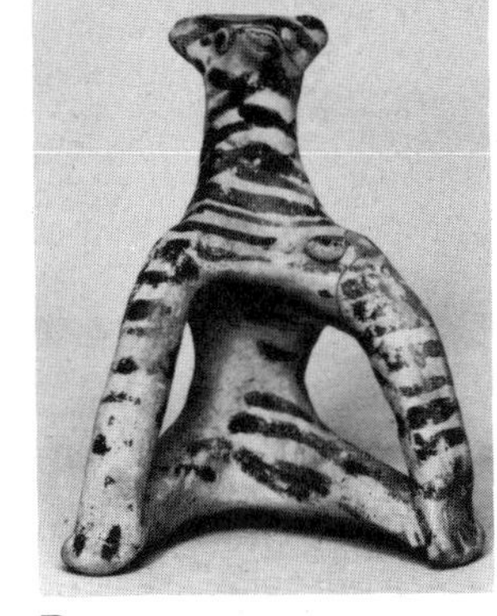

D

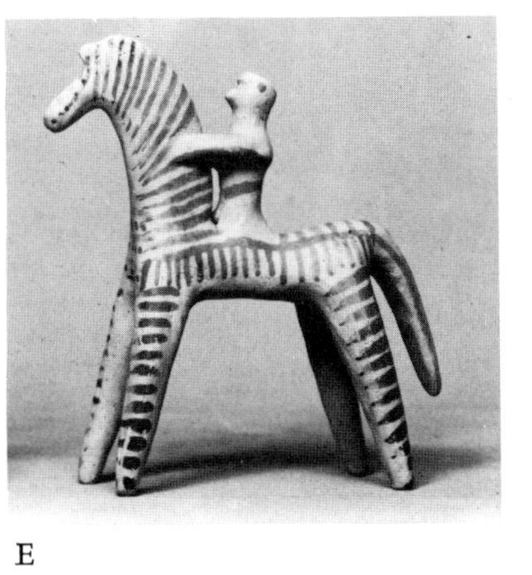

E

F

20 Corinth, seventh and sixth centuries B.C.

A

B

C

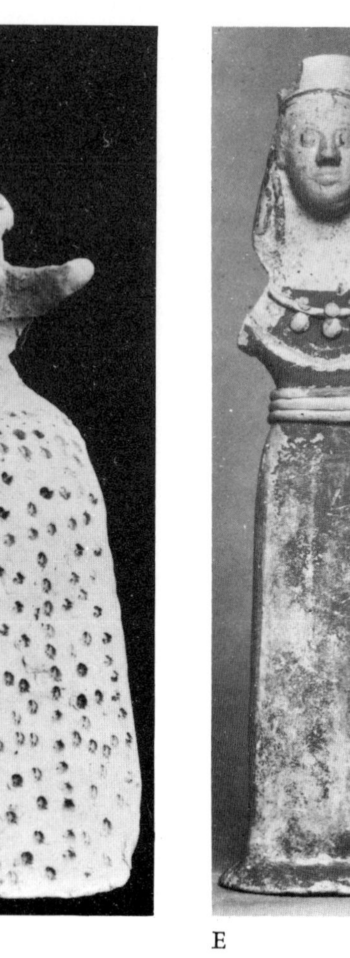

D

E

F

A

B

C

D

E

F

G

22 South Italy, seventh and sixth centuries B.C.

A

B

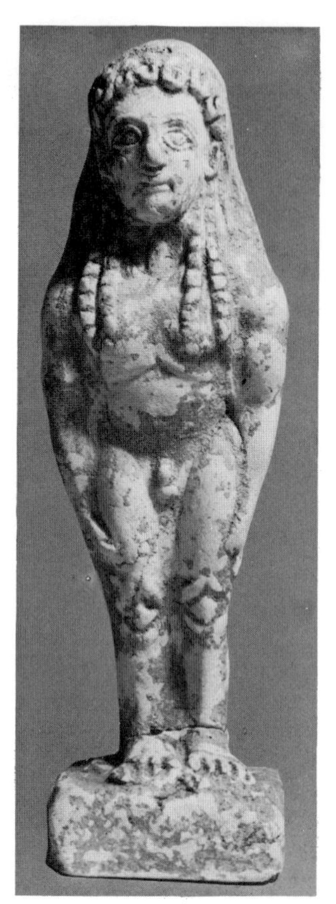

C

D

E

F

A B C

D E F

 Ionia (?) and Rhodes, fifth century B.C.

A

B

C

D

E

F

A

B

C

D

E

F

26 Rhodes, fifth century B.C.

A

B

C

D

A

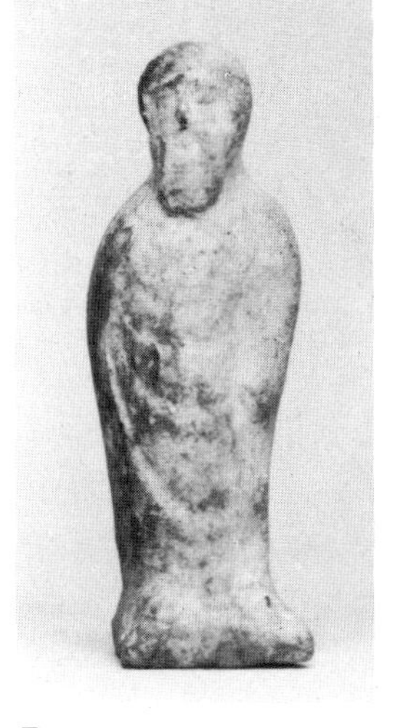

B

C

D

E

F

G

H

A

B

30 Attica, fifth century B.C.

A

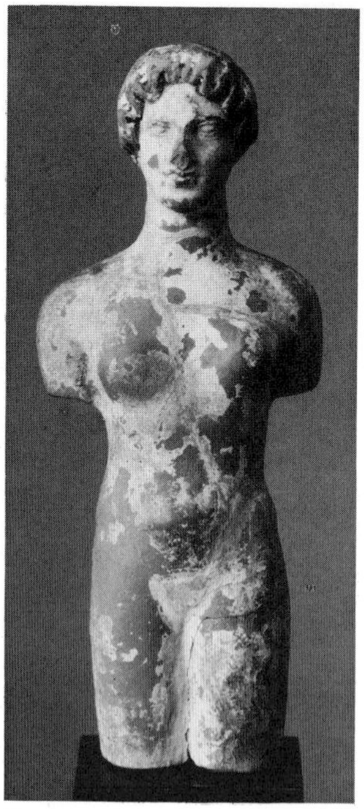

B

C

D

E

F

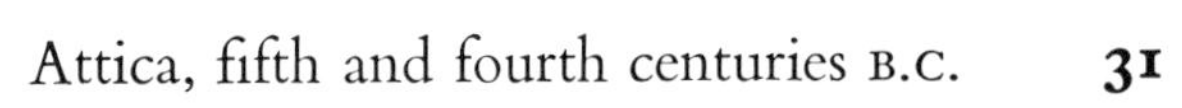

A

B

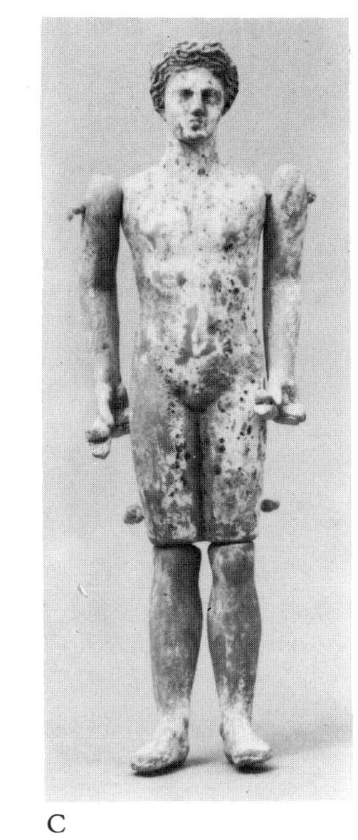
C

D

E

F

Boeotia, around 500 B.C.

A

B

C

D

E

F

G

A

B

C

D

E

34 Boeotia, fourth century B.C.

A

B

C

D

E

F

A

B

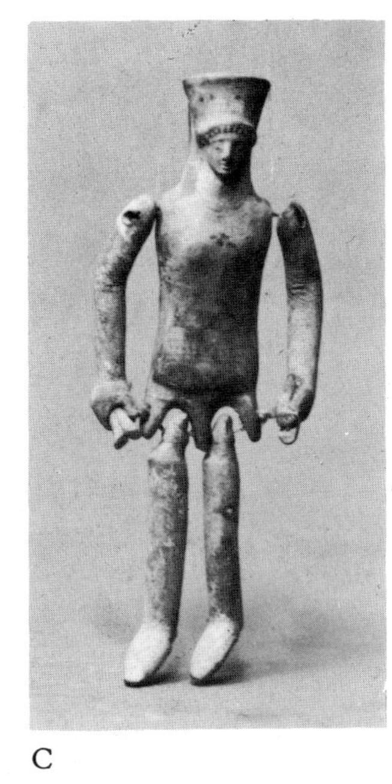

C

D

E

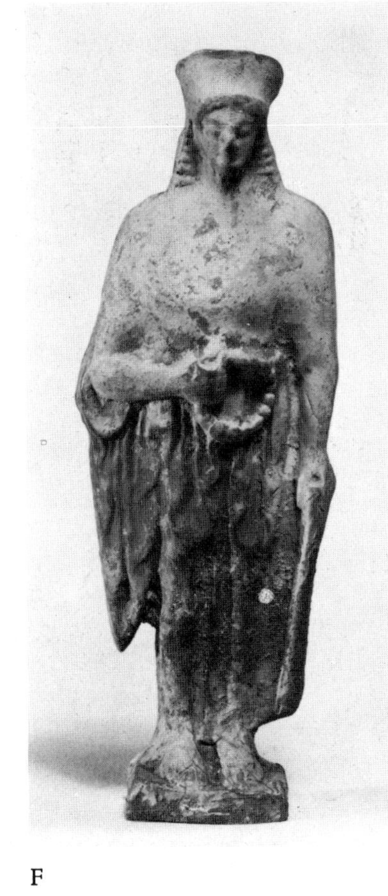

F

A

B

C

D

E

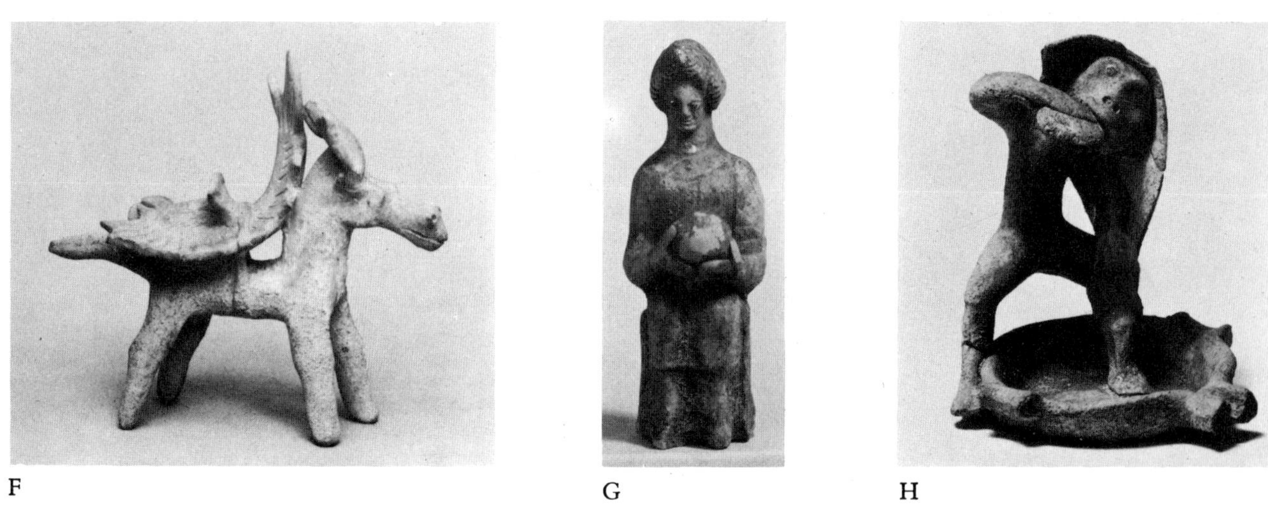

F

G

H

A B C

D E F

 Locri, fifth century B.C.

A

B

C

D

A

B

C

D

A

B

C

D

E

F

A

B

C

D E F

A

B

A

B

C

D

E

A

B

C

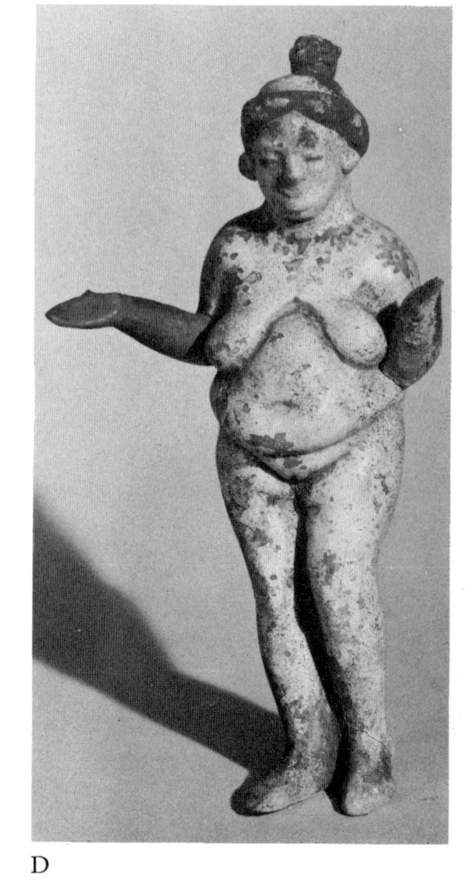

D

E

A

B

C

D

E

F

A

B

C

A

B

C

D

E

F

A

B

C

D

E

F

A

B

C

D

E

F

50 Delos, early first century B.C.

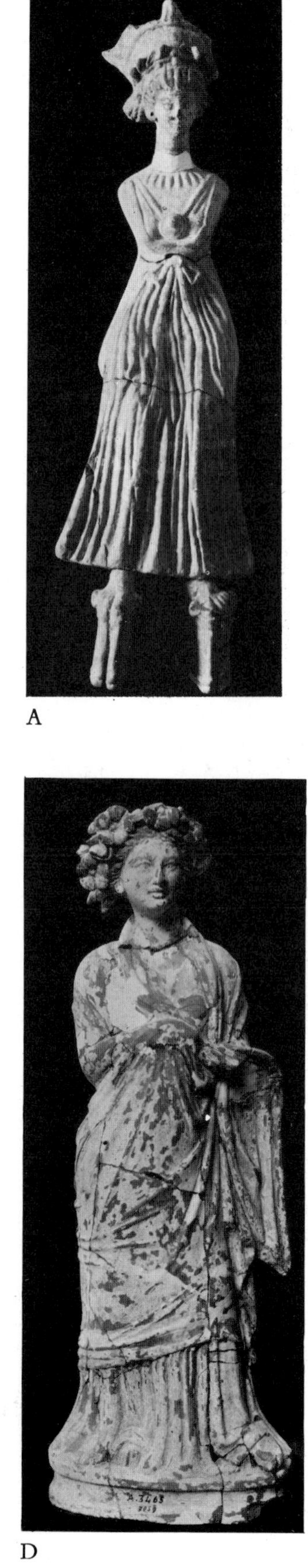

A

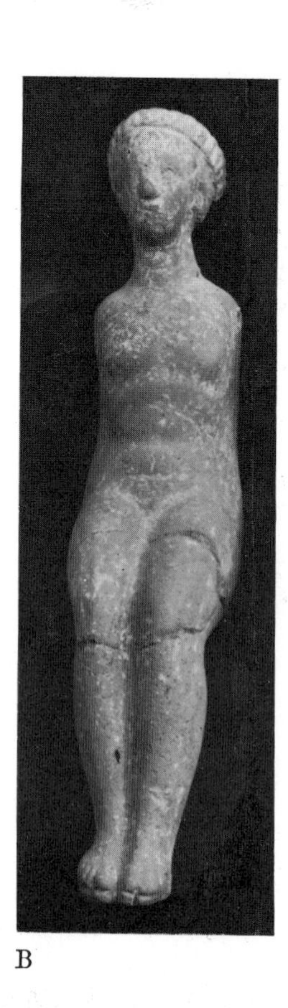

B

C

D

E

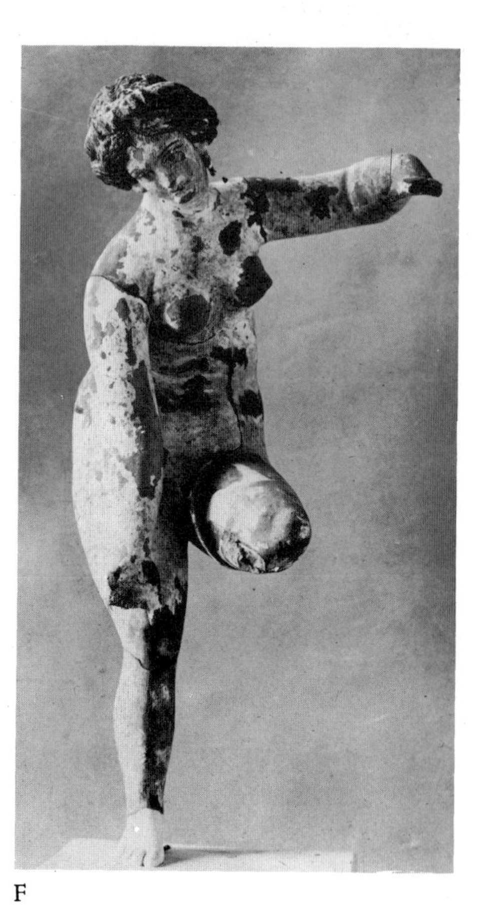

F

A

B

C

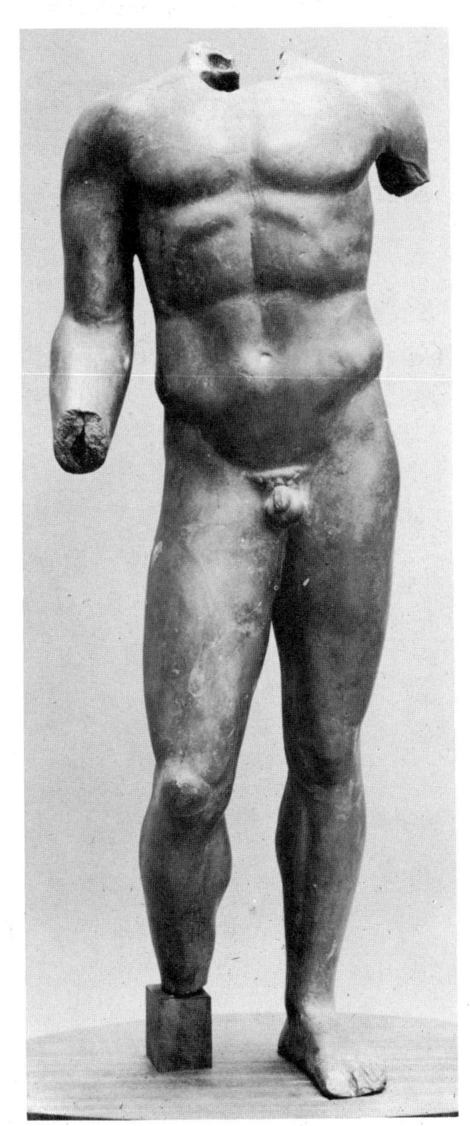
D

E

A

B

C

D

E

F

A B C D E

A

B

C

D

A

B

C

D

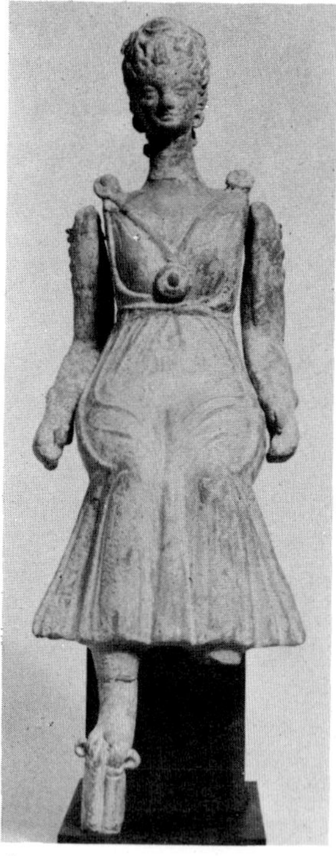

A

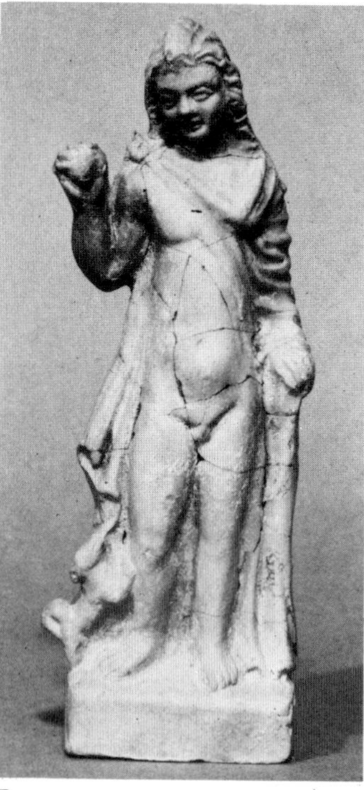

B

C

D

E

A B C

D E F

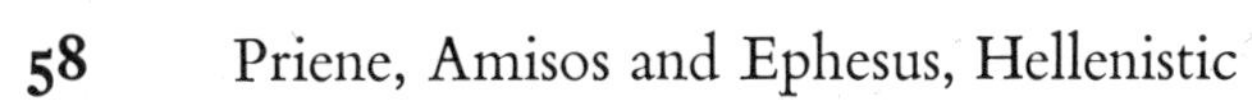

A

B

C

D

E

A

B

C

D

E

A

B C D

A

B

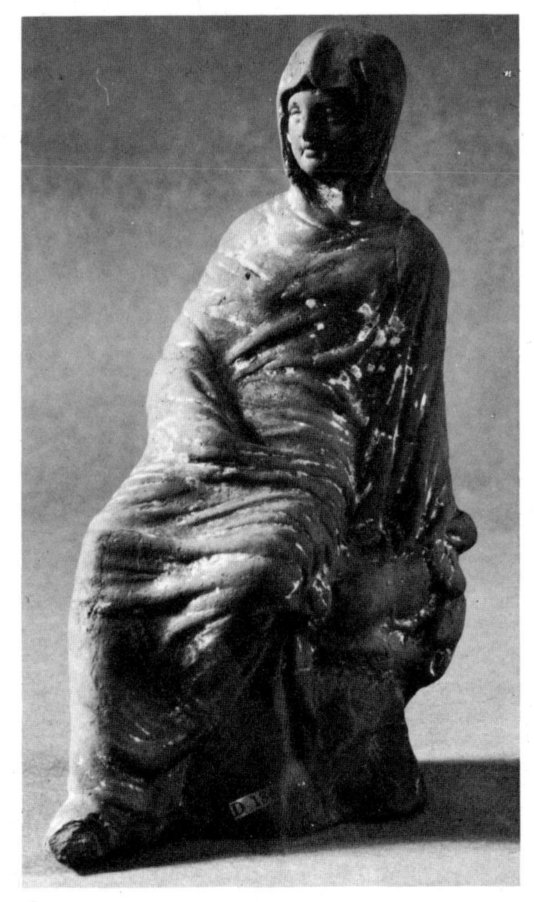

C

A

B

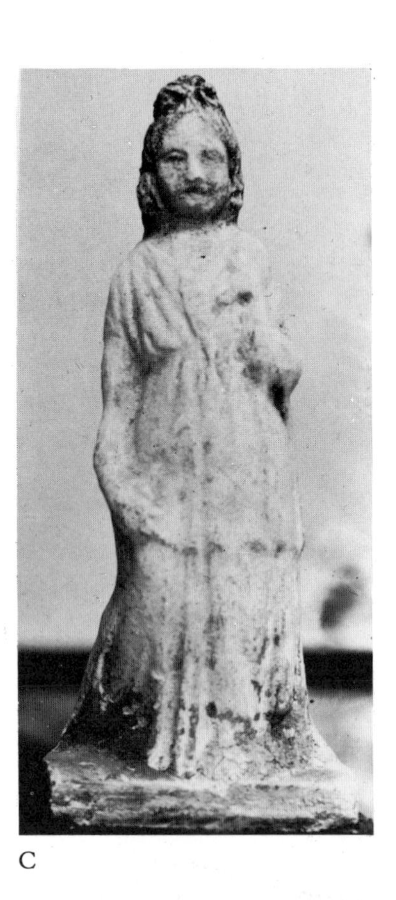

C

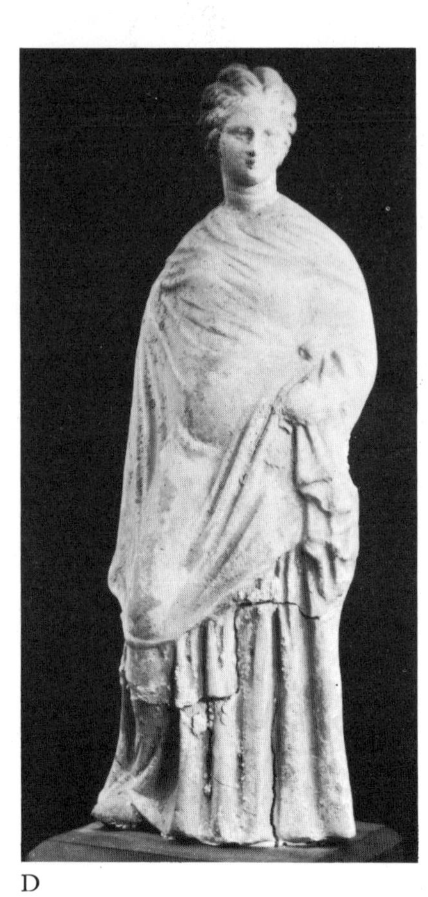

D

E

F

A

B

C

D

E

F

A

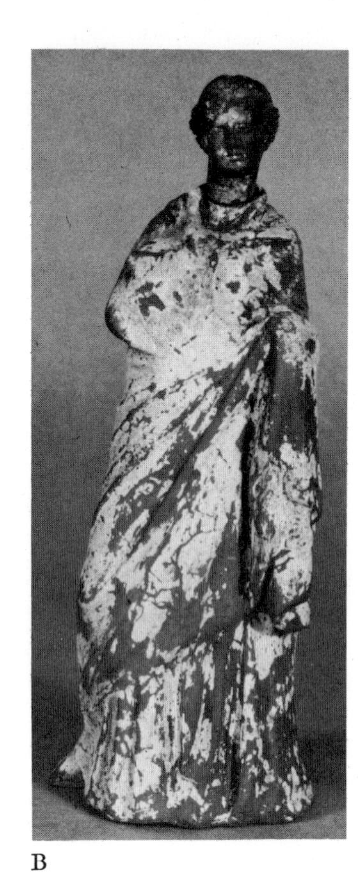

B

C

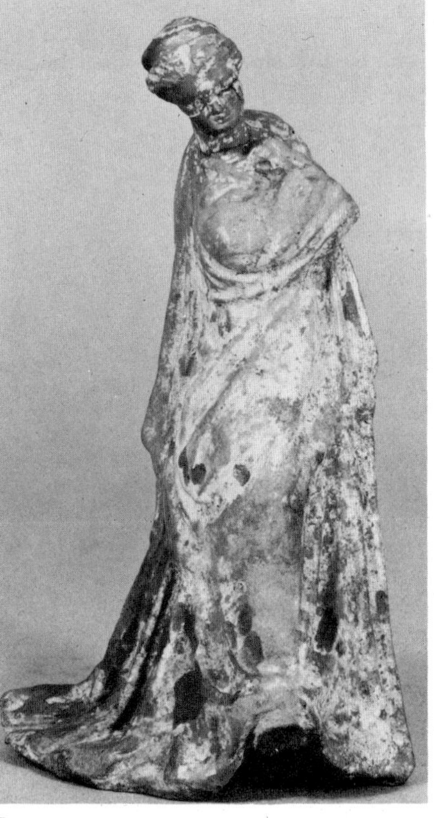

D

E

F